Authenticity, Language and Interaction in Second Language Contexts

SECOND LANGUAGE ACQUISITION

Series Editor: **Professor David Singleton**, *University of Pannonia, Hungary* and Fellow Emeritus, *Trinity College, Dublin, Ireland* and **Dr Simone E. Pfenninger**, *University of Zurich, Switzerland*

This series brings together titles dealing with a variety of aspects of language acquisition and processing in situations where a language or languages other than the native language is involved. Second language is thus interpreted in its broadest possible sense. The volumes included in the series all offer in their different ways, on the one hand, exposition and discussion of empirical findings and, on the other, some degree of theoretical reflection. In this latter connection, no particular theoretical stance is privileged in the series; nor is any relevant perspective – sociolinguistic, psycholinguistic, neurolinguistic, etc. – deemed out of place. The intended readership of the series includes final-year undergraduates working on second language acquisition projects, postgraduate students involved in second language acquisition research, and researchers, teachers and policy-makers in general whose interests include a second language acquisition component.

Full details of all the books in this series and of all our other publications can be found on http://www.multilingual-matters.com, or by writing to Multilingual Matters, St Nicholas House, 31–34 High Street, Bristol BS1 2AW, UK.

SECOND LANGUAGE ACQUISITION: 96

Authenticity, Language and Interaction in Second Language Contexts

Edited by
Rémi A. van Compernolle and
Janice McGregor

MULTILINGUAL MATTERS
Bristol • Buffalo • Toronto

Library of Congress Cataloging in Publication Data
Names: Compernolle, Rémi A. van, editor. |McGregor, Janice, editor.
Title: Authenticity, Language and Interaction in Second Language Contexts/Edited by Rémi A. van Compernolle and Janice McGregor.
Description: Bristol; Buffalo: Multilingual Matters, [2016] | Series: Second Language Acquisition: 96 | Includes bibliographical references and index.
Identifiers: LCCN 2015044275 | ISBN 9781783095308 (hbk : alk. paper) | ISBN 9781783095292 (pbk : alk. paper) | ISBN 9781783095315 (ebook)
Subjects: LCSH: Second language acquisition—Study and teaching. | Language and languages—Study and teaching. | Communicative competence—Evaluation.|Social interaction. | Interlanguage (Language learning) | Applied linguistics.
Classification: LCC P118.15.A88 2016 | DDC 418.0071—dc23 LC record available at http://lccn.loc.gov/2015044275

British Library Cataloguing in Publication Data
A catalogue entry for this book is available from the British Library.

ISBN-13: 978-1-78309-530-8 (hbk)
ISBN-13: 978-1-78309-529-2 (pbk)

Multilingual Matters
UK: St Nicholas House, 31–34 High Street, Bristol BS1 2AW, UK.
USA: UTP, 2250 Military Road, Tonawanda, NY 14150, USA.
Canada: UTP, 5201 Dufferin Street, North York, Ontario M3H 5T8, Canada.

Website: www.multilingual-matters.com
Twitter: Multi_Ling_Mat
Facebook: https://www.facebook.com/multilingualmatters
Blog: www.channelviewpublications.wordpress.com

Copyright © 2016 Rémi A. van Compernolle, Janice McGregor and the authors of individual chapters.

All rights reserved. No part of this work may be reproduced in any form or by any means without permission in writing from the publisher.

The policy of Multilingual Matters/Channel View Publications is to use papers that are natural, renewable and recyclable products, made from wood grown in sustainable forests. In the manufacturing process of our books, and to further support our policy, preference is given to printers that have FSC and PEFC Chain of Custody certification. The FSC and/or PEFC logos will appear on those books where full certification has been granted to the printer concerned.

Typeset by Nova Techset Private Limited, Bengaluru and Chennai, India.
Printed and bound in Great Britain by Short Run Press Ltd.

Contents

	Contributors	ix
1	Introducing Authenticity, Language and Interaction in Second Language Contexts	1
	Rémi A. van Compernolle and Janice McGregor	
	Aim and Rationale of the Volume	1
	Key Concepts and Challenges	2
	Overview of the Contributions	5
	Final Comments	8
2	Evaluating L2 Pragmatic Appropriateness and Authenticity in Synchronous Computer-mediated Strategic Interaction Scenarios	10
	Rémi A. van Compernolle and Ashlie Henery	
	Introduction	10
	Conceptual Background	11
	French *Tu* and *Vous*	16
	Context of the Research and Methods	17
	Analyses and Findings	21
	Discussion and Conclusion	31
3	Authenticity and Pedagogical Grammar: A Concept-based Approach to Teaching French Auxiliary Verbs	35
	Lawrence Williams	
	Introduction	35
	Explanations of French Auxiliary Verb Choice in Selected Textbooks	37
	Creating a Didactic Tool	43
	Implementing Concept-based Instruction	47
	Conclusions	54
	Appendix A: Worksheet 1	55
	Appendix B: Worksheet 2	57

4　Sociolinguistic Authenticity and Classroom L2 Learners: Production, Perception and Metapragmatics　61
Rémi A. van Compernolle
　Introduction　61
　Conceptualizing L2 Sociolinguistic Authenticity　62
　Focus of the Chapter and Research Questions　66
　Methods　67
　Findings and Analysis　69
　Discussion and Conclusions　75
　Appendix A: Interview Questions　77
　Appendix B: Narrative Prompt Worksheet　77
　Appendix C: Language Awareness Interview Questions　78
　Appendix D: Oral Appropriateness Judgment Task　79

5　Learning Speech Style in Japanese Study Abroad: Learners' Knowledge of Normative Use and Actual Use　82
Naoko Taguchi
　Introduction　82
　Methods　88
　Results　93
　Conclusions and Implications　101
　Appendix A: Oral DCT Scenarios　105
　Appendix B: Abbreviations in the Oral DCT Excerpts　106

6　Gender, Youth and Authenticity: Peer Mandarin Socialization Among American Students in a Chinese College Dorm　109
Wenhao Diao
　Introduction　109
　Background　110
　The Study　114
　Findings　115
　Discussion　125
　Appendix A: Transcription Conventions　127
　Appendix B: Grammar Glossary　128

7　Authenticating Language Choices: Out-of-Class Interactions in Study Abroad　131
Julieta Fernández
　Introduction　131
　The Study　133
　Findings　136
　Discussion and Conclusions　147

8	Authenticating Practices in Chinese Homestay Interactions *Sheng-Hsun Lee and Celeste Kinginger*	151
	Introduction	151
	Literature	152
	The Current Project	157
	Study Design	157
	Analytic Approach and Research Questions	161
	Findings	161
	Discussion and Conclusions	170
	Appendix A: Transcription Conventions	173
	Appendix B: Grammatical Glosses	173
9	Metapragmatic Talk and the Interactional Accomplishment of Authenticity in Study Abroad *Janice McGregor*	177
	Introduction	177
	L2 Interaction in Study Abroad	179
	L2 Competence	180
	Data Collection and Analysis	185
	Findings	186
	Discussion	192
	Conclusions	194
	Appendix: Transcription Conventions	194
10	Focus on Form in the Wild *Gabriele Kasper and Alfred Rue Burch*	198
	Introduction	198
	Authenticity	200
	Interactional Competence	201
	Method	203
	Analysis	205
	Discussion and Conclusions	223
	Appendix A: Transcription Conventions	225
	Appendix B: Japanese Language	226
11	Conclusions and Future Directions *Rémi A. van Compernolle and Janice McGregor*	233
	Introduction	233
	Patterns of Language and Patterns of Meaning	233
	Agency, Identity and Culture	235
	Future Directions	236
	Final Thoughts	240
Index		242

Contributors

Alfred Rue Burch is a PhD candidate in second language studies at the University of Hawai'i at Mānoa. His interests include re-examining traditional topics in second language acquisition such as motivation, communication strategies and task-based language learning/teaching through the lens of conversation analysis. He has worked on Japanese and English as second languages and with data from both pedagogical and non-pedagogical contexts. He has published in *Language Learning* and co-authored a chapter to appear in Prior and Kasper, *Emotion in Multilingual Interaction* (John Benjamins, in press).

Wenhao Diao is Assistant Professor in the Department of East Asian Studies and an affiliated faculty member in the program of second language acquisition and teaching at the University of Arizona. She is interested in the sociolinguistic and sociocultural aspects of language learning and use among study abroad students. Her work has been funded by the US Department of Education and the Chinese Language Teachers Association (USA). Her articles have appeared in journals such as *Applied Linguistics* and *Frontiers: The Interdisciplinary Journal of Study Abroad*.

Julieta Fernández is Assistant Professor of Applied Linguistics in the Department of English at Northern Arizona University. Her research interests include second language pragmatics, language learning in study abroad and second language development and pedagogy.

Ashlie Henery is currently a lecturer at the University of Pennsylvania, USA, in the Department of Romance Languages, French Section and the Graduate School of Education, Educational Linguistics Division. She holds a PhD in second language acquisition from Carnegie Mellon University, USA. Her research focuses on language learning in the study abroad context, second language pragmatic development, and French language pedagogy from a Vygotskian sociocultural perspective.

Gabriele Kasper is Professor of Second Language Studies at the University of Hawai'i at Mānoa. Her current research is concerned with social interaction in multilingual contexts, including second language learning and assessment, the social side of cognition and emotion, and the application of conversation analysis to standard social science research methods. Her most recent co-edited volumes are *Assessing Second Language Pragmatics* (Palgrave Macmillan, 2013) and *Emotion in Multilingual Interaction* (John Benjamins, in press).

Celeste Kinginger is Professor of Applied Linguistics at the Pennsylvania State University (USA), where she teaches courses in second language acquisition and education as well as advanced seminars, most recently, narrative approaches to multilingual identity, second language pragmatics, and approaches to language in use. She is affiliated with the Center for Advanced Language Proficiency Education and Research, funded by the United States Department of Education, and with the Center for Language Acquisition in the University's College of Liberal Arts. Her research has examined telecollaborative, intercultural language learning, second language pragmatics, cross-cultural life writing, teacher education and study abroad.

Sheng-Hsun Lee is a PhD candidate at the Department of Applied Linguistics, Pennsylvania State University. His research draws insights from sociocultural theory and linguistic anthropology to explore language learning processes in and beyond study abroad. He also studies communication in Chinese medicine clinics.

Janice McGregor is Assistant Professor of German in the Department of Modern Languages at Kansas State University, where she coordinates the basic German language program and teaches in the MA program in second language acquisition. Her research focuses on language use and identity in language learning contexts, especially during study abroad.

Naoko Taguchi is Associate Professor of Japanese and Second Language Acquisition at Carnegie Mellon University. Her research interests include second language pragmatics, English-medium education and classroom-based research. Among her book publications are *Context, Individual Differences and Pragmatic Development* (2012), *Developing Interactional Competence in a Japanese Study Abroad Context* (2015), *Technology in Interlanguage Pragmatics Research and Teaching* (2013) and *Pragmatic Competence in Japanese as a Second Language* (2009). She is the co-editor of a new journal, *Journal of Multilingual Pragmatics*.

Rémi A. van Compernolle is Assistant Professor of Second Language Acquisition and French and Francophone Studies at Carnegie Mellon University. His research centers primarily on extensions of sociocultural psychology to second language development and instruction, with specific focus on the sociolinguistic, pragmatic and interactional competencies of language learners. He is the author of *Sociocultural Theory and L2 Instructional Pragmatics* (Multilingual Matters, 2014), *Interaction and Second Language Development: A Vygotskian Perspective* (John Benjamins, 2015), and numerous journal articles and book chapters.

Lawrence Williams is Professor of French and Applied Linguistics in the Department of World Languages, Literatures and Cultures at the University of North Texas. His research and teaching interests are centered around sociolinguistic and pragmatic dimensions of language and the use of new technologies as tools for communication and language learning and teaching.

1 Introducing Authenticity, Language and Interaction in Second Language Contexts

Rémi A. van Compernolle and Janice McGregor

Aim and Rationale of the Volume

The notion of authenticity has been a central, if variably interpreted, construct in much applied linguistics and second language (L2) research since the early 1980s, when Canale and Swain (1980) proposed an extension of Hymes's (1972) concept of communicative competence to the domain of L2 teaching and testing (see also Celce-Murcia, 2007; Leung, 2005; van Lier, 1996; Widdowson, 2007). In broad terms, discussions of authenticity typically center around the extent to which some use of language aligns with the lexicogrammatical conventions and/or sociolinguistic and pragmatic practices of native speakers of the language that learners are studying, in contrast to the (perceived) less-than-authentic representation of the language in pedagogical materials and classroom discourse. In addition, some treatments of authenticity in L2 contexts focus more on origins of language use: for example, pedagogical language is authentic classroom language, and L2 learner language is authentically the learner's language.

Drawing on work in philosophy, MacDonald *et al.* (2006) discuss these two broad types of authenticity as *authenticity of correspondence* and *authenticity of genesis* (see Cooper, 1983), respectively.[1] Authenticity of correspondence refers to the extent to which the use of language corresponds to some perceived (and perhaps idealized) norm or convention. Authenticity of genesis refers to the idea that the use of language is authentic in terms of its origins, irrespective of its correspondence to some notion of norms or conventions. MacDonald *et al.* argue, however, that applied linguistics research has for too long focused on one or the other of these conceptualizations of what authentic language is, and that it is time for the field 'to synthesize these two accounts of authenticity' (MacDonald *et al.*, 2006: 251). The objective of this volume is to respond to MacDonald *et al.*'s (2006: 251) critique of the 'one-sidedness' of L2 and applied linguistics research by showcasing original scholarship that synthesizes the concepts of authenticity of correspondence and authenticity of genesis as a dialectic – that is, as a unified whole – with specific focus on language teaching and communicative interaction in which at least one participant is using an L2/additional language.

An understanding of what counts as authentic language and interaction has important implications for L2 teaching and assessment, and the question of who counts as an authentic (native and/or L2) speaker can help researchers and teachers to understand learners as people (van Compernolle, 2014). Indeed, in our own research in classroom language teaching and pragmatics (van Compernolle) and study abroad (McGregor), we have often had to resolve (perceived) tensions between authenticities of correspondence and genesis (Cooper, 1983; MacDonald *et al.*, 2006) with regard to the following questions: Does authentic learning in the classroom or in study abroad mean that students approximate native speaker conventions, or do they contribute to the authenticity of their language use and interactional practices in ways that may diverge with, but are no less authentic than, their native speaker counterparts? Can we conceive of L2 learners as authentic speakers of the language even if, in comparison to idealized conceptions of monolingual native speakers, they do not fully 'master' the grammatical, phonological, pragmatic and sociolinguistic aspects of the language they are studying? Can classrooms and language learning materials be conceptualized as authentic in their own right, or must they correspond to some type of language used beyond formal educational settings? This volume is an attempt to answer some of these questions by bringing together different scholars working in a variety of contexts and with several languages (i.e. Chinese, English, French, German, Japanese and Spanish).

The remainder of this introductory chapter has two principal objectives. First, we present a brief overview of some of the key concepts and challenges of exploring authenticity in language and interaction in L2 contexts. Secondly, we contextualize the contributions included in the volume in relation to these concepts and challenges.

Key Concepts and Challenges

Although the contributions to this volume address the issue of authenticity from a variety of theoretical and methodological approaches, three principal themes are common across all of them in one way or another: (1) What is authentic language? (2) Who is an authentic speaker? and (3) How is authenticity achieved?

What is authentic language?

As noted above, the view of authentic language that we adopt in this volume is one that attempts to unify the traditional, and bifurcated, notions of authenticity of correspondence and authenticity of genesis (Cooper, 1983; MacDonald *et al.*, 2006). We can summarize our position as follows: authentic language entails patterns of language and meaning that are recognizable within and across communities of speakers and that are appropriated as one's own. This perspective recognizes that language users certainly have ownership over their language and the linguistic choices they make (authenticity of genesis), but at the same time, any speaker's linguistic practices can only be meaningful to the extent that they are interpretable by one's interlocutors (authenticity of correspondence). Language users have agency, but agency is socioculturally mediated (Ahearn, 2001) and is therefore afforded and constrained by historical, contextual and material circumstances, including what counts as a recognizable (or acceptable, appropriate, correct, etc.) pattern of language (van Compernolle, 2014).

This perspective on authenticity certainly poses challenges for language learning and teaching scholarship and practice. As Leung (2005) has pointed out, although approaches to communicative language teaching have since the 1970s emphasized contextually sensitive language use in authentic contexts, language-learning materials still typically follow a structural syllabus. This means that even if so-called communicative tasks (e.g. role plays) are included, grammatical forms – and a perceived correct sequencing of their teaching – typically determine the content of such materials. While Hymes's (1972) ideas regarding communicative competence, and their appropriation in L2 teaching and testing by such scholars as Canale and Swain (1980) and Bachman (1990), advocated for the investigation and understanding of language use in specific social and cultural contexts, Leung (2005: 127) notes that we have arrived at a 'scaled-down universalism' compared to what was originally intended. The social realm 'now resides in pedagogic projects of the "authentic" (native) speaker and "expert knower"' (Leung, 2005: 127). In this way, what constitutes real language in communicative language teaching approaches, and who speaks this real or authentic language, has been simplified and flattened as an idealized version of the L2, a version that often ignores geographic, social and stylistic variation in communicative practices (van Compernolle, 2014). We echo Leung's (2005) concern over reductive conceptions of authenticity that idealize a single form of language as the authentic variety. There are certainly many different patterns of language and meaning that are recognizable within and across communities. And there are certainly many ways in which these recognizable patterns may be appropriated and challenged by language learners.

Who is an authentic speaker?

A common conception of an authentic speaker – both in linguistic scholarship and outside the academy – is the monolingual native speaker of a given language. This is certainly the view that Chomsky (1965) at least indirectly espoused in his formulation of generative linguistics, which has been highly influential in several domains of linguistic inquiry for the past five decades. The problem with this view is that the idealized monolingual native speaker does not reflect sociolinguistic reality (Eckert, 2003). Variation in language across time, community and context is a linguistic fact. Likewise, native speakers do not hold a monopoly on authenticity (Leung, 2005). Our view of authentic speakers, therefore, is an extension of our conception of authentic language. An authentic speaker is a person who has appropriated patterns of language and meaning that are recognizable within and across communities of speakers of the language. Learners do not become authentic by emulating perfectly an idealized native speaker of the language they are learning, but instead forge their identities as authentic speakers in multiple and variable ways that may align with, or diverge from, expected norms from one individual to the next, and from one context to the next.

How is authenticity achieved?

Authenticity is not a state of being that is achieved once and for all time; rather, it is a non-telic process – *authentication* (Bucholtz, 2003) – which is achieved between people from moment to moment. Consequently, authentic speakers do not exist as such. Rather, they authenticate themselves, and are authenticated by others, in their communicative practices. This is because the individual life project must be viewed as a perpetually modifiable and dynamic process, not a bounded product (Blommaert & Varis, 2013). Speakers collaboratively manage talk-in-interaction and therefore interpret, and make judgments about, their interlocutors' utterances. Speakers' interpretations and judgments necessarily inform their own language choices in interaction. In this way, individuals orient to particular sets of features (i.e. recognizable patterns of language and meaning) that are representative of particular identities when aligning with, or rejecting, particular ways of being. An important part of L2 development therefore involves the appropriation of socioculturally relevant metapragmatics (Silverstein, 2001) – that is, knowledge and understanding of the social-indexical meanings of linguistic practices – in addition to developing the ability to use L2 patterns.

We use the term *appropriation* here as a shorthand device for the process of picking up a resource and making it one's own. Our understanding of authentication in this sense is inspired by the maxim found in Vygotsky's (1986) work that sign meaning develops. Put simply, humans may acquire signs (e.g. linguistic forms) quickly and rather easily in a first step, but the real work of development involves 'a process of coming to understand the meaning and functional significance of the sign forms that one has been using' (Wertsch, 2007: 186). L2 authenticity develops as learners connect the patterns of language (i.e. sign forms) they have appropriated to the meanings and functional significance of those patterns (i.e. metapragmatics) in different sociocultural contexts.

Overview of the Contributions

In addition to this Introduction and our Conclusion at the end of the book, the current volume includes nine original chapters that address L2 authenticity in a variety of second (or additional) languages – Chinese, French, German, Japanese and Spanish. The contributions are arranged from those that focus on classroom language learners to contexts of study and residence abroad.

Rémi A. van Compernolle and Ashlie Henery's chapter describes and explores the challenges of evaluating L2 French pragmatic appropriateness and authenticity in computer-mediated strategic interaction scenarios. Focusing on second-person address patterns (i.e. *tu* versus *vous*), they respond to MacDonald *et al.*'s (2006) call to conceptualize authenticity as involving both correspondence and genesis, arguing that pragmatic authenticity is achieved when the performance corresponding to a recognizable pattern of language is mediated by a recognizable metapragmatic meaning that a learner has appropriated as his or her own (i.e. authenticity of genesis).

The next chapter, by Lawrence Williams, examines the authenticity of L2 French textbook grammatical explanations and reports on a pilot project involving concept-based instruction. In a first step, the author analyzes several textbooks' presentations of auxiliary verb choice for compound past tense (i.e. *avoir* 'to have' versus *être* 'to be' in the *passé composé*), finding that the explanations are unsystematic and reflect neither authentic uses of auxiliary verbs nor the meanings they create in communication. In a second step, Williams shows how a concept-based approach to teaching auxiliary verb choice in relation to transitivity can improve students' understanding of appropriate auxiliary verb choice in terms of meaning and increase their confidence in choosing between *avoir* and *être*.

In the last chapter dealing with classroom language learners, Rémi A. van Compernolle explores the concept of sociolinguistic authenticity by presenting two contrastive case analyses of advanced US university-level learners of French. Expanding on recent work in variationist sociolinguistics, the author argues that sociolinguistic authenticity involves three dimensions: (1) performance abilities, including quantitative patterns of variation; (2) metapragmatic knowledge of social rules and evaluations of linguistic variants; and (3) attitudes toward, and personal preferences for, variable speech forms. The analysis – which focuses on the two learners' variable speech patterns, performances on a sentence versions task and responses during a language awareness interview – shows that authenticity can be achieved in divergent ways because learners can orient to, and evaluate, variable speech patterns differently.

The focus on contexts of learning beyond the classroom begins with Naoko Taguchi's chapter, which explores the learning of Japanese speech styles during study abroad. She begins by problematizing the authenticity of discourse completion tasks as an instrument for measuring pragmatic competence, and then moves on to compare study abroad participants' performances on an oral discourse completion task with their verbalizable knowledge of normative, or conventional, pragmatic practices. Taguchi reports that the learners made strong gains during their sojourn abroad in terms of appropriate speech act performance. However, she also takes a critical look at several discrepancies between pragmatic performance and pragmatic knowledge. Drawing on interview data, Taguchi addresses two common sources of such discrepancies: linguistic difficulty and dynamicity of language in interaction. In some cases, pragmatic norms are known, but are not used in online speech because learners find them too linguistically challenging, and they therefore opt for simpler forms, even if they are less appropriate. In other cases, learners' performances do not align with perceived, or idealized, conventions because they recognize that language is dynamic, and variable, both across and within contexts.

In the following chapter, Wenhao Diao investigates peer Mandarin socialization in a Chinese college dorm. Her focus is on how gender, sexuality and youth are authenticated in and through linguistic practices between American students and their Chinese peers. Through close analysis of recorded interactions, Diao shows how the social meaning of sociolinguistic practices, such as affective sentence-final particles, is made visible to the American students by their Chinese interlocutors (e.g. men using too many affective sentence-final particles 'sound gay'). This is the kind of language use and knowledge of language that is typically not taught in formal, structured educational environments. Rather, as Diao points out, students are socialized into these culturally based understandings of the social-indexical functions of language, and they can be used as ways of authenticating L2 identities.

Julieta Fernández's chapter offers a critical perspective on the perceived authenticity of out-of-class interactions during study abroad. Her study focuses on US university learners who were studying in Argentina and who had access to local hosts and conversational partners. Fernández shows that learners may not always be positioned as legitimate (viz. 'authentic') Spanish speakers by their local hosts, who engage in accommodation strategies in order to mitigate perceived deficiencies in the language. In addition, learners themselves can resist patterns of language that may be authentic in terms of correspondence but do not align with their desired L2 identities (i.e. authenticity of genesis).

In their chapter, Sheng-Hsun Lee and Celeste Kinginger explore authenticating practices in homestay contexts during Chinese study abroad. Their focus is on interactions between US learners of Chinese and members of their host families. They provide three examples of authenticating practices. The first centers on phonology – namely, the perceived 'Chineseness' (viz. authenticity) of the retroflex vowel [ɻ] in Beijing Mandarin that is approximated by one of the learners. The second involves the appropriate use of conceptual metaphors as authenticating communicative practices. The third centers on discussions of cultural practices and negotiating cultural differences. Their analysis shows that authentication can occur along several dimensions, including the use of L2 forms, thinking through culturally appropriate metaphors, and engagement in metatalk about culture.

Janice McGregor's chapter focuses on metapragmatic talk and authentication among American university students in a German study abroad context. Drawing on self-recorded conversations between a student and his German friend, McGregor looks at the ways in which knowledge of language rules (i.e. metapragmatics) is talked about and authenticated in interaction. The case presented in the chapter centers on the participant's retelling of a pragmatic faux pas – using the familiar *du* 'you' address pronoun with his friend's parents, where the more formal *Sie* 'you' would have been more appropriate. Although the interaction begins with the German native speaker positioned as the expert, it turns later to a cross-cultural comparison of address practices in Germany and the United States, and consequently the learner is authenticated as an expert as well. In this way, metapragmatic talk is a way of legitimizing the learner's own knowledge while at the same time creating opportunities to develop his understanding of German pragmatic practices and the meaning of *du* and *Sie*.

The final contribution, by Gabriele Kasper and Alfred Rue Burch, offers a different perspective on language and learning while living abroad. In contrast to the preceding chapters, Kasper and Burch's focal participant is an L2 speaker of Japanese living and working in Tokyo rather than a student participating in a school-organized study abroad program of a predetermined length. Their focus is on how focus-on-form is achieved 'in the wild' – that is, in authentic, naturalistic contexts outside of a formal space for learning, such as a classroom. Adopting a conversation analysis perspective, the authors show how a lexical understanding problem in an everyday conversation prompts the interlocutors to shift from achieving intersubjectivity in talking about a mundane topic to the spoken and written forms of the lexical item and its synonyms.

Our concluding chapter synthesizes the findings of the nine original contributions, with a focus on two principal themes that recur throughout this book: (1) authenticity in relation to patterns of language and meaning; and (2) authenticity in relation to agency, identity and culture. Based on our synthesis, we then propose several implications for theory, method and pedagogy that we hope will inform future scholarship in this important domain.

Final Comments

The present volume provides, we believe, a rich collection of perspectives on authenticity as it can be evaluated, achieved and questioned or challenged in a variety of second language contexts. A common theme running throughout the volume is the tension between what may be essentialized as authentic by virtue of correspondence to an expected norm, and what may be particularized as authentic when we take into account individuals' own orientations to language and learning, their histories as learners and the affordances that are made available in pedagogical materials as well as in the local context of L2-mediated interactions. We also see clearly that authenticity in language and interaction is not limited to the linguistic forms that learners use. Indeed, knowledge of language (e.g. metapragmatics) and cultural values are routinely authenticated, or challenged and questioned, in interactions. Authenticity lies at the intersection of many facets of L2 development, including linguistic competence, sociolinguistic and pragmatic capacities, agency, identity and cultural knowledge. It is our hope that the contributions to this volume will serve as a point of departure for stimulating much-needed further reflection on, and research into, the relationship between authenticities of correspondence and genesis in L2 development as well as the various domains of L2 development subject to authentication.

Note

(1) The concepts of authenticity of correspondence and authenticity of genesis originate in the writings of Cooper (1983) in his discussion of Nietzsche's educational philosophy. MacDonald *et al.* (2006) appropriated Cooper's take on authenticity, and the need to overcome one-sided views (i.e. as either correspondence or genesis), in the context of second language learning and teaching and intercultural communication. In this book, we engage with MacDonald *et al.*'s interpretation of Cooper's writings as they apply to contexts of second language use and development.

References

Ahearn, L. (2001) Language and agency. *Annual Review of Anthropology* 30, 109–137.
Bachman, L. (1990) *Fundamental Considerations in Language Testing.* Oxford: Oxford University Press.

Blommaert, J. and Varis, P. (2013) Enough is enough: The heuristics of authenticity in superdiversity. In J. Duarte and I. Gogolin (eds) *Linguistic Superdiversity in Urban Areas: Research Approaches* (pp. 143–160). Amsterdam: John Benjamins.

Bucholtz, M. (2003) Sociolinguistic nostalgia and the authentication of identity. *Journal of Sociolinguistics* 7, 398–416.

Canale, M. and Swain, M. (1980) Theoretical bases of communicative approaches to second language teaching and testing. *Applied Linguistics* 1, 1–47.

Celce-Murcia, M. (2007) Rethinking the role of communicative competence in teaching. In E. Alcon Soler and M.P. Safront Jorda (eds) *Intercultural Language Use and Language Teaching* (pp. 41–57). Dordrecht: Springer.

Chomsky, N. (1965) *Aspects of a Theory of Syntax*. Cambridge, MA: MIT Press.

Cooper, D.E. (1983) *Authenticity and Learning: Nietzsche's Educational Philosophy*. London: Routledge and Keagan Paul.

Eckert, P. (2003) Elephants in the room. *Journal of Sociolinguistics* 7, 392–397.

Hymes, D. (1972) On communicative competence. In J.B. Pride and J. Holmes (eds) *Sociolinguistics* (pp. 269–293). Harmondsworth: Penguin.

Leung, C. (2005) Convivial communication: Recontextualizing communicative competence. *International Journal of Applied Linguistics* 15, 119–144.

MacDonald, M.N., Badger, R. and Dasli, M. (2006) Authenticity, culture, and language learning. *Language and Intercultural Communication* 6 (3–4), 250–261.

Silverstein, M. (2001) The limits of awareness. In A. Duranti (ed.) *Linguistic Anthropology: A Reader* (pp. 382–401). Oxford: Blackwell.

van Compernolle, R.A. (2014) *Sociocultural Theory and L2 Instructional Pragmatics*. Bristol: Multilingual Matters.

van Lier, L. (1996) *Interaction in the Language Curriculum: Awareness, Autonomy, and Authenticity*. New York: Longman.

Vygotsky, L.S. (1986) *Thought and Language*. Cambridge, MA: MIT Press.

Wertsch, J. (2007) Mediation. In H. Daniels, M. Cole and J. Wertsch (eds) *The Cambridge Companion to Vygotsky* (pp. 178–192). Cambridge: Cambridge University Press.

Widdowson, H. (2007) Un-applied linguistics and communicative language teaching: A reaction to Keith Johnson's review of *Notional Syllabuses*. *International Journal of Applied Linguistics* 17, 214–220.

2 Evaluating L2 Pragmatic Appropriateness and Authenticity in Synchronous Computer-mediated Strategic Interaction Scenarios

Rémi A. van Compernolle and
Ashlie Henery

Introduction

In this chapter, we explore the nature and complexities of evaluating second language (L2) pragmatic appropriateness and authenticity within the context of synchronous computer-mediated communicative tasks modeled after Di Pietro's (1987) strategic interaction scenario (SIS) approach. SISs involve three basic stages: (i) a planning stage in which learners reflect on appropriate uses of language; (ii) a performance stage in which learners perform the scenario among themselves; and (iii) a reflection stage in which learners self-assess their performance. Grounded in Vygotskian sociocultural psychology (Vygotsky, 1978, 1986) as it has been extended to L2 research in general (Lantolf & Poehner, 2014; Lantolf & Thorne, 2006) and to instructional pragmatics in particular (van Compernolle, 2014), the data analyzed in this chapter come from a study focusing on teaching learners of French the concepts of self-presentation, social distance and power in relation to the second-person pronouns *tu* and *vous* (see van Compernolle & Henery, 2014). Our chapter focuses on problematizing the relationship between *authenticity of correspondence* and *authenticity of genesis* (e.g. Cooper, 1983; MacDonald *et al.*, 2006) in evaluations of appropriate choices (planning) and uses (performance) of French *tu* and *vous*.

The first part of our chapter provides an overview of the Vygotskian approach to L2 instructional pragmatics and its take on appropriateness in language learning and teaching (van Compernolle, 2014) in relation to the dual nature of authenticity (i.e. as correspondence and genesis; Cooper, 1983; MacDonald *et al.*, 2006). In particular, we problematize the use of idealized native speaker conventions as a benchmark for L2 pragmatic appropriateness: native speaker conventions are not always stable or constant and students' informed, agentive language choices are just as relevant and important. Secondly, we describe the methods and data collected during the larger study, focusing specifically on the SISs. Thirdly, our analysis delves into learners' planning and performance data in order to evaluate each in terms of different forms of authenticities. In concluding our chapter, we discuss our findings in relation to assessing L2 pragmatics, and we offer a number of recommendations for classroom pedagogy.

Conceptual Background

Mediation through patterns of language and patterns of meaning

Mediation is the core concept in Vygotskian sociocultural psychology. Briefly put, higher forms of human mental functioning are mediated by culturally based tools. Thus, as Vygotsky (1978) argued, the direct stimulus-response process is inhibited, and the psychological function takes on a new quality because it is accomplished indirectly via some meditating artifact. Memory, for example, has a biological (neuroanatomical) basis, but the internalization of language – our most powerful cultural tool – makes it possible to recall memories intentionally, to remember things and events in different ways, and to recount and color past experiences to other persons from various perspectives, as individuals and as societies (Wertsch, 1985, 1998). In other words, while the brain provides a substructure for memory processes, the higher function of remembering (and remembering for specific purposes and in particular contexts) is mediated by a cultural tool: language.

L2 development entails the internalization of new mediating artifacts and the growth and/or modification of existing artifacts (Lantolf & Thorne, 2006) that expand our capacities to think and act in the world. Broadly speaking, two types of interrelated artifacts are involved: patterns of language and patterns of meaning. Patterns of language include vocabulary, morphosyntax, grammatical constructions, and so on. Patterns of meaning refer to the particular ways in which things, events, experiences and so forth in the material world can be represented or construed through language. A large part of L2 development involves forging a link between the various patterns of language that are available in the L2 and the patterns of meaning that are indexed through linguistic choices. For instance, in internalizing active and passive grammatical constructions, learners not only need knowledge of the patterns of language (e.g. *The dog [agent] bit [active verb] the man [patient]* versus *The man [patient] was bitten [passive verb] by the dog [agent in prepositional phrase]*), but also knowledge of how the different constructions construe an event – focusing attention on the agent of the action in an active construction versus focusing attention on the patient in a passive construction, and potentially effacing the agent as in an agentless passive (e.g. *The man was bitten*) (see, for example, Swain *et al.*, 2009). To recall the brief discussion of memory from the preceding paragraph, we can see that the same event (e.g. a dog biting a man) may be remembered for the self and/or for others in various ways – language choices point to particular meanings or construals of the event, which mediates the psychological function of remembering.

Some recent L2 pedagogical work falling under the broad label of concept-based instruction (Negueruela, 2003) has attempted to design instructional interventions, sometimes called enrichment programs, around the internalization of patterns of meaning, with guidance on how patterns of meaning link to patterns of language (see Lantolf & Poehner, 2014, for a recent review and summary of exemplar studies).[1] The argument put forward in such work is that the patterns of meaning function as psychological tools that mediate the choice of available patterns of language for constructing meanings in motivated and thoughtful ways. Thus, use of the L2 is driven by an orientation to meaning rather than rules. Our own research in pragmatics (e.g. Henery, 2014; van Compernolle, 2014; van Compernolle & Henery, 2014; van Compernolle & Williams, 2012a), discussed in more detail below, has focused on patterns of meaning in the sociopragmatic domain – namely, identity and social relationship qualities – that mediate the selection of available pragmalinguistic resources (i.e. patterns of language). Consequently, our interest has centered around the ways in which sociopragmatic knowledge may be developed through interventive action (i.e. concept-based instruction) to mediate the development of pragmatic capacities. Our perspective holds several important implications for how we conceptualize L2 pragmatics, on the one hand, and the notions of appropriateness and authenticity, on the other. We address these issues in turn in the following two subsections.

Pragmatics as mediated action

Let us begin with a simple definition of pragmatics and its development in an L2, following Bardovi-Harlig's (2013: 68) 'cocktail party' explanation: 'pragmatics is the study of how-to-say-what-to-whom-when'. L2 pragmatics is, therefore, 'the study of how [L2] learners come to know how-to-say-what-to-whom-when' (Bardovi-Harlig, 2013: 68–69). And, in essence, this is what the study of pragmatics and its development is all about. The 'how-to-say-what' part refers to the various patterns of language that are available for creating different patterns of social meaning depending on the 'whom' and the 'when'. It is in this sense that pragmatics is seen as mediated action within Vygotskian sociocultural psychology (van Compernolle, 2014).

The mediated action perspective assumes three expanding spheres of activity. The core is social action – essentially, a goal to be accomplished. Social action is mediated by the pragmalinguistic domain – these are the patterns of language available in the L2. The choice of one pattern of language over another is in turn mediated by the sociopragmatic domain – these are the patterns of meaning available in the culture. The relationship between social action, pragmalinguistics and sociopragmatics has been represented elsewhere (van Compernolle, 2014) as three interlocking ovals (Figure 2.1). Sociopragmatic knowledge mediates pragmalinguistic choices, which mediate social action. The reader will also note that the two-way arrows within the pragmalinguistic and sociopragmatic domains, which indicate choices a speaker can choose to create more conventional meanings via conventional forms, or alternatively, a speaker may wish to create less conventional meaning via alternative pragmalinguistic practices. We will address the concept of conventionality in relation to appropriateness and authenticity in the following section, so for now it suffices to say that the mediated action perspective conceptualizes L2 pragmatic development as the internalization of patterns of meaning (i.e. sociopragmatics) as motives for choosing a pattern of language (i.e. pragmalinguistics) from among the available options in order to accomplish some social action. Accordingly, we would modify Bardovi-Harlig's (2013)

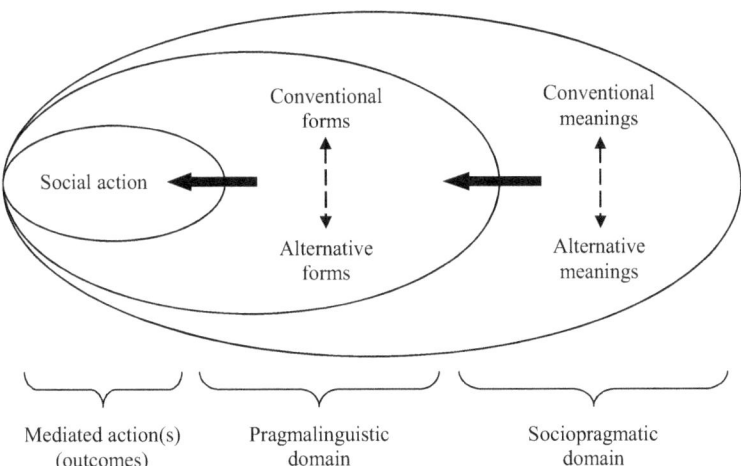

Figure 2.1 Pragmatics as mediated action
Source: van Compernolle (2014: 42).

definition of L2 pragmatics as learning 'how-to-say-what-to-whom-when-for-creating-a-particular-meaning' – that is, not as rules for 'proper' pragmatic behavior but as motivated pragmatic meaning making.

In our work (van Compernolle, 2014; van Compernolle & Henery, 2014), the mediated action perspective has served as a theoretical framework for developing a concept-based approach to instructional pragmatics in formal, structured educational settings (and see Henery, 2014 for an extension of the framework to L2 pragmatic development in study abroad). Our focus has been on guiding learners toward the internalization of patterns of meanings in the sociopragmatic domain through the teaching of the concepts of self-presentation, social distance and power in relation to illustrative pragmalinguistic forms (e.g. the French second-person pronouns *tu* and *vous*). Essentially, the idea is that by focusing on sociopragmatic concepts (i.e. patterns of meaning), learners develop a systematic framework for making pragmalinguistic choices (i.e. patterns of language) as they engage in social actions. And because we focus on patterns of meaning rather than rules, learners gain flexibility in manipulating their pragmatic resources in order to create the meanings they want to create. In an important sense, what we are doing is to make explicit the culturally relevant meanings that can be indexed by pragmatic practices. Whether such meanings, and the patterns of language used to create them, align with social conventions is a separate issue (see below).

Appropriateness and authenticity

A consequence of conceptualizing pragmatics and its development as mediated action is that traditional notions of what counts as appropriate language use need to be rethought in recognition of the ways in which mediating artifacts – especially internalized patterns of meaning – impact upon the motives for engaging in pragmatic actions. Van Compernolle (2014: 29) cites Crystal's (1997) definition of appropriateness as a useful starting point: appropriate language use is 'any use of language considered to be compatible with a given social situation' (Crystal, 1997: 421).

This definition is attractive because it is rather open, and it is flexible enough to allow multiple uses of language to be seen as appropriate rather than relying on a doctrinal interpretation of appropriateness. However, this also creates a challenge in L2 pragmatics inasmuch as appropriateness judgments may be highly variable from one person to the next. Consequently, it becomes difficult to say whether a learner's use of language is appropriate or not (or somewhere in between these two extremes of the appropriateness continuum) unless appropriateness is reduced to simplistic and idealized rules, as is often done in L2 pragmatics research. In an attempt to resolve this issue, van Compernolle (2014), echoing Hymes's (1972) well-known parameters of communicative competence, proposes that appropriateness should be judged in terms of '[the] degree to which a particular instance of language use – whether conventional or unconventional – is interpretable by one's interlocutor(s) or audience given the discourse situation in which language is being used' (van Compernolle, 2014: 40) and '[the] degree to which a particular instance of language use – whether conventional or unconventional – is effective in reflecting and (re)shaping activity types, social relationships and/or social identities' (van Compernolle, 2014: 41). This is an emic, or participant-relevant, perspective on appropriateness, rather than an etic, or externally imposed, yardstick for making appropriateness judgments (see also Dewaele, 2008).

This perspective on appropriateness has interesting consequences for how pragmatic authenticities are evaluated because of the need to understand both learner intentions and what is recognizable in the language. As discussed in the Introduction to this volume (van Compernolle & McGregor; see also Cooper, 1983; MacDonald et al., 2006), the concept of authenticity has been operationalized in two, often opposing, ways in applied linguistics and L2 research. The first, and dominant, perspective referred to by MacDonald et al. (2006) in their extension of Cooper's (1983) work in educational philosophy is *authenticity of correspondence*, that is, use of language that aligns with an external, normative benchmark (e.g. native speaker practices). The second perspective is *authenticity of genesis*, which conceives of language use as being authentically the speaker's, regardless of the degree to which it corresponds to a normative benchmark (e.g. learner language is authentic learner language). Accordingly, pragmatic authenticity may be judged in relation to its correspondence to a set of normative pragmatic practices or in relation to its genesis as a learner's pragmatic practices.

Following MacDonald et al.'s (2006) general argument, we believe that this is an unnecessary, and ultimately counterproductive, dichotomous view of pragmatic authenticity. Instead, we prefer to view authenticity as the dialectical relationship between correspondence and genesis. This entails a need to understand the motives for learner's pragmatic choices (i.e. the patterns of meaning they intend to emulate through the use of particular patterns of language) in relation to some set of recognizable patterns of meaning and language within the second *languaculture* (Agar, 1994: 64) they are appropriating. This view of authenticity complements the concept of appropriateness as proposed by van Compernolle (2014) in two ways. First, it extends the emic perspective because it recognizes that one side of pragmatic authenticity is the genesis of pragmatic language within the learner – authentic learner pragmatic practices need not align with conventions of appropriateness. Secondly, it recognizes the etic, or externally referenced, dimension of authenticity as involving patterns of meaning and language shared by a culture that are available for use.

Sociolinguistic agency

We would like to touch briefly on the concept of sociolinguistic agency, defined by van Compernolle and Williams (2012a: 237) as 'the socioculturally mediated act of recognizing, interpreting, and using the social and symbolic meaning-making possibilities of language'. This notion of agency draws on sociocultural psychology and anthropology (see Ahearn, 2001; Lantolf & Thorne, 2006; van Lier, 2008; Wertsch, 1998) where agency is not seen as co-equivalent with free will or an 'anything goes' type of behavior; rather, agentive human action – including language use – is variably afforded and constrained by available mediational means. Accordingly, and as elaborated in van Compernolle (2014), sociolinguistic agency develops as learners internalize relevant languacultural concepts and their link with sociolinguistic and pragmatic practices, and in the process make these cultural tools their own. The possibility of being a sociolinguistic agent therefore depends on the qualities of the concepts that a learner has internalized. We extend this argument to note that authenticity of genesis cannot exist without sociolinguistic agency since unagentive actions – including pragmatic behavior – do not originate in the learner but rather in externally referenced rules or norms for acting in the world. Such behavior can certainly be appropriate on a superficial level, but it is, as Vygotsky (1986) would have argued, the result of mindless or non-thoughtful activity and cannot be considered the person's own. We refer the reader to van Compernolle (2014, Chapter 3) for further details, including a conceptualization of internalization as inward growth and personalization, as elaborated by scholars such as Frawley (1997) and Zinchenko (2002), rather than acquisition of ready-made tools.

French *Tu* and *Vous*

As we consider appropriateness and authenticity in the context of learners' sociolinguistic choice between the French second-person pronouns *tu* and *vous*, we must consider the nature of this sociolinguistic choice as understood and documented through the sociolinguistic literature as well as the problems it presents to learners.

In a recent review of *tu/vous* research, Coveney (2010: 127) described these pronouns as 'the most salient of all sociolinguistic phenomena in French'. Early work focused predominately on the expression of power and solidarity (Brown & Gilman, 1960) or social-psychological variables in *tu/vous* preferences (Lambert & Tucker, 1976). Although these first studies have been influential, they have also been critiqued for representing social relationships and identities as inauthentically static and/or without sufficient theoretical explanation of empirical observations. More recently, Morford (1997) has reinvigorated *tu/vous* research from an anthropological perspective, drawing on Silverstein's (e.g. Silverstein, 2003) argument that sociolinguistic phenomena are indexical in two ways: they point to aspects of the social context, including social relationships on the one hand, and to dimensions of the speaker's social identity on the other. Importantly, the indexicality framework conceives of the meaning of *tu/vous* as a dynamic process of semiosis that is contextually contingent and locally emergent (van Compernolle, 2011).

Consider the following example from the French film *Entre les murs* (Cantet, 2008): in a difficult, socio-economically disadvantaged Parisian middle school, students say *tu* to each other, teachers use *tu* toward students and among themselves, but students are expected to say *vous* to teachers. Accordingly, the convention in the school is for students and teachers to express something like solidarity or social-relational equality through *tu* use within their own groups, but to express deference between the groups, with students being positioned as subordinates to their teachers. This code is strictly enforced as well: in one scene, a student, Souleymane, is taken to the head teacher for insubordination, including using *tu* toward his teacher, Monsieur Marin, which is treated as an inappropriate and disrespectful way to speak to a person deserving of respect. Thus, we see that within the space of a single scene of the film the pronoun *tu* has at least three different contextually contingent and emergent meanings: it expresses (1) solidarity and/or 'social sameness' (i.e. between students or among teachers); (2) power over a person of 'lower' social standing (i.e. a teacher to a student); and (3) impoliteness, disrespect and insubordination (i.e. a student to a teacher). *Tu*, therefore, has no inherent or stable meaning; it simply indexes aspects of different categories of meanings that are oriented to, and interpreted within, a larger communicative, social, ideological, etc. system of indexical orders (Silverstein, 2003; van Compernolle, 2011).

Quite understandably, then, the French *tu/vous* system is challenging for L2 learners (e.g. Belz & Kinginger, 2002; Dewaele, 2004; Kinginger, 2008; van Compernolle, 2014; van Compernolle *et al.*, 2011). Indeed, while many pedagogical materials at first present *tu* and *vous* as straightforwardly expressing familiarity and politeness (van Compernolle, 2010, 2014), learners often report perceiving the system as increasingly difficult as they gain experience in a greater number and range of novel social-interactive contexts, many of which are ambiguous (Dewaele & Planchenault, 2006). It seems that L2 development in the domain of *tu/vous* is marked by a growing appreciation for the complexity and ambiguity of the second-person address system. Elsewhere, Dewaele (2004) has used the metaphor of a 'sociolinguistic tightrope' in reference to the difficulties that learners and native speakers alike experience at times when choosing between the two pronouns.

Context of the Research and Methods

This chapter draws data from a larger project in which an adaptation of van Compernolle's (2014) sociocultural theory framework for L2 instructional pragmatics was integrated into a second-semester US university French classroom (we will refer to the class simply as 'French 2'). We have reported our general findings in a previous publication (van Compernolle & Henery, 2014), so they will not be repeated here. Instead, we focus on some of the theoretical and methodological issues surrounding judgments of the appropriateness and authenticity of learners' pragmatics choices in one type of task used in the study: computer-mediated SISs. In what follows, we present a brief overview of the research design of the study and data collection, a description of the computer-mediated SISs and a brief sketch of our approach to data analysis.

Overview of the research design and data collection

Our study was conducted over the course of a regular 16-week academic term in a French 2 class taught by Mrs Hanks (a pseudonym). We focused on teaching the concepts of self-presentation, social distance and power in relation to the French second-person pronouns *tu* and *vous*. We used the concept-based pedagogical materials developed by van Compernolle (2014), including several pedagogical diagrams intended to serve as visual shorthand devices that capture the essential characteristics of the concepts in relation to relevant pragmatic choices (e.g. *tu* versus *vous*) (see Figures 2.2–2.4).

The term was divided into four parts for data collection purposes: a pre-enrichment period (i.e. prior to pedagogical intervention), two enrichment periods (i.e. enrichment 1 and 2), and a post-enrichment period. Each period involved several different tasks, outlined in Table 2.1. We will forego detailed descriptions of each of these tasks and refer the reader to our previous publication for more information (van Compernolle & Henery, 2014). Briefly put, our study involved the collection of a variety of types of data aiming to tap into learners' conceptual knowledge of *tu/vous* practices (i.e. language awareness questionnaires, concept reflections), strategies for making appropriate *tu/vous* choices (i.e. appropriateness judgments tasks), classroom interactions

Figure 2.2 Diagram for self-presentation

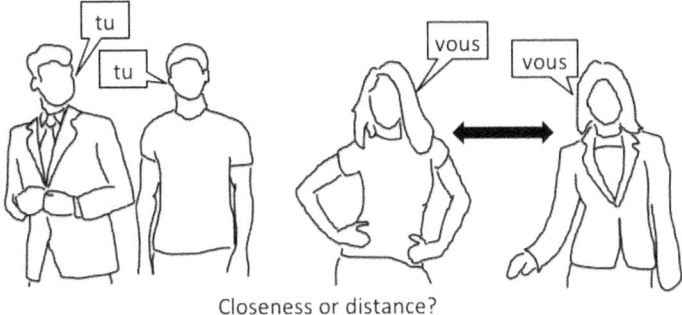

Closeness or distance?

Figure 2.3 Diagram for social distance

Relative status?

Figure 2.4 Diagram for power

(i.e. instructional conversations) in which concepts and other tasks were discussed and feedback provided by Mrs Hanks, and use of *tu* and *vous* in communication (i.e. scenarios). In the following sections, we will discuss the specific use of computer-mediated SISs, which is the focus of the chapter.

Computer-mediated strategic interaction scenarios

SISs (Di Pietro, 1987) involve communicative interaction in a fictional situation in which students are assigned roles with particular agendas that are in conflict in some way with the agendas of their interlocutors. (Roles are not shared in advance of the scenario performance, so students are not aware of the conflicts until it becomes relevant in the interaction.) For instance, one scenario from our study involved two friends planning a short trip to Montreal, and the goal was to outline an itinerary, which involved compromising certain preferences for site seeing and other activities. The tasks are

Table 2.1 Outline of research design

Period	Weeks	Tasks
Pre-enrichment	3–4	• Language awareness questionnaire • Appropriateness judgment task • Scenarios 1 and 2
Enrichment 1	5–7	• Concept reflection • Instructional conversation • Appropriateness judgment task • Instructional conversation • Scenarios 3 and 4
Enrichment 2	8–10	• Concept reflection • Instructional conversation • Appropriateness judgment task • Instructional conversation • Scenarios 5 and 6
Post-enrichment	11–12	• Language awareness questionnaire • Appropriateness judgment task • Scenarios 7 and 8

designed in three parts. First, there is a planning stage in which learners reflect on the kind of language they might need or want to use in the scenario. Secondly, there is the performance of the scenario (i.e. communicative interaction). And thirdly, there is a debriefing stage in which learners can discuss and reflect on the performance. Such scenarios were used previously in van Compernolle's (2014) research as a way of promoting the growth of pragmalinguistic features of French in the context of teacher–learner interaction, focusing principally on the planning and performance stages.

In our study, we adapted these tasks for use in the classroom, which involved two principal modifications of the procedures outlined in van Compernolle (2014). First, the tasks were conducted online rather than face-to-face. Secondly, scenarios were performed between students rather than between a learner and a tutor. The planning- and debriefing-stage reflections were completed via Blackboard, and the performance stage took place via Google Chat, a synchronous computer-mediated communication (SCMC) application that is freely available with a Google account. The rationale for using SCMC rather than face-to-face interaction was related to efficiency – namely, all pairs (and one group of three students) were able to participate simultaneously during a single course meeting and simply copy and paste the SCMC transcript into an email to their teacher once they had completed the task. It would not have been possible to assign as many face-to-face scenarios, which would require much more class time than was available. As noted above, eight scenarios were performed during four different periods. Each pair of scenarios included one that took place in a conventionally informal context (e.g. friends talking on the phone) and one that took place in a conventionally formal context (e.g. a job interview). Thus, we expected to elicit different levels of discourse from each scenario in the data collection period, where in one scenario *tu* would likely be preferred and *vous* preferred in the other.

Approach to data analysis

Since our goal in this chapter is to spur discussion of the issue of pragmatic authenticity and its relationship with pragmatics, we approached data analysis from a grounded, or bottom-up, perspective rather than deciding in advance how to code instances of *tu* and *vous* in the scenarios from an etic perspective. In fact, as we will discuss below, we intentionally avoided judgments of appropriateness during the initial phase of data analysis in order to focus more specifically on the issues of authenticity of correspondence and authenticity of genesis. This approach also aligns with the general idea proposed in van Compernolle (2014) of judging appropriateness from a participant-relevant perspective that recognizes the dialectics of communicative intent and interpretation. We therefore included in our analysis pretask planning data (i.e. students' plans for *tu/vous* use and rationales for their choices) as well as students' scenario performances (i.e. use of *tu* and *vous* in SCMC) in order to compare learners' stated communicative intentions and the execution of their communicative practices. As we will explain in greater detail in the analysis, we developed three categories of authenticity: (1) correspondence without genesis; (2) genesis without correspondence; and (3) a dialectic of correspondence and genesis.

Analyses and Findings

We approach the presentation of our findings in a three-tiered fashion in which category definitions, examples and discussion are presented and elaborated in turn, first for the category 'correspondence without genesis', then for 'genesis without correspondence', and lastly for 'the dialectics of correspondence and genesis'. We would like to remind the reader that when we refer to the notion of correspondence, we mean to suggest correspondence to any pattern of meaning in *tu/vous* choice that is recognizable as such. Consequently, correspondence – in our view at least – is not co-equivalent with *convention* or *appropriateness* because pragmatic practices can certainly correspond to unconventional, inappropriate or impolite, yet recognizable, patterns of meaning.

Correspondence without genesis

In our previous research (van Compernolle, 2014; van Compernolle & Henery, 2014; van Compernolle & Williams, 2012a), we have argued that a common finding in L2 pragmatics research is that language learners often approximate patterns of language without sociolinguistic agency. This means, in essence, that they may emulate pragmatic practices without really understanding what they are doing or why. The concept of *correspondence without genesis* therefore refers to a learner's pragmatic behavior that happens to match some recognizable pattern of language but for which the motive does not derive from the learner's own internalized mediational-conceptual system. Thus, correspondence without genesis may result from (a) a lack of knowledge and/or (b) knowledge of rules or 'rules of thumb' (e.g. use *tu* with friends) that externally regulate the learner's behavior but have not been internalized (or personalized; see van Compernolle, 2014) as his or her own. Consequently, we argue that the authenticity of such pragmatic behavior is quite superficial because the learner is simply using L2 resources without the resources having some personally significant meaning for the learner.

A frequent phenomenon in our data is that, prior to the enrichment program, learners tended not to orient to *tu/vous* use as a language feature relevant for discussion in their planning task, but they did sometimes use *tu* and *vous* in ways that aligned with expected social conventions. For example, Rashid noted the following:

> The language I use can show what stage in friendship I think I am with this person. (Rashid)

While Rashid recognized that language might communicate information about his relationship with his interlocutor, he did not note any specific practices. Such was also the case in van Compernolle's (2014) research, which included more in-depth interview-style planning phases: learners often displayed some general orientation to more 'informal' or more 'formal' language, but they were unaware of specific L2 practices that would accomplish their goals. Nonetheless, as we see in Excerpt 2.1, Rashid did indeed use *tu* in a way that corresponded to a recognizable pattern (i.e. young age peers, friends, classmates, etc. tend to use *tu* with each other). We note that Rashid also used *vous* once in the interaction (not shown here), which is a common type of pragmatic gaff among students (Belz & Kinginger, 2002; van Compernolle *et al.*, 2011). We therefore conclude that, although Rashid's pragmatic behavior more or less corresponded to a recognizable pattern of language, his motive was probably not derived from much more than a learned 'rule' for *tu* use with friends, a point we explore in the next example.

Excerpt 2.1

1 **Rashid:** Ok. Let's start.
2 Bonjour Sally!
    Hi Sally!

3		Est-que tu aimes CMU?
		Do you [T] like CMU?
4	**Sally:**	Bonjour!
		Hello!
5		Oui, je l'aime!
		Yes, I like it!
6		mais il est tres different
		but it's very different
7	**Rashid:**	Oui, je sais.
		Yes, I know.
8		Quelle difference? Qu'est-ce qu'il y a sur tu campus en France.
		What difference? What is there on your [T] campus in France?

As we have pointed out elsewhere (van Compernolle, 2010, 2014; van Compernolle & Henery, 2014), pedagogical materials typically present lists of rules of thumb that are to guide learners' choice of *tu* and *vous* according to very specific categories of persons (e.g. use *tu* with friends; use *vous* with a person to whom you owe respect). Although they are not incorrect, van Compernolle and Williams (2012b) have characterized such rules of thumb as 'narrowly empirical representations of abstracted language use' (van Compernolle & Williams, 2012b: 185) that tend to 'become confused with invariable rules (e.g. a deterministic "either/or" application of a rule) and, thus, are detached from their probabilistic underpinnings, as well as any notion of the meanings created through their use' (van Compernolle & Williams, 2012b: 186). Accordingly, following a rule of thumb, it is argued, lacks agency because it is not thoughtful or meaning based, and hence the choice to use *tu* or *vous* derives from something external to the learner. Therefore, while a choice may correspond to a recognizable pattern of language, its genesis is not in the learner, but rather in an external rule of thumb.

We see this in the following example, in which Virginia was playing the role of a student applying for a work-study program in France and who would be speaking with the program's director over the telephone.

> Using the vous form would show respect to the program director and make me seem more professional and reliable. Using the tu form could be disrespectful if the director is older. (Virginia)

Here, Virginia certainly understood a common rule of thumb: *vous* can be used to show respect. She also remarked that, given the program director's age status (i.e. older than Virginia), *tu* would be disrespectful. The problem with this knowledge is not that it is categorically wrong, but rather it does not point to a more systematic understanding of the underlying principles (e.g. creating closeness or distance, and how degrees of social distance are in turn interpreted). The reader will note that neither *tu* nor *vous* is inherently respectful or disrespectful; rather, conceptual categories of meaning such as distance (*vous*) and closeness (*tu*) are variably interpreted as more or less respectful, polite, friendly, etc. depending on the context and interlocutor relationship qualities.

In any event, as we see in Excerpt 2.2, Virginia's pragmatic behavior certainly corresponded to the recognizable, and expected, pattern of language that the rule of thumb happened to align with. However, and this should be emphasized, because of her stated rationale for using *vous* in the planning stage, we cannot say that Virginia demonstrated authenticity of genesis.

Excerpt 2.2

1 **Lucas:** Bonjour Virginia. Comment allez-vous?
Hello Virginia. How are you? [V]
2 **Virginia:** Bonjour! Je suis bien. Et vous?
Hello! I'm well. And you? [V]
3 **Lucas:** Tres bien. Quand est-ce que vous avez une heure ou une heure et demie sur le semain?
Very well. When do you [V] have an hour or an hour and a half this week?
4 **Virginia:** Je suis libre de dix heures du matin a un heure de l'apres-midi. Est-ce que vous avez besoin de parler avec moi?
I'm free from 10 o'clock in the morning until 1 in the afternoon. Do you [V] need to talk to me?
5 **Lucas:** Je suis libre lundi
I'm free Monday.
6 Oui, oui, je voudrais avoir une interview officielle.
Yes, yes, I'd like to have an official interview
7 **Virginia:** Nous n'avon assez de temp lundi. Pouvez-vous retrouver mardi du deux heures a cinq heures?
We don't have enough time Monday. Can you [V] meet Tuesday from 2 o'clock to 5 o'clock?

We would like to acknowledge at this point a potential weakness in our argumentation regarding correspondence without genesis. It is certainly often difficult to say if learners were not operating with an internalized/

personalized conceptual system that mediated their choices or if they simply happened not to explain their rationales in a verbose manner in the planning task. It could be the case that, as concepts are internalized, learners may not happen to verbalize their content at all times. However, other research (e.g. van Compernolle, 2014) has shown that learners often start out relying heavily on rules of thumb that enable them to perform in expected ways before they develop a deeper, more systematic understanding of underlying principles that they make their own, and hence develop their sociolinguistic agency.

Genesis without correspondence

Our second category – *genesis without correspondence* – involves authenticity in the sense that a learner's use of *tu/vous* derives from his or her own sociolinguistic agency but which does not match, or approximate, a recognizable pattern of language. In other words, there is some mismatch between what the learner intends to do and how the learner's use of language would likely be interpreted in the situation. As mentioned earlier, one common example cited in the literature is the overreliance on using *vous* as the so-called 'polite' form of address with age-peers and potential friends among university-aged students (e.g. Belz & Kinginger, 2002; van Compernolle, 2014). Contrary to learners' internalized conceptual system in which *vous* indexes politeness and respect, in such instances it is often perceived as inappropriate, or even rude, because *vous* introduces an unnecessary and undesirable degree of social distance between interlocutors who are expected to share a sense of solidarity. In our data, we also observed examples of students attempting to use the concept of social distance as a justification for using *tu* to create closeness in contexts in which the interpretation of *tu* would more likely be seen as an extension of power. We note, however, that because of the rather unambiguous nature of the scenarios in our study, very few examples were found in our data.

For instance, in the following scenario involving a French travel agent and an American student planning a trip to Paris, Adan (the travel agent) noted in his plan that he would use *tu* to create closeness, but that *vous* was also a viable option as a display of his professionalism:

> This could go either way as I want myself to appear friendly and close in age to the student to appeal to her better side using tu to close the social distance. however, our relationship is strictly professional and I could also use vous to express my professionalism. (Adan, Time 4, Travel agent scenario plan)

We note here that Adan's orientation to the scenario certainly derives from his internalized mediational-conceptual system, hence authenticity of genesis, but the use of *tu* in this context would not likely map onto his intended pattern of meaning (i.e. social closeness). Instead, the use of *tu* by a service employee to a client would typically be seen as rude or condescending, and hence there is a lack of authenticity of correspondence. It is worth noting, however, that Adan did indeed recognize the possibility of using *vous*, and as we pointed out in a previous publication (van Compernolle & Henery, 2014), he was sensitive to his interlocutor's, Katie, use of *vous*, switching from *tu* to *vous* in the interaction in order to establish a symmetrical *vous–vous* relationship with Katie, which was maintained for the remainder of the scenario. This is shown in Excerpt 2.3.

Excerpt 2.3

1 **Adan:** Bonjour Katie, qu'est ce que je peux t'aider?
              Hello Katie, what can I help you [T] with?
2 **Katie:** Je voudrais une salle pas cher a Paris...
              quelles sont vos suggestions? C'est pour moi et une amie.
              I would like an inexpensive room in Paris...
              what are your [V] suggestions? It's for me and a friend.
   ((5 lines not shown where Adan lists hotel options))
3 **Adan:** Quel chambre voulez vous
              Which room would you [V] like?

Our evaluation of Adan's example is somewhat mixed. We note that his original plan fitted into our concept of genesis without correspondence, but he recognized an alternative, and one that did correspond to a recognizable pattern of meaning (using *vous* reciprocally), and it was this pattern of language that he adopted once his interlocutor used *vous*, in contrast to Adan's initial use of *tu*. However, his motive for using *vous*, while certainly corresponding to expectations, was not clearly derived from his personal preference: it was his second choice, for one thing, and we also note that his phrasing 'I could use vous' is hedged, indicating some hesitation here.

A second example is shown below. Carly was playing the role of an employer who was arranging an interview with a job candidate. In her plan, she opted to use *tu*, which is certainly unconventional, but her reasoning shows that this choice was guided by her conceptual knowledge. However, in this case, Carly was misguided: while *tu* use would certainly put her (the employer) in a position of authority over her interlocutor (the job candidate), her caveat that this would not be disrespectful does not correspond to a recognizable pattern of meaning in this kind of context.

I will use 'tu' when addressing the other person. This will put me in a position of authority without being disrespectful. (Carly)

We would like to note, however, that Carly never actually used *tu* in her scenario performance; rather, she maintained a reciprocal *vous* relationship with her interlocutor despite her stated plan to create a power hierarchy.

An interesting point to make here is that genesis without correspondence may be a necessary part of the developmental process as learners' understandings of rules of thumb are destabilized. As noted above with reference to correspondence without genesis, learners are often able to perform in pragmatically acceptable ways without having developed a systematic, personalized conceptual-mediational system. However, following the sociocultural observation that development is nonlinear, dynamic and revolutionary (Lantolf & Thorne, 2006), it is not surprising that, as learners begin to internalize conceptual categories of meaning, their performances become destabilized. This is because they are appropriating new mediational means, but this takes time, and during the process it is understandable that they would happen to get things wrong from time to time. It other words, we believe that, at least under certain circumstances (e.g. concept-based pedagogical intervention), genesis without correspondence may in fact point to the development-in-progress of a conceptual-mediational system.

Dialectics of correspondence and genesis

Our final category refers to a dialectic perspective on authenticities of correspondence and genesis. By this we mean overcoming the potential tension between favoring one or the other aspect of authenticity in order to view them as an integral whole (MacDonald *et al.*, 2006; van Compernolle & McGregor, this volume). In practical terms, this means that a learner's pragmatic behavior corresponds to some recognizable pattern of meaning and, at the same time, derives from his or her sociolinguistic agency. Although the two examples from our data presented here focus on what would be typically evaluated as conventionally appropriate pragmatic behavior, we hasten to remind the reader that our view of authenticity is not coequivalent with 'pragmatic convention' or anything like expected appropriate behavior. Unexpected, even impolite, pragmatic behaviors can certainly be authentic insofar as they correspond to a recognizable pattern of meaning (e.g. intentional impoliteness) and have their genesis in the learner's internalized conceptual-mediational system (i.e. agency). We simply did not observe this unexpected behavior in our data (but see van Compernolle, 2014; van Compernolle & Williams, 2012a, which we discuss below). Our data do, however, include examples that feature more expected behavior.

Our first example is from Virginia, who was adopting the role of a student traveler calling a French travel agent in Paris. In the planning stage, she opted to use *vous* with the travel agent in order to present 'a professional distance' and to avoid 'a power hierarchy' (see below). We note that these comments directly index her developing conceptual system which included the concepts of social distance (i.e. creating distance through *vous*) and power (i.e. maintaining an equal, but distant, relationship through *vous* use). We also believe that Virginia was operating with a personalized concept of distance in this instance that was a synthesis of 'suit-and-tie self-presentation' (i.e. professional) and distant relationships (see also van Compernolle & Kinginger, 2013). This evidence points to Virginia's developing sociolinguistic agency, and hence authenticity of genesis. It is also important to note that her plan to use *vous*, as well as her explanation of her motive for this choice, corresponds to a recognizable pattern of meaning and language use in customer–employee interaction (i.e. reciprocal *vous* use to establish and maintain a distant but mutually respectful relationship), and that the plan was carried out in the performance (Excerpt 2.4) in an expected way. Accordingly, we argue, Virginia's thinking about and performance of *tu/vous* pragmatics in this instance

Excerpt 2.4

1 **Virginia:** Scenario B
2 **Lucas:** Allo?
  Hello?
3 **Virginia:** Bonjour! Je voudrais un hotel por deux personnes
  a Paris por dix jours.
  Hello! I'd like a hotel for two people
  in Paris for 10 days.
4 **Lucas:** Tres bien mademoiselle. J'ai une hotel pour
  60€ cette soir dans Quartier Latin.
  Very well ma'am. I have a hotel for
  60€ this evening in the Latin Quarter.
6 **Virginia:** Est-ce que vous avez un endroit moins cher?
  Do you [V] have a less expensive place?
7 **Lucas:** J'ai une hotel pour 45€ cette soir sur le côté nord de paris.
  I have a hotel for 45€ this evening on the north side of Paris.
8 **Virginia:** C'est bien!
  That's great!
9 **Lucas:** Tres bien madameoiselle, je reserverai vos chamber.
  Very well ma'am. I'll reserve your [V] room.

Table 2.2 Katie's planning responses

Relationship	Self-presentation	Language
They are close enough friends that they have lunch together, definitely a 't-shirt and jeans' equal power relationship.	I'm going to present myself casually using *tu* because of the reasons stated above.	It can show how close a relationship the two people have and what kind of situation they are in.

derived from the dialectic relationship between authenticities of correspondence and genesis.

> I would use the vous form to keep myself at a professional distance and not establish a power hierarchy. (Virginia's plan)

Similarly, Katie's plan and performance in a scenario in which she was inviting a friend to go to lunch demonstrates the dialectics of correspondence and genesis in pragmatic authenticity. In her plan (Table 2.2), Katie centered her explanations of her choice to use *tu* around recognizable patterns of meaning embodied in the concepts she was appropriating (i.e. self-presentation,

Excerpt 2.5

1 **Katie:** Bonjour!
Hello!
2 **Adan:** Bonjour
Hello
3 **Katie:** est-ce que tu es toujours libre de se reunir pour le dejeuner? a midi?
are you [T] still free to meet for lunch?
at noon?
4 **Adan:** Oui je pense
mais je suis très occupe aussi
parce que j'ai un examan demain et je veux étudier
a la bibliothèque audjord'hui
Yes, I think so
but I'm very busy too
because I have an exam and I want to study
at the library today
5 **Katie:** Genial! A quelle heure est-ce que tu es tres occupe?
Je ne suis pas occupe avant tres heures de l'apres midi
Great! What time are you [T] very busy?
I'm not busy until 3 o'clock in the afternoon

social closeness and equal power). We note that this is also authenticity of genesis because Katie was drawing on her understanding of the social and symbolic meaning-making potential of *tu* – that is, aspects of her sociolinguistic agency. Katie's performance (Excerpt 2.5), where she used *tu* systematically with her interlocutor, shows that she was able to follow through with her stated plan.

As noted earlier, our conception of the dialectic relationship between authenticity of correspondence and authenticity of genesis does not refer specifically to expected, conventionally appropriate or polite pragmatic behaviors. Rather, authenticity is simply about pragmatic behaviors corresponding to some recognizable pattern of meaning, whether polite or impolite, conventional or unconventional, and that pragmatic choices derive from the learner's sociolinguistic agency. To illustrate this point, we have excerpted a portion of an interaction between two intermediate-level US university learners of French, Casey and Joan, which was published in van Compernolle and Williams (2012a) (Excerpt 2.6).

Excerpt 2.6 (van Compernolle & Williams, 2012a: 241)

Casey: Alles dans le chambre de fumes
Go to the smoking section
Joan: Pas!
No!
je ne veux pas
I don't want to
Casey: et ne parle pas avec moi sauf si tu utilises 'vous'!!!
and don't talk to me unless you use vous [you-formal]

Here, Casey and Joan were having a (playful) argument in their role play as a restaurant manager (Casey) and a server (Joan), who was smoking in the restaurant's non-smoking area. Casey instructed Joan to move to the smoking section, but Joan refused. In response to this insubordinate behavior, Casey reprimanded Joan, stating that Joan was not allowed to speak to Casey unless she used *vous*. The authors note that Casey continued to use *tu* with Joan, but expected *vous* in return, a type of impolite behavior that demonstrated Casey's 'understanding of the roles the pronouns [*tu*] and [*vous*] play in extending constructs of power' (van Compernolle & Williams, 2012a: 241). Through her use of *tu* and demand for *vous*, Casey positioned herself above Joan in an explicit, and unexpected, manner, and this would be the recognizable pattern of meaning in an employee–employer interaction. In short, this example illustrates how authenticity – as we conceived of the concept – is independent of whether a particular pragmatic behavior is expected, normative or conventionally appropriate.

Discussion and Conclusion

In this chapter, we have examined the notion of authenticity as it relates to correspondence to recognizable patterns of meaning and language, on the one hand, and genesis in the learner's conceptual-mediational system, on the other. The specific focus of our analysis was on French language learners' planning and use of the second-person pronouns *tu* and *vous* in computer-mediated strategic interactions scenarios (SISs). We identified and discussed three categories of authenticity: correspondence without genesis, genesis without correspondence, and a dialectical relationship of correspondence and genesis. Briefly put, while the first two categories include important aspects of authenticity – either in terms of corresponding to recognizable patterns or generating within the learner – we argue that authenticity ought to be evaluated in relation to the extent that correspondence and genesis form an integral whole.

Although we have more or less eschewed explicit judgments of appropriateness in this chapter, we turn now to a brief discussion of this important concept. As noted earlier, our perspective on appropriateness (van Compernolle, 2014) differs from common or traditional conceptualizations in the L2 pragmatics literature. Namely, we do not see appropriateness as a shorthand device for describing idealized conventions for polite behavior, community-wide normative behavior, and so on – that is, as a substitute for saying 'the right or proper way' to behave. Rather, appropriateness is simply about the degree to which a particular use of language is compatible with its context of use (Crystal, 1997). And because contexts involve people, their relationships and their goals for interactions, appropriateness cannot be judged on the basis of idealized pragmatic conventions linked to static conceptions of context as the physical situation in which one is communicating. Instead, we must recognize that what is compatible with a given context depends on speaker intention and interlocutor interpretation, independent of any notion of polite, proper, conventional, etc. language.

As we have shown in our data analysis, our students tended to perform in more or less conventional ways. However, we do not believe that all of these examples could be evaluated as appropriate because they were not authentic in terms of correspondence and genesis. For example, Rashid's lack of planning but conventional use of *tu* with an age-peer (see *Correspondence without genesis*), could be seen as lacking appropriateness because he simply used a tool (*tu*) without understanding the situation, having an intent, and so on. Likewise, Adan's unconventional plan to use *tu* to create social closeness with a customer (see *Genesis without correspondence*) could be judged as inappropriate not only because *tu* would generally be interpreted as impolite in this situation, but because his understanding of its meaning potential, and thus his intent, did not actually match the situation. Thus, we argue that appropriateness and authenticity – seen as a dialectic of correspondence and genesis – are integrally related. Appropriateness depends on authenticity, and authenticity depends on a learner's orientation to, and intentions for, using language in a way that is recognizable in a particular situation. We note here that what is recognizable is so precisely because it is compatible with a given situation. Accordingly, while appropriateness and authenticity are not the same, neither is independent of the other because they are linked through the concept of recognizable and contextually compatible patterns of meaning and language. This is why van Compernolle and Williams (2012a) present Casey's demand for *vous* while using *tu* with her employee as appropriate (see above): Casey's intention, her practice and the effect it had on the situation and her interlocutor were all recognizable as something a boss could do in order to correct the behavior of an insubordinate employee, and hence Casey's pragmatic behavior can be seen as compatible with that context, even if it was 'impolite'.

We recognize that our study is limited in scope since we have focused only on a limited number of examples from our previous research (e.g. van Compernolle & Henery, 2014; van Compernolle & Williams, 2012a). This is especially true since the study was not originally designed as an exploration of authenticity. Nonetheless, we believe that the examples presented above are sufficient for stimulating further discussion in the field of L2 pragmatics in particular and in L2 development more generally. We agree with MacDonald *et al.* (2006) that authenticity needs to be a more central concept in applied linguistics, and one that is not limited to discussions of 'authentic materials' (e.g. using movies or newspaper articles) in pedagogy (see van Compernolle & McGregor, this volume). We also agree with these authors that the field needs to overcome one-sided perspectives on authenticity that focus solely on correspondence or genesis. We hope that the preliminary arguments laid out in our chapter regarding authenticity and its relationship with appropriateness will be taken up in future scholarship, which has the potential to provide much needed insight into L2 (pragmatic) development and pedagogy.

Note

(1) It is beyond the scope of this chapter to delve into the details of concept-based instruction, but it is important to recognize two sources of inspiration for the approach. The first is the work of Galperin (1989, 1992), one of Vygotsky's most important pedagogical interpreters, and the second is the work of Davydov (2004), one of Galperin's students. Galperin and Davydov worked in Soviet schools developing Vygotskian approaches to education through the teaching of scientific concepts, and their work has had an important influence on the ways in which concept-based instruction has been conceptualized and carried out in L2 instructional contexts in the West. The reader is referred to Lantolf and Thorne (2006) and Lantolf and Poehner (2014) for more discussion.

References

Agar, M. (1994) *Culture Shock: Understanding the Culture of Conversation.* New York: Morrow.
Ahearn, L. (2001) Language and agency. *Annual Review of Anthropology* 30, 109–137.
Bardovi-Harlig, K. (2013) Developing L2 pragmatics. *Language Learning* 63 (Suppl. 1), 68–86.
Belz, J. and Kinginger, C. (2002) The cross-linguistic development of address form use in telecollaborative language learning: Two case studies. *Canadian Modern Language Review* 59, 189–214.
Brown, R. and Gilman, A. (1960) The pronouns of power and solidarity. In T. Sebeok (ed.) *Style in Language* (pp. 253–276). Cambridge, MA: MIT Press.
Cantet, L. (ed.) (2008) *Entre les Murs* [film]. Paris: Haut et Court.
Cooper, D.E. (1983) *Authenticity and Learning: Nietzsche's Educational Philosophy.* London: Routledge and Keagan Paul.
Coveney, A. (2010) *Vouvoiement* and *tutoiement*: Sociolinguistic reflections. *Journal of French Language Studies* 20, 127–150.
Crystal, D. (1997) *The Cambridge Encyclopedia of Language* (2nd edn). Cambridge: Cambridge University Press.
Davydov, V.V. (2004) *Problems of Developmental Instruction: A Theoretical and Experimental Psychological Study* (trans. P. Moxay). Moscow: Akademyia Press.
Dewaele, J.-M. (2004) *Vous* or *tu*? Native and non-native speakers of French on a sociolinguistic tightrope. *International Review of Applied Linguistics* 42, 383–402.
Dewaele, J.-M. (2008) Appropriateness in foreign language acquisition and use: Some theoretical, methodological and ethical considerations. In R. Manchón and J. Cenoz (eds) *Doing SLA Research: Theoretical, Methodological, and Ethical Issues. Special Issue of the International Review of Applied Linguistics* 46 (4), 235–255.
Dewaele, J.-M. and Planchenault, G. (2006) 'Dites-moi tu?!' La perception de la difficulté du système des pronoms d'adresse en français ['Say tu to me?!' Perceptions of difficulty in the French system of address pronouns]. In M. Faraco (ed.) *La Classe de Langue: Théories, Méthodes, Pratiques [The Language Classroom: Theories, Methods, Practice]* (pp. 153–171). Aix-en-Provence: Publications de l'Université de Provence.
Di Pietro, R.J. (1987) *Strategic Interaction: Learning Languages Through Scenarios.* Cambridge: Cambridge University Press.
Frawley, W. (1997) *Vygotsky and Cognitive Science. Language and the Unifiation of the Social and Computational Mind.* Cambridge, MA: Harvard University Press.
Galperin, P.I. (1989) Organization of mental activity and the effectiveness of learning. *Soviet Psychology* 27 (3).
Galperin, P.I. (1992) Stage-by-stage formation as a method of psychological investigation. *Journal of Russian and East European Psychology* July/August, 30 (4).
Henery, A. (2014) Interpreting 'real' French: The role of expert mediation in learners' observations, understandings, and use of pragmatic practices while abroad. Doctoral thesis, Carnegie Mellon University, Pittsburgh, PA.
Hymes, D. (1972) Models of the interaction of language and social life. In J.J. Gumperz and D. Hymes (eds) *Directions in Sociolinguistics: The Ethnography of Communication* (pp. 35–71). New York: Holt, Rinehart & Winston.
Kinginger, C. (2008) Language learning in study abroad: Case studies of Americans in France. *Modern Language Journal* 92 (1).
Lambert, W.E. and Tucker, G.R. (1976) *Tu, vous, usted: A Social-psychological Study of Address Patterns.* Rowley, MA: Newbury House.
Lantolf, J.P. and Poehner, M.E. (2014) *Sociocultural Theory and the Pedagogical Imerative in L2 Education.* New York: Routledge.

Lantolf, J.P. and Thorne, S.L. (2006) *Sociocultural Theory and the Genesis of Second Language Development*. Oxford: Oxford University Press.

MacDonald, M.N., Badger, R. and Dasli, M. (2006) Authenticity, culture, and language learning. *Language and Intercultural Communication* 6 (3–4), 250–261.

Morford, J. (1997) Social indexicality in French pronominal address. *Journal of Linguistic Anthropology* 7, 3–37.

Negueruela, E. (2003) A sociocultural approach to teaching and researching second language: Systemic-theoretical instruction and second language development. Unpublished PhD thesis, Pennsylvania State University, University Park, PA.

Silverstein, M. (2003) Indexical order and the dialectics of sociolinguistic life. *Language and Communication* 23, 193–229.

Swain, M., Lapkin, S., Knouzi, I., Suzuki, W. and Brooks, L. (2009) Languaging: University students learn the grammatical concept of voice in French. *Modern Language Journal* 93, 5–29.

van Compernolle, R.A. (2010) Towards a sociolinguistically responsive pedagogy: Teaching second-person address forms in French. *Canadian Modern Language Review* 66, 445–463.

van Compernolle, R.A. (2011) Developing a sociocultural orientation to variation in language. *Language and Communication* 31, 86–94.

van Compernolle, R.A. (2014) *Sociocultural Theory and L2 Instructional Pragmatics*. Bristol: Multilingual Matters.

van Compernolle, R.A. and Henery, A. (2014) Instructed concept appropriation and L2 pragmatic development in the classroom. *Language Learning* 64, 549–578.

van Compernolle, R.A. and Kinginger, C. (2013) Promoting metapragmatic development through assessment in the zone of proximal development. In R.A. van Compernolle and L. Williams (eds) *Sociocultural Theory and Second Language Pedagogy*. Special issue of *Language Teaching Research* 17 (3), 282–302.

van Compernolle, R.A. and Williams, L. (2012a) Reconceptualizing sociolinguistic competence as mediated action: Identity, meaning-making, agency. *Modern Language Journal* 96, 234–250.

van Compernolle, R.A. and Williams, L. (2012b) Teaching, learning, and developing L2 French sociolinguistic competence: A sociocultural perspective. *Applied Linguistics* 33, 184–205.

van Compernolle, R.A., Williams, L. and McCourt, C. (2011) A corpus-driven study of second-person pronoun variation in L2 French synchronous computer-mediated communication. *Intercultural Pragmatics* 8, 67–91.

van Lier, L. (2008) Agency in the classroom. In J.P. Lantolf and M.E. Poehner (eds) *Sociocultural Theory and the Teaching of Second Languages* (pp. 163–186). London: Equinox.

Vygotsky, L.S. (1978) *Mind in Society: The Development of Higher Mental Processes*. Cambridge, MA: Harvard University Press.

Vygotsky, L.S. (1986) *Thought and Language*. Cambridge, MA: MIT Press.

Wertsch, J. (1985) *Vygotsky and the Social Formation of Mind*. Cambridge, MA: Harvard University Press.

Wertsch, J. (1998) *Mind as Action*. Oxford: Oxford University Press.

Zinchenko, V.P. (2002) From classical to organic psychology. *Journal of Russian and East European Psychology* 39, 32–77.

3 Authenticity and Pedagogical Grammar: A Concept-based Approach to Teaching French Auxiliary Verbs

Lawrence Williams

Introduction

This study examines the authenticity of grammar explanations in textbooks designed for beginning learners of French in the United States, focusing specifically on auxiliary verb choice in compound past verbal constructions. The main objective of the analysis presented in this study is to explore one way for learners to be able to engage in authentic meaning-making activity, which does not seem possible if they do not understand the role of the concept of transitivity in French auxiliary verb choice.

For compound past verbal constructions, French has two auxiliary verbs: *avoir* 'to have' and *être* 'to be'. Choosing the appropriate auxiliary verb can become a source of frustration for learners and teachers alike because the so-called 'rules' for auxiliary verb choice are far from systematic. For the most part, and for a number of possible reasons, textbooks designed for US learners of French provide incomplete and/or misleading explanations of auxiliary verb choice. A notable example is the use of mnemonic devices, such as 'DR & MRS VANDERTRAMPP'[1] and the illustration of the house of *être*,[2] which are intended to assist learners in memorizing which lexical verbs 'take' which auxiliary verb in compound past constructions (e.g. the lexical verb *aller* takes *être*).

Although the two aforementioned pedagogical tools – and any accompanying explanations or notes – can provide some guidance to learners, they raise serious concerns regarding the authenticity of correspondence (Cooper, 1983; MacDonald *et al.*, 2006). Their applicability is limited to the structures and discourse provided within each specific textbook. These explanations do not address the authentic meanings of the verbs, but typically provide guidance only in terms of superficial French–English translations where English meanings are highlighted. For example, the verb *sortir* is usually translated as the equivalent of English 'to exit' or 'to go out', an intransitive use of the verb, which takes *être* as an auxiliary verb in compound past constructions. However, the authentic (French) meaning of *sortir* is more conceptual: it entails a person or object moving from the inside of a real or metaphorical container to the outside. This movement can be either uncaused, as in *il est sorti du bâtiment* 'he exited the building', which is intransitive in French and takes *être*, or it can be facilitated, as in *il a sorti la poubelle* 'he took out the trash', which is transitive in French and takes the auxiliary verb *avoir*. In both cases, however, the authentic meaning remains the same at a conceptual level, and the only difference is in how the verb is being used (i.e. intransitive versus transitive), which determines auxiliary verb choice in compound past constructions. It should be noted that in non-compound past constructions there is no morphosyntactic difference between intransitive and transitive uses of such verbs, a fact that is typically not addressed in pedagogical materials.

As a remedy, this study proposes a concept-based approach to teaching French auxiliary verb choice – centered around the concept of transitivity – following the pedagogical framework developed by Galperin (1989, 1992), which has led to a growing body of research in concept-based foreign/second language education (see Lai, 2012; Negueruela, 2003; Negueruela & Lantolf, 2006; van Compernolle, 2012; Williams *et al.*, 2013; Yáñez-Prieto, 2008). Such an approach offers authenticity of correspondence since the concept of transitivity is not only central to gaining control of auxiliary verb choice in French, but it is also a concept that is closely related to other language/communication concepts of French and many other languages. A concept-based approach to teaching/learning French auxiliary verbs also affords learners an authenticity of genesis (Cooper, 1983; MacDonald *et al.*, 2006) since the appropriation of the concept of transitivity enables learners to make authentic meaning(s) rather than being constrained by a partial or inaccurate representation of language structures. This implies that authenticity has its genesis in the learner, not in a 'rule of thumb' represented by an inauthentic mnemonic device or illustration.

In line with Heidegger's writings on authenticity, which have been echoed and redirected by MacDonald *et al.* (2006), among others, this study demonstrates a way to build on each student's knowledge base in order to expand it while at the same time transforming it so that 'existing sets of beliefs and values are restructured and extended rather than torn down root and branch' (MacDonald *et al.*, 2006: 260).

Explanations of French Auxiliary Verb Choice in Selected Textbooks

The analysis in this section offers a detailed description of the presentation of the passé composé (PC) with *avoir* and PC with *être* in various introductory French textbooks published in the United States in 2010 or later. In all, eight textbooks were analyzed, four of which were selected for detailed review. Some of the main features used in explanations of PC are presented together in Tables 3.1 and 3.2 for the sake of comparison. Table 3.1 displays the features found in the textbooks reviewed in this section, and Table 3.2 provides a list of the same features in other introductory textbooks that have not been described in detail in the present study.

In Tables 3.1 and 3.2, there is a clear trend toward providing students with an imprecise rule of thumb that conflates the number of verbs with the frequency of verbs in discourse since the phrases 'most verbs use *avoir* as the auxiliary' and 'a few verbs use *être* as the auxiliary' can be interpreted in two ways (i.e. a decontextualized list of all verbs or a tally of verbs used in a given text or corpus). Thus, if verbs that use *être* as an auxiliary happen to be frequently used in a given text or corpus, the rule of thumb provided by

Table 3.1 Explanations of PC in introductory French textbooks analyzed in this chapter

Textbook feature	T1	T2	T3	T4
Use of 'most verbs/usually' for *avoir* explanation	X	X	X	X
Use of 'some/only a few verbs' for *être* explanation	X	X	X	X
Use of 'motion/movement' for *être* explanation	X	X	X	X
Use of 'state of being' for *être* explanation	X	X		
# of verbs with *être*	15	17	17	17
# of verbs with choice of *avoir* or *être* (student's edn)	0	0	0	1
# of verbs with choice of *avoir* or *être* (teacher's edn)	4	[same]	2	[same]

Table 3.2 Explanations of PC in other introductory French textbooks

Textbook feature	T5	T6	T7	T8
Use of 'most verbs/usually' for *avoir* explanation	X	X	X	X
Use of 'some/only a few verbs' for *être* explanation	X	X	X	X
Use of 'motion/movement' for *être* explanation	X	X	X	X
Use of 'state of being' for *être* explanation				
# of verbs with *être*	14	14	17	17
# of verbs with choice of *avoir* or *être* (student's edn)	1	1	4	0
# of verbs with choice of *avoir* or *être* (teacher's edn)		[same in all]		

textbooks would make no sense to learners. The textbooks reviewed for the present study also demonstrate the consistent use of the rule of thumb suggesting that any 'motion' or 'movement' verb will use *être* as the auxiliary. This explanation is also misleading because there are many lexical verbs that convey or express some type of motion or movement, yet do not use *être* as the auxiliary (e.g. *boire* 'drink', *danser* 'dance', *fuir* 'flee', *gifler* 'slap', *marcher* 'walk', etc.). A comparison of line 3 (motion/movement) and line 4 (state of being) in Tables 3.1 and 3.2 indicates that textbooks focus primarily on motion and movement as a rationale for the use of *être* as an auxiliary, and there is much less emphasis placed on the expression of a 'state of being' as the rationale.

Table 3.3 provides a list of verbs associated with the use of *être* in the eight textbooks reviewed for this study. Although there is a great deal of overall consistency among these textbooks, only four of them provide the same set of verbs. Moreover, this consistency is undermined by the seemingly intentional lack of information provided about these verbs, many of which can use *avoir* or *être* as an auxiliary. As shown in Tables 3.1 and 3.2, four of these textbooks do not explain (in the students' edition) that some verbs can use *avoir* or *être* as an auxiliary, and three of these textbooks only mention one such verb.

Table 3.3 Verbs listed for PC with *être*

Verb	T1	T2	T3	T4	T5	T6	T7	T8	Total
aller 'go'	X	X	X	X	X	X	X	X	8
arriver 'arrive'	X	X	X	X	X	X	X	X	8
décéder 'die'							X		1
descendre 'descend'	X	X	X	X	X	X	X	X	8
devenir 'become'	X	X	X	X			X		5
entrer 'enter'	X	X	X	X	X	X	X	X	8
monter 'go up'	X	X	X	X	X	X	X	X	8
mourir 'die'	X	X	X	X	X	X	X	X	8
naître 'be born'	X	X	X	X	X	X	X	X	8
partir 'leave'	X	X	X	X	X	X	X	X	8
passer 'stop by'		X	X	X	X	X	X	X	7
rentrer '(re)enter'	X	X	X	X	X	X	X	X	8
rester 'remain'	X	X	X	X	X	X	X	X	8
retourner 'return'	X	X	X	X	X	X	X	X	8
revenir 'come back'		X	X	X			X	X	5
sortir 'go out'	X	X	X	X	X	X	X	X	8
tomber 'fall'	X	X	X	X	X	X	X	X	8
venir 'come'	X	X	X	X			X	X	6
Total	15	17	17	17	14	14	17	17	

In the following sections, a review of specific introductory French textbooks is provided as a way to illustrate a lack of uniformity and detail in explanations provided to learners. This critique of textbooks is not intended to be criticism of the authors or publishers. Instead, the objective is to demonstrate that using rules of thumb accompanied by lists of exceptions as a coherent and effective way to explain compound past constructions is actually an impossible task.

Français-Monde (Ariew & Dupuy, 2011)

In this introductory French textbook, examples of the passé composé are first presented in bold in a dialog at the beginning of a section on 'the **passé composé** with **avoir**' (p. 152) in Chapter 5. An explanation of the PC with *avoir* below the dialog includes the following: (1) formation of the PC; (2) negation with the PC; and (3) position of the adverb with the PC. The next set of explanations of PC is found in Chapter 6, which focuses on PC with *être* and includes three sections (including discourse samples and exercises): (1) regular *-re* verbs and the PC of regular *-re* verbs; (2) asking questions in the PC; and (3) the PC with *être*. The initial explanation of PC with *être* in this section of Chapter 6 is the following: 'Most verbs use *avoir* as an auxiliary verb in the *passé composé*, but some use *être*' (p. 177).

In addition to the rules (and examples) provided in the version of the textbook published for students, there are some additional teaching tips in the annotated instructor's edition. One of these is for 'Implementation of verbs conjugated with *être* in the *passé composé* – Memory aids can help students remember these verbs. One such aid is the *maison d'être*: All the verbs using *être* are depicted around a house' (p. 178). After this main explanation of PC on pp. 177–178 of this chapter, some additional information is provided on irregular past participles (p. 184), and students are introduced to pronominal verbs in the PC (structure and agreement) (p. 186).

Since the PC with *avoir* and *être* has been explained in Chapters 5 and 6, respectively, this textbook does not dedicate specific sections to PC in subsequent chapters; however, whenever new verbs (i.e. infinitives) are introduced, there is always a brief mention of how any new verbs would be used in the PC. In Chapter 7, for example, when the verbs *sortir, partir* and *dormir* are presented for the first time, the version of the textbook published specifically for students indicates that 'the verbs *sortir* and *partir* are conjugated with *être*. The verb *dormir* is conjugated with *avoir*' (p. 222). However, in the margin of the annotated instructor's edition, there is a teaching tip in blue font related to auxiliary verb choice for the PC: 'Implementation for the *passé composé* – The verbs *sortir, rentrer, monter,* and *descendre* can also be conjugated with *avoir*, but this textbook does not present those instances' (p. 222).

The only additional information about the PC presented later in this textbook is in Chapter 10, where object pronouns and the PC are the focus of study and practice. Although some information is provided about the PC in Appendix 3, this includes only verb conjugations with a column dedicated to the PC.

En Avant (Anderson *et al.*, 2012)

In this introductory French textbook, information about both auxiliary verbs used for the PC is presented in two different sections of the same chapter (7.3: 206–208; 7.4: 208–211). Before any rules for PC with *avoir* are given, the use of *avoir* as an auxiliary is shown in a brief paragraph followed by some questions that give students an opportunity to explore the forms. Next, some specific rules are provided. The explanation of PC with *avoir* in this textbook also introduces PC structures with negation and provides students with opportunities to negate PC sentences in addition to other types of practice activities.

In the section on PC with *être*, students are introduced to structures with *être* in a brief series of sentences before specific rules are presented. The main problem related to the explanation of PC with *être* provided in this textbook is the lack of any indication that some of the verbs provided in the mnemonic device 'Dr. & Mrs. Vandertrampp' (p. 209) can use *avoir* as an auxiliary, depending on the intended meaning of the lexical verb (which appears in the form of a past participle). However, it is worth noting, for example, that when the verb *sortir* is introduced in an earlier chapter, there is at least a brief mention of the different possible meanings of *sortir*. Nonetheless, there is no attempt made to link the different meanings of a verb like *sortir* to the need to choose *avoir* or *être* as the appropriate auxiliary verb.

Chez Nous (Valdman *et al.*, 2010)

In this textbook, PC with *avoir* and PC with *être* are also presented and explained in different sections of the same chapter. A note to teachers (in blue font) in the annotated instructor's edition suggests the following: 'This topic can be presented inductively in class. Begin by describing your own activities during, for example, the past weekend. Then ask students about their own weekend using yes/no, either/or, and short-answer questions' (p. 196). Such an introduction to the topic would require preparation on the teacher's part since no discourse sample is provided before rules and comments are offered.

PC with *être* is presented as one of the main grammar features in the next lesson (i.e. unit) of Chapter 5. The explanation of PC with *être* offers, among other information, the following: 'To tell what you did in the past, you have already learned that most French verbs form the *passé composé* with the present tense of *avoir*. However, some verbs use the present tense forms of *être* as an auxiliary. These are usually the verbs of motion' (p. 206). The same list of verbs provided by Anderson *et al.* (2012) are given here, albeit in a different order. Nonetheless, a tip for students in the margin states the following: 'The list of verbs conjugated with *être* in the *passé composé* is easy to remember if you use a mnemonic device such as the acronym "Dr & Mrs Vandertrampp" (each letter stands for a verb conjugated with *être*' (p. 206). The suggestion for teachers (in blue font) in the annotated instructor's edition includes the following statement: 'The learning strategy focuses on mnemonic devices: display, explain, and distribute the illustration of the "house of être," included in the [Instructor's Resource Manual]; help students organize the list of verbs according to the "Dr & Mrs Vandertrampp" mnemonic' (p. 206).

In the margin of the annotated instructor's edition, the main suggestion (in blue font) recommends that teachers do the following:

> Point out that verbs that form the *passé composé* with *être* do not take a direct object, only adverbial complements. In fact, if a direct object does follow, the verb *avoir* must be used: *Je suis sorti ce matin* vs. *J'ai sorti le chien*; *Il est monté au bureau* vs. *Il a monté les ordinateurs au bureau*. Also, not all verbs of motion form the *passé composé* with *être*: *J'ai marché une heure*; *Nous avons traversé la rue*; *Tu as quitté l'université?* (p. 206)

Unfortunately, teachers who simply read these particular suggestions out loud in class will be providing misleading information to their students. First, this lesson offers students conflicting information about PC when a direct object is present. If teachers tell their students that verbs using *être* 'do not take a direct object' (p. 206), the students may take this literally and erroneously apply this to pronominal verbs too (since, according to what students have also learned in this lesson, a sentence with a pronominal verb can include a direct object). Secondly, if students were to interpret 'only adverbial complements' to mean that a PC structure formed with *être* will necessarily include an adverbial complement, they would have a skewed understanding of implications related to the absence or presence of adverbial complements. Thirdly, these suggestions (in blue font) in the annotated instructor's edition (p. 206) give the false impression that there are only three exceptions (i.e. *j'ai marché, nous avons traversé* and *tu as quitté*) to this textbook's rule that implies that verbs using *être* to form the PC are 'usually verbs of motion' (p. 206). Since these comments are in the margin of the annotated instructor's edition, teachers will be able to decide on specific wording as they explain how direct objects and adverbial complements can influence the structure of a sentence with PC and as they explain that a rule printed in a textbook (e.g. 'usually verbs of motion') is not necessarily an accurate or authentic representation of the grammar of a language.

Horizons (Manley *et al.*, 2015)

In this textbook, the PC with *avoir* is introduced in the first unit (*Compétence 1*) of Chapter 5 in a table with the title 'Saying what you did'

(p. 184). In addition to some rules provided in a table, there is a checklist of questions (*Pour vérifier*) that students could ask themselves after they have previewed the content at home or once the PC with *avoir* has been explained in class. The second item in this list asks the following questions: 'What verb is usually used as the auxiliary verb? Do you conjugate it?' (p. 184). These particular questions correspond to a specific sentence in the table that introduces PC with *avoir* to the students: 'The auxiliary verb, usually *avoir*, is conjugated' (p. 184). Unfortunately, this statement – and those that are similar in other textbooks – has the potential to be misleading. Even though there are hundreds of French verbs that always use *avoir* to form the PC and few that always use *être*, this does not necessarily mean that in a given text, PC structures formed with *avoir* will always occur more frequently than PC structures formed with *être*.

Another supplement to this lesson is a box of text with grammar-related information (*Note de grammaire*) in the margin next to the table that explains PC with *avoir*. This box includes the following statements: 'Some verbs expressing *going, coming,* and *staying,* such as *aller, sortir, rentrer,* and *rester,* have *être,* not *avoir,* as their auxiliary verb. You will learn about them in the next *Compétence*' (p. 184). The use of three specific English verbs (*going, coming, staying*) here seems to be an attempt to create synonyms for 'verbs of motion/ movement', a phrase that seems to be used in most other textbooks. Unfortunately, the use of these specific English verbs might lead students to anticipate that only the close or seemingly exact French equivalents of these verbs will be presented in the next unit when the PC with *être* is introduced. Moreover, the use of *sortir* and *rentrer* as examples seems problematic since these two verbs can have *avoir* or *être* in PC structures. Likewise, the verb *passer* is introduced in the first two exercises following the rules for PC with *avoir* (in the expression *passer la matinée chez elle/moi* [to spend the morning at her place/my place]); however, there is no indication that the PC structure for this verb can also be formed with *avoir* or *être*.

The PC with *être* is introduced at the beginning of *Compétence* 2 of the same chapter in a table that includes a series of examples followed by a printed dialog that is also available as an audio file. Next, there are a few exercises that provide students with some additional exposure to the PC with *être*; then a formal explanation of the PC with *être* is provided on the third page of this unit in a table with the title 'Telling where you went' (p. 190).

Additional information related to PC structures is also provided in a box (*Note de grammaire*) in the margin: 'Passer takes *être* in the *passé composé* when it means *to pass by. Je suis passé(e) chez toi.* It takes *avoir* when it means *to spend time. J'ai passé la soirée avec mes amis*' (p. 190). In the explanations of PC in this textbook, this is the only verb identified as one that uses *avoir* or *être* in a compound past construction, even though the grammar summary (*Résumé de grammaire*) at the end of the chapter might have been an ideal place to include at least a basic explanation about the need to make a choice between *avoir* or *être* for a specific set of verbs. Instead, only a reminder about *passer* is provided here: '[In the box below] are some verbs that have *être* as their auxiliary verb. Use *être* only when it means *to pass by* and not when it means *to spend time*' (p. 212). Although there are other meanings and expressions associated with the verb *passer*, this reminder to students only happens to include the specific meanings that it is necessary to know in order to be able to complete the exercises provided in this textbook.

Summary

The inconsistencies and lack of information in textbooks for beginning learners of French demonstrate a need to reconsider how auxiliary verb choice is being taught and learned. Although explanations in textbooks provide learners with basic information about auxiliary verb choice, there is a clear pattern to provide students with explanations that include just enough information to allow them to complete the exercises in their textbook (and workbook). Such a model calls into question the authenticity of current textbook explanations of French auxiliary verb choice. One way to reorganize the teaching and learning of French auxiliary verb choice is to establish the *être*-or-*avoir* (as auxiliary) group of verbs as a category in its own right instead of simplifying all verbs into two groups (i.e. *être*-only and *avoir*-only) with various random verbs explained as exceptions in some – very few, in fact – textbooks. The model provided in the next section for teaching and learning French auxiliary verb choice has as its centerpiece the concept of transitivity, since understanding transitivity is the only way for students to determine how to use the French language as a meaning-making system when faced with the *être*-or-*avoir* (as auxiliary) group of verbs.

Creating a Didactic Tool

Concept-based instruction[3] (Galperin, 1989, 1992; see also Lantolf & Thorne, 2006) offers a framework for teaching and learning (grammar, in this case) that is centered around an underlying scientific (theoretical) concept. This contrasts sharply with attempts to create a series of rules and exceptions that represent everyday (spontaneous) concepts, or rules of thumb, as we saw above in the review of the textbook explanations of auxiliary verb choice. Lantolf (2007: 38) – drawing on Vygotsky – offers the following summary of the importance of concepts in language learning:

> This type of highly structured knowledge, or what Vygotsky (1986) refers to as 'scientific concepts', should be the primary focus of classroom instruction. Because of their abstract and coherent properties, control of

scientific concepts leads to the ability to freely and voluntarily use the object of study, in the case at hand, language, in a much wider array of circumstances than is permitted by spontaneous concepts, which are often invisible and closely connected to specific contexts. (Vygotsky, 1986: 148)

It is important to note that the difference between scientific concepts and everyday concepts is not parallel to the distinction made by Vygotsky (1986) between knowledge acquired in educational versus non-educational contexts, respectively, since everyday concepts and scientific concepts can be used in either type of setting. The present study focuses on improving learning (and development) by identifying an everyday concept that can be replaced with a scientific concept for a specific structure in French.

According to the pedagogical framework developed by Galperin (1989, 1992), scientific concepts can be provided to students in a number of different forms that serve as mediational means for promoting development. Galperin's approach, an extension and expansion of earlier work by Vygotsky, is 'based in elaborating the support material and procedures needed to perform a specific task, providing the students with this material, guiding them through learning, and then documenting their progress in solving the tasks' (Arievitch & Haenen, 2005: 159). This pedagogical framework proposes the notion of a cycle with five levels through which learners progress: orienting at a basic level; acting at the material level; acting at the verbal level; acting at the mental level; and orienting at a more advanced level (see Arievitch & Haenen, 2005: 160).

At the end of each cycle, students come to better understand the actions they have learned, because they have internalized verbal generalizations and formed mental images that allow for performing the actions in the abbreviated form. As a result of the activity at the preceding levels, the students become more knowledgeable and come to understand the actions' content in their operative, figurative, verbal, and conceptual dimensions. (Arievitch & Haenen, 2005: 160)

In order for learners to engage in orienting at a basic level, they have to understand why, for example, rules of thumb (along with a list of related exceptions) are inadequate and why gaining an understanding of a scientific concept (e.g. transitivity) will be far more effective. 'First (while orienting at a basic level), students have to understand and accept the motivational and cognitive value of the to-be-acquired knowledge, before the actual appropriation and ability to use it can take place' (Arievitch & Haenen, 2005: 160). Next, learners need some type of representation of the scientific concept such as an image (or a set of images), a diagram or a flowchart that 'reflect[s] the properties and relationships essential for the action' (Arievitch & Haenen, 2005: 161). The third stage in this pedagogical model involves acting at the verbal level, and this could be done through spoken verbalization (i.e. overt speech), written verbalization or computer-mediated verbalization.[4] Regardless of the type of verbalization used, this reflective activity 'pushes learners to represent actions in external speech, which allows learners to generalize the action beyond familiar contexts (i.e. abstraction of the concept as meaning) and to form new psychological functions (i.e. to restructure thinking processes through the concept)' (van Compernolle, 2014: 97). Arievitch and Haenen explain that 'when the action has been developed almost to the point of becoming automatic, there can be a transition to acting mentally, "in the mind"' (Arievitch & Haenen, 2005: 161). At this point in the five-stage cycle, action is abbreviated and 'transformed into a mental phenomenon – a chain of images and concepts. ... [T]he action attains a new form: It becomes a "pure thought"' (Arievitch & Haenen, 2005: 161). The final stage of the cycle is once again orienting activity; however, the orienting has become more advanced since students at this stage of the process have a better retrospective understanding of what they have learned, and they 'are more knowledgeable about [actions they have learned] as the result of prior activities at the preceding levels. ... Putting it somewhat differently, Galperin viewed the ability of looking ahead (orientation) as a precondition to and even a prime aspect of learning' (Arievitch & Haenen, 2005: 161–162). Since the use of a didactic tool and engagement in verbalized reflection are key components of Galperin's model, they are the focus of the pilot study reported on in the remainder of this chapter.

For the present study, a flowchart was selected as the type of learning tool[5] that could most effectively reflect the scientific concept of transitivity, an understanding of which is indispensable for the *être*-or-*avoir* (as auxiliary) group of French verbs. This flowchart (see Figure 3.1) guides learners through a decision-making process with a series of five questions, but it is not necessary to answer all of these questions for every verb. For example, if a learner is trying to determine the appropriate auxiliary for the pronominal use of *précipiter* ('to precipitate'), there is no need to continue past the first question (*Pronominal use of verb?*). The only instance when all the questions must be answered occurs when the learner is trying to determine the appropriate auxiliary for a verb in the *être*-or-*avoir* group, and the only way to make the correct decision is to understand the concept of transitivity.

The only part of Figure 3.1 that may seem quite strange to learners is the third question related to *paraître* ('to appear') and its prefixed forms. A separate question (with a separate list) has been created for this group of verbs since the choice of the auxiliary depends primarily on semantic nuances or, in some cases, a preference for a form that 'sounds' better (e.g. avoiding hiatus between two vowels). In the online version of the *Trésor de la langue française*, for example, there is a note indicating that the use of *être* as the auxiliary of *apparaître* 'to appear' is much more frequent than the use of *avoir*, especially in contemporary texts; however, some authors – not all – use both auxiliaries, in which case *avoir-apparaître* indicates the action of having appeared, and *être-apparaître* indicates the state of being or condition resulting from the action. The point to reinforce here is that the purpose of the task is to allow the students to focus on transitivity without being temporarily distracted by other concepts that will be addressed at a later point in time. In the flowchart developed for the present study, creating a separate question with a separate list of verbs seems to be the only systematic way to account for a group of verbs that (some) authors enjoy using in different ways for primarily stylistic reasons, some of which are closely related to verbal aspect.

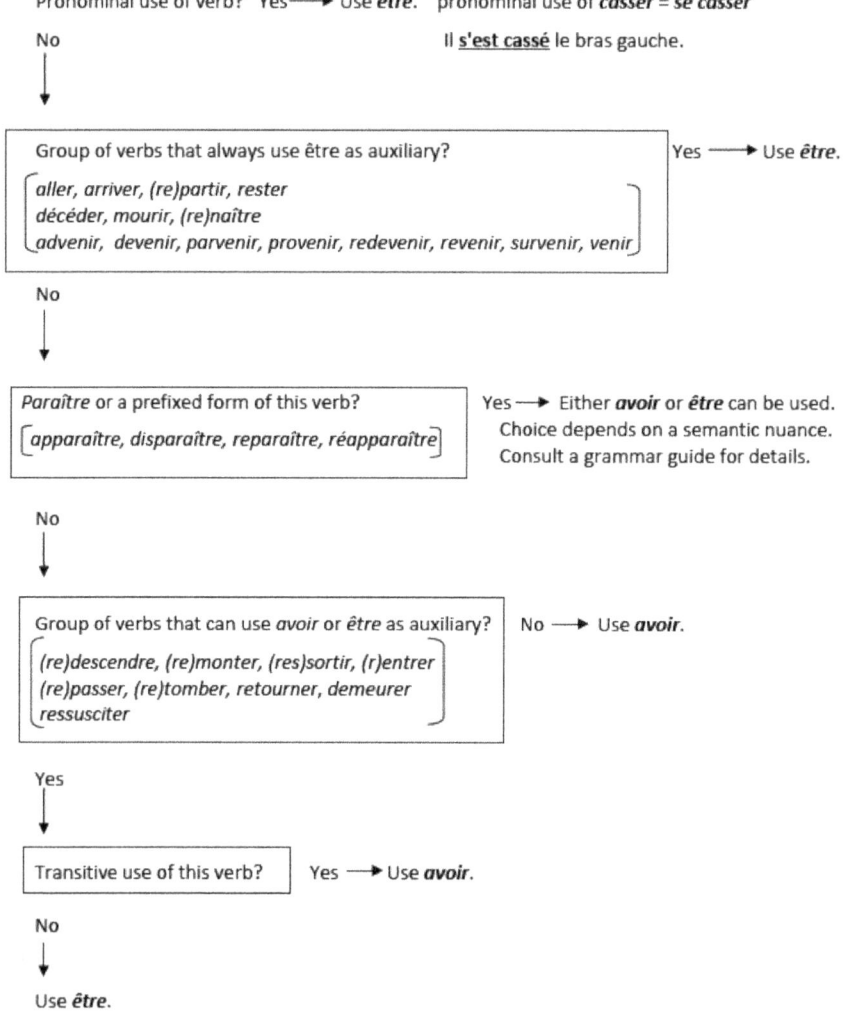

Figure 3.1 Flowchart for auxiliary verb choice in French

Implementing Concept-based Instruction

Participants and procedures

In order to evaluate the didactic tool created for teaching French auxiliary verb choice using concept-based instruction, a pilot study was conducted with 12 participants in their first semester of intermediate (i.e. second-year) French. Auxiliary verb choice had already been covered during their first year of French, so this content was being presented during the second year for review and reinforcement. Several instructors expressed willingness to have their students participate in this pilot study. Eventually, the class with the fewest students was selected in order to have maximum flexibility for scheduling a computer classroom (since not all of them can accommodate larger classes) on the day of the project. The class met for 80 minutes twice a week, which was also preferable to other classes that met three times a week with shorter regularly scheduled class periods.

The steps of the pilot study and the amount of time dedicated to each of these steps are shown in Table 3.4. The review of French auxiliary verb choice was taught by the instructor. Then, Worksheet 1 (see Appendix A) was given to the students as an individual task. The worksheet included different kinds of structures and a range of verbs; it also prompted students to report their level of confidence for each answer (i.e. *être* or *avoir* as the auxiliary verb) and to provide a brief written explanation of their reasoning (i.e. written verbalization). Students who followed the explanations of French auxiliary verb choice typically provided in textbooks would be able to select the correct auxiliary verb for more than half of the items, but not all of them.

During the next step of the pilot study (i.e. the explanation of transitivity and the presentation of the flowchart), students were asked to decide if they would change – without doing so – any of their answers on Worksheet 1 based on the new explanation of French auxiliary choice demonstrated by the flowchart. This part of the task allowed students to see that even if their understanding of French auxiliary verb choice (i.e. based on typical explanations found in textbooks) was complete, the explanations found in textbooks only provide just enough information for students to be able to complete the practice exercises in a specific textbook (or workbook).

Table 3.4 Pilot project details

Step	Minutes	Description
1	10	Review of French AUX choice as (typically) provided in textbooks
2	10	Worksheet 1: French AUX choice, 9 items; confidence level; individual
3	30	Explanation of transitivity and its role in the flowchart (Figure 3.1)
4	30	Worksheet 2: French AUX choice, 10 items; confidence level; chat dyads

In the final part of this pilot study, students completed Worksheet 2 in pairs, and each pair worked in its own live online chat room on the Chatzy[6] website. Since, in the context of the classroom, students often seem to focus on finding each answer quickly in order to complete the task in as little time as possible, each dyad of learners was instructed to agree on each answer before moving to the next item so that they were forced to share their thinking and reasoning with each other (i.e. computer-mediated verbalization). Worksheet 2 featured the verbs *retourner, tomber, passer* and *monter*, all of which are part of the *être*-or-*avoir* group. The decision-making process and the thinking involved in this task required students to go through each part of the flowchart in order to arrive at the last question, which forced them to encounter (and, ideally, discuss) the concept of transitivity with one another in their live chat room.

Results

A vertical (i.e. column) analysis of the results of Worksheet 1 (nine items; see Appendix A) provided in Table 3.5 reveals that Items (C) and (I) were relatively more difficult for these students. The verb in Item (C) on Worksheet 1, *devenir*, was presented as an *être*-only verb in the textbook used for first-year French at the university where this study was conducted; however, given the large transfer student population, it is likely that many students had learned auxiliary verb choice with a different textbook, and it is also quite possible that they had simply not remembered *devenir* as an *être*-only verb. The verb in Item (I) on Worksheet 1, *décéder* ('to die'), is often neglected

Table 3.5 Worksheet 1: Auxiliary verb choice

Student	(A)	(B)	(C)	(D)	(E)	(F)	(G)	(H)	(I)
				(Incorrect answers shaded)					
1	e	a	e	e	a	e	a	e	e
2	e	a	e	a	a	e	a	e	a
3	e	e	a	e	a	a	a	e	e
4	e	a	e	a	e	e	a	e	e
5	e	a	a	a	a	e	e	a	e
6	e	a	a	a	a	e	e	e	a
7	e	a	e	a	a	e	a	e	a
8	e	a	e	a	a	e	a	e	a
9	e	a	a	a	a	e	a	e	e
10	e	a	a	a	a	e	a	e	a
11	a	a	a	a	a	e	a	e	a
12	a	e	a	a	a	a	a	e	e

in textbooks in favor of the synonym *mourir*. A horizontal (i.e. row) analysis of the results in Table 3.5 indicates that Students 3 and 12 struggled considerably with this task. Once again, however, it is impossible to know if their lack of understanding is due to poor memory ability, misleading explanations in their previous textbook(s), or some other mitigating factor particular to the period of the project.

The students' self-reported confidence levels (see Table 3.6) for Worksheet 1 indicate a greater range of means among students than among individual items, which reflects the ability of a mean to absorb and balance out high ratings mixed with low ratings. Moreover, it is important to note that a high confidence level rating or mean does not necessarily correlate with a high score. For example, Student 5 produced the highest confidence level mean (4.6), yet this student's score on the task was one of the lowest of the entire class (see Table 3.7). Nonetheless, the students with the two lowest scores (3 and 12) did indeed self-report the lowest confidence level means of the class (2.0).

A vertical analysis of the scores for Worksheet 2 (10 items; see Appendix B) in Table 3.8 indicates that Items (E) and (F) were relatively more difficult than the other items, with (F) being slightly more challenging (i.e. only two groups selected the correct auxiliary verb). A close reading of the computer-mediated verbalizations of each group showed that, although the students were able to use the flowchart as it was intended to be used, they stumbled when trying to determine the grammatical function of *plus d'un homme* 'more than one man' since they did not recognize this as a direct object of the verb *tomber* (meaning *to seduce* in this context). In other words, once each of these groups had incorrectly decided that *plus d'un homme* was not a noun phrase

Table 3.6 Worksheet 1: Confidence levels

Student	(A)	(B)	(C)	(D)	(E)	(F)	(G)	(H)	(I)	Mean
1	2	2	2	4	2	4	2	2	3	2.6
2	5	4	5	3	3	5	3	5	4	4.1
3	2	2	2	2	2	2	2	2	2	2.0
4	2	4	5	5	4	4	2	2	4	3.6
5	5	5	4	5	5	4	4	4	5	4.6
6	5	4	4	5	3	5	3	3	4	4.0
7	4	4	4	3	5	5	4	4	4	4.1
8	5	5	4	5	2	5	4	5	4	4.3
9	4	3	3	4	5	4	4	4	4	3.9
10	5	5	3	4	4	4	4	5	4	4.2
11	3	3	3	3	3	4	2	2	3	2.9
12	2	2	2	2	2	2	2	2	2	2.0
Mean	3.8	3.7	3.5	3.9	3.5	4.1	3.2	3.5	3.7	

50 Authenticity, Language and Interaction in Second Language Contexts

Table 3.7 Worksheet 1: Scores and confidence level means

Student	Score	Score as %	Conf. Mean
1	7	77.8%	2.6
2	9	100.0%	4.1
3	4	44.4%	2.0
4	7	77.8%	3.6
5	5	55.6%	4.6
6	7	77.8%	4.0
7	9	100.0%	4.1
8	9	100.0%	4.3
9	7	77.8%	3.9
10	8	88.9%	4.2
11	7	77.8%	2.9
12	4	44.4%	2.0

(functioning as a direct object), they incorrectly chose *être* as the auxiliary verb. (Incidentally, *tomber* is one of the verbs presented in textbooks as an *être*-only verb.) Likewise, the students seem to have used the flowchart in an appropriate way for Item (F); however, the chat transcripts revealed specific gaps in their understanding of basic categories of verbs in French (e.g. auxiliary, copular, lexical), which it is necessary to understand for the concept of transitivity.

Table 3.8 Worksheet 2: Auxiliary verb choice

Student	Group	(A)	(B)	(C)	(D)	(E)	(F)	(G)	(H)	(I)	(J)
						(Incorrect answers shaded)					
1	1	e	a	e	a	e	e	a	a	e	a
2	1	e	a	a	a	e	e	a	a	e	a
3	2	a	a	e	a	e	a	e	a	e	a
4	2	a	a	e	a	e	a	e	a	e	a
5	3	e	a	a	a	a	a	a	a	e	a
6	3	e	a	a	a	a	a	a	a	e	a
7	4	e	a	a	a	a	a	a	a	e	a
8	4	e	a	a	a	a	a	a	a	e	a
9	5	e	a	a	a	a	e	a	a	e	a
10	5	e	a	a	a	a	e	a	a	e	a
11	6	a	a	a	a	e	a	a	a	e	a
12	6	a	a	a	a	e	a	a	a	e	a

Additional close reading of the computer-mediated verbalizations of each group revealed that the scores for Item (F) were the result of guessing, an unwillingness to spend much time on certain items, and unfamiliarity with French syntax. This is demonstrated in the brief excerpt between Tom and Sandy (Group 1) reproduced below:

Michael (referring to Item E): im thinking etre for some reason but im not sure
Mary: i think so too
Mary (referring to Item F): same with the next one
Michael: yeah i think so
Mary: cool

The other groups were not all so quick to guess (based on a feeling or some other impression), but this type of exchange is quite prevalent in the transcripts of all the groups in this class. A brief example of this is from Group 2 is shown below:

Julie: I think that C is etre
Mark: Confirmed.
Julie: k

Even though the instructions on Worksheet 2 clearly indicated that the students were supposed to determine *why* they agreed on *être* or *avoir* (after they had actually agreed on one or the other), completing the task as quickly as possible (i.e. to find the answers and submit their work) seems to have become their main priority. In fact, none of the groups reviewed their answers in any kind of substantial or systematic way during the last 10 minutes of the class period; the students chose instead to leave since the assignment had – from their perspective – been completed. This type of situation highlights the need, in some cases, for a teacher or tutor to push 'learners to consider the qualities of the concepts in greater depth and to (re)mediate their understandings of them and of their existing … knowledge and socialization experiences' (van Compernolle, 2014: 109).

A horizontal analysis of Table 3.8 shows that two groups in particular (2 and 6) had relatively more difficulty than the other groups in selecting appropriate auxiliary verbs. It is most likely not a coincidence that one member of each of these groups (Students 3 and 12) also had the lowest score on Worksheet 1, and that these same participants also self-reported the lowest confidence level means of all the students in this class. Nonetheless, some students with relatively low scores on Worksheet 1 (an individual task) showed clear improvement on Worksheet 2 (working in dyads).

Table 3.9 Worksheet 2: Confidence levels

Student	Group	(A)	(B)	(C)	(D)	(E)	(F)	(G)	(H)	(I)	(J)	Mean
1	1	5	4	5	5	4	4	5	4	5	5	4.6
2	1	5	5	5	5	5	5	5	5	5	5	5.0
3	2	4	4	4	4	4	4	4	4	5	4	4.1
4	2	5	5	5	5	5	5	5	5	5	5	5.0
5	3	5	5	3	4	5	5	5	5	5	5	4.7
6	3	5	5	3	3	4	4	4	5	4	4	4.1
7	5	5	5	3	5	4	4	5	5	4	3	4.3
8	5	5	5	4	5	5	4	5	5	5	4	4.7
9	6	3	4	3	4	3	2	3	4	3	5	3.4
10	6	5	5	5	4	4	4	4	4	4	5	4.4
11	7	4	4	4	4	2	4	4	4	4	4	3.8
12	7	4	4	4	4	2	4	4	4	4	4	3.8
Mean		4.5	4.6	3.9	4.3	3.8	3.9	4.4	4.5	4.4	4.4	

The results provided in Tables 3.9 and 3.10 show that all confidence level means except one are very close to 4.0 or higher (out of five) for each learner. From a vertical perspective (Table 3.9), looking at each item, the lowest mean is 3.8; however, the top of the range is only as high as 4.6. A greater range of means among students than among individual items was also found in the results for Worksheet 1, and this once again demonstrates how means for items can absorb high ratings mixed with low ratings. Nonetheless, the range differential is noticeably less for Worksheet 2 than it is for Worksheet 1, which suggests that the students not only have more confidence in themselves, but they are also more confident moving from item to item when different patterns, structures and forms are encountered.

Since one of the best indicators of successfully implementing a new approach accompanied by a new type of learning tool might be the confidence that learners have in understanding how to use this tool, a comparison of learners' confidence level means for Worksheet 1 and Worksheet 2 is provided in Table 3.11. The results in this table suggest that the participants, with the exception of Student 9, benefited from a noticeable increase in confidence during a single class period focused on French auxiliary verb choice. Moreover, between Worksheet 1 and Worksheet 2, a paired-samples *t*-test indicated a statistically significant increase of students' confidence levels, $t(11) = 3.24$, $p < 0.05$, and a d value of 1.09 revealed an effect size that is large (Cohen, 1992).[7]

Although Student 9's overall self-reported level of confidence decreased slightly, this particular student chose seven (out of nine) correct auxiliary verbs on Worksheet 1, and her dyad chose 10 (out of 10) correct auxiliary

Table 3.10 Worksheet 2: Scores and confidence level means

Student	Score (/10)	Score as %	Conf. mean (1–5 scale)
1	8	80.0%	4.6
2	9	90.0%	5.0
3	5	50.0%	4.1
4	5	50.0%	5.0
5	9	90.0%	4.7
6	9	90.0%	4.1
7	9	90.0%	4.3
8	9	90.0%	4.7
9	10	100.0%	3.4
10	10	100.0%	4.4
11	7	70.0%	3.8
12	7	70.0%	3.8

verbs on Worksheet 2. Conversely, Student 3's overall self-reported confidence level means showed the greatest increase among all participants, yet her performance on both tasks resulted in the lowest scores of the class. These apparently conflicting results can be at least partially explained by the decision on the part of many students to finish the tasks quickly and to leave the classroom without undertaking a thorough review of their answers in order to understand why they had chosen a specific auxiliary verb. In many cases, students had encountered problems on some of the first few items of Worksheet 2, and then they had collectively resolved these problems while

Table 3.11 Summary of learners' confidence level means

Student	Worksheet 1	Worksheet 2	Change
1	2.6	4.6	+2.0
2	4.1	5.0	+1.9
3	2.0	4.1	+2.1
4	3.6	5.0	+1.4
5	4.6	4.7	+0.1
6	4.0	4.1	+0.1
7	4.1	4.3	+0.2
8	4.3	4.7	+0.4
9	3.9	3.4	−0.5
10	4.2	4.4	+0.2
11	2.9	3.8	+0.9
12	2.0	3.8	+1.8

discussing subsequent items, yet they never returned to review their answers on any of the items that had proven difficult initially. Such a problem underscores the need for additional time to model the use of the flowchart and to explain the purpose of verbalizations (i.e. as something that is more than just a way to know whether or not someone else agrees with an answer so that the dyad can move on to the next item and complete the task quickly).

Conclusions

The review of textbooks (published in the United States) for beginning learners of French suggests that over time, a great deal of similarity has emerged in explanations of French auxiliary verb choice, most likely because authors compare new editions of textbooks and possibly because textbook reviewers have come to expect things to be explained in certain ways. A lack of authenticity becomes apparent when students are asked to choose auxiliary verbs in samples of discourse that are not taken directly from a textbook (or workbook). Therefore, current explanations of French auxiliary verb choice in introductory textbooks provide a false sense of achievement and confidence in students who believe that they have indeed learned the French auxiliary verb system. Some teachers might find this lack of authenticity to be acceptable if, for example, they do not wish to present a concept that could be perceived as potentially confusing to their students. However, an argument can be made in favor of presenting the concept of transitivity to students at all instructional levels and in many different types of lessons and tasks, as transitivity is a fundamental part of grammar as a meaning-making system, and its scope extends beyond auxiliary verb choice in French.

The learning tool – in the form of a flowchart – proposed in the present study oriented the students in this class toward a perspective of grammar that diverged in many ways from their previous experiences which created a reliance on inaccurate rules of thumb (including exceptions to these rules) and misleading mnemonic devices (e.g. DR. & MRS. VANDERTRAMPP) or diagrams (e.g. the house of *être*). This concept-based model also revealed gaps in the students' understanding of the dynamic nature of grammar and semantics, specifically the notion that the same verb (e.g. *passer*) can have two different functions (i.e. copular or lexical), depending on the meaning that is being conveyed. Nonetheless, the type of pedagogical intervention proposed in the present study is not intended as a one-time experience for learners. Instead, this initial use of a learning tool to represent the concept of transitivity can form the foundation for ongoing development that will occur at a different rate (and in different trajectories) for each learner.

Since the scope of the present study was limited to raising students' awareness of the importance of the concept of transitivity, learning was only measured indirectly. Future research could go further by including an additional step that would require participants to explain how they arrived at choosing one auxiliary instead of another, especially in cases where verbalizations did not include such details. In addition, increasing the longitude of the study would create greater potential for direct measures of learning followed by development since individual participants do not necessarily follow the same trajectory or progress at the same rate.

Although a concept-based approach to learning grammar requires memorization, Negueruela and Lantolf (2006: 98) point out that 'the goal ... is not simply the internalization of concepts, in the banal sense of memorization, but also development of the learner's capacity to use the concepts to mediate (i.e. self-regulate) their language performances'. In foreign/second language education, where learning grammar can easily and inadvertently become an end in and of itself, this is an important reminder that 'the ability to engage in effective communicative (spoken and written) activity where conceptual understanding of grammar in the service of the user's efforts to construct appropriate meaning is the goal of instruction' (Negueruela & Lantolf, 2006: 99). In other words, the objective of learning or memorizing conceptual information, definitions, vocabulary and so on is to develop a systematic orienting basis for using the language learners are studying in creative, meaningful and personally significant ways.

Concept-based instruction offers much more to learners and teachers than a systematic approach to understanding French auxiliary verb choice through the use of a flowchart representing the concept of transitivity. It is fundamentally more authentic in terms of correspondence to 'real' language (i.e. how French actually works) and in terms of genesis: internalizing concepts mediates agency. Consequently, this offers a clear and convincing argument for resituating authenticity at the center of pedagogical materials development and, more globally, as part of the core of foreign/second language education.[8]

Appendix A: Worksheet 1

Auxiliary verb choice in French: *avoir* or *être*

NAME: _____

I. Pierre Lissou
Here are the past participles that you will need: *entré, obtenu, devenu, été, reçu.*
(A) Pierre Lissou _____ (entrer) au bataillon en septembre 2007 à Marseille.
How confident are you that you have chosen the correct auxiliary verb (*avoir* or *être*)?
1–Not at all confident 2–Not really confident 3–Neutral 4–Somewhat confident 5–Very confident
Why did you chose {*avoir/être*}? _____

(B) Au début de l'année 2008, il _____ (obtenir) sa première décoration.
How confident are you that you have chosen the correct auxiliary verb (*avoir* or *être*)?
1–Not at all confident 2–Not really confident 3–Neutral 4–Somewhat confident 5–Very confident
Why did you chose {*avoir/être*}? _____

(C) En juillet 2008, il _____ (devenir) capitaine de la 1re Cie.
How confident are you that you have chosen the correct auxiliary verb (*avoir* or *être*)?
1–Not at all confident 2–Not really confident 3–Neutral 4–Somewhat confident 5–Very confident
Why did you chose {*avoir/être*}? _____

(D) Il _____ (être) muté à Saint-Germain-en-Laye sous le commandement de la 1re Cie.
How confident are you that you have chosen the correct auxiliary verb (*avoir* or *être*)?
1–Not at all confident 2–Not really confident 3–Neutral 4–Somewhat confident 5–Very confident
Why did you chose {*avoir/être*}? _____

(E) Après le commandement d'une année, il _____ (recevoir) la *Médaille du mérite militaire*.
How confident are you that you have chosen the correct auxiliary verb (*avoir* or *être*)?
1–Not at all confident 2–Not really confident 3–Neutral 4–Somewhat confident 5–Very confident
Why did you chose {*avoir/être*}? _____

II. Pierre Mamboundou

Here are the past participles that you will need: *né, passé, rentré, décéder.*

(F) Pierre Mamboundou _____ (naître) le 6 novembre 1946 à Mouila, dans le sud du Gabon.
How confident are you that you have chosen the correct auxiliary verb (*avoir* or *être*)?
1–Not at all confident 2–Not really confident 3–Neutral 4–Somewhat confident 5–Very confident
Why did you chose {*avoir/être*}? _____

(G) Il _____ (passer) toute sa vie politique dans l'opposition.
How confident are you that you have chosen the correct auxiliary verb (*avoir* or *être*)?
1–Not at all confident 2–Not really confident 3–Neutral 4–Somewhat confident 5–Very confident
Why did you chose {*avoir/être*}? _____

(H) En 2010, après un séjour médical en France, il _____
(rentrer) au Gabon pour continuer son combat politique.
How confident are you that you have chosen the correct auxiliary verb (*avoir* or *être*)?
1–Not at all confident 2–Not really confident 3–Neutral 4–Somewhat confident 5–Very confident
Why did you chose {*avoir/être*}? _____

(I) Il _____ (décéder) le 15 octobre 2011.
How confident are you that you have chosen the correct auxiliary verb (*avoir* or *être*)?
1–Not at all confident 2–Not really confident 3–Neutral 4–Somewhat confident 5–Very confident
Why did you chose {*avoir/être*}? _____

Appendix B: Worksheet 2

Auxiliary verb choice in French

NAME: _____

- Choose the appropriate auxiliary verb (*avoir* or *être*) for each sentence below. Here are the past participles you will need: *fracturé, retourné, tombé, passé, monté*.
  In some cases, you may need an extra -*e* or -*s*, but don't worry about that too much right now.
- Work with a chat partner to discuss why you **both** agree on the auxiliary verb that should be used, according to the flowchart provided in class. Use your assigned Chatzy room.
- After you have decided why you agree on each auxiliary verb, rate your level of confidence for each sentence.

(A) L'ex-premier ministre François Fillon _____ (se fracturer) une cheville dans un accident de scooter sur l'île de Capri.
How confident are you that **you and your chat partner** have chosen the correct auxiliary (*avoir* or *être*)?
1–Not at all confident 2–Not really confident 3–Neutral 4–Somewhat confident 5–Very confident

(B) Les cambrioleurs _____ (retourner) l'appartement.
How confident are you that **you and your chat partner** have chosen the correct auxiliary (*avoir* or *être*)?
1–Not at all confident 2–Not really confident 3–Neutral 4–Somewhat confident 5–Very confident

(C) Le gouvernement _____ (retourner) sa veste sur la question de la neutralité de l'internet.
How confident are you that **you and your chat partner** have chosen the correct auxiliary (*avoir* or *être*)?
1–Not at all confident 2–Not really confident 3–Neutral 4–Somewhat confident 5–Very confident

(D) Le lutteur favori _____ (tomber) son adversaire très tôt dans l'affrontement.
How confident are you that **you and your chat partner** have chosen the correct auxiliary (*avoir* or *être*)?
1–Not at all confident 2–Not really confident 3–Neutral 4–Somewhat confident 5–Very confident

(E) Notre cousine _____ (tomber) plus d'un homme.
How confident are you that **you and your chat partner** have chosen the correct auxiliary (*avoir* or *être*)?
1–Not at all confident 2–Not really confident 3–Neutral 4–Somewhat confident 5–Very confident

(F) Pierre Lissou _____ (passer) lieutenant avec la mention *très bien*.
How confident are you that **you and your chat partner** have chosen the correct auxiliary (*avoir* or *être*)?
1–Not at all confident 2–Not really confident 3–Neutral 4–Somewhat confident 5–Very confident

(G) En 2001, il _____ (passer) son permis de conduire.
How confident are you that **you and your chat partner** have chosen the correct auxiliary (*avoir* or *être*)?
1–Not at all confident 2–Not really confident 3–Neutral 4–Somewhat confident 5–Very confident

(H) Il _____ (monter) un site Web sur un serveur gratuit.
How confident are you that **you and your chat partner** have chosen the correct auxiliary (*avoir* or *être*)?
1–Not at all confident 2–Not really confident 3–Neutral 4–Somewhat confident 5–Very confident

(I) Il _____ (monter) jusqu'au sommet de la colline.
How confident are you that **you and your chat partner** have chosen the correct auxiliary (*avoir* or *être*)?
1–Not at all confident 2–Not really confident 3–Neutral 4–Somewhat confident 5–Very confident

(J) Il _____ (monter) la tente sur des cailloux.
How confident are you that **you and your chat partner** have chosen the correct auxiliary (*avoir* or *être*)?
1–Not at all confident 2–Not really confident 3–Neutral 4–Somewhat confident 5–Very confident

Notes

(1) Each letter of this acronym represents the first letter of a verb that uses *être* (and *être* only, presumably) as an auxiliary verb in compound past constructions. Some textbooks and other pedagogical materials used 'DR & MRS VANDERTRAMP' (one *P* instead of two) or 'DR & MRS VANDERTRAMP(P)' (a second *P* in parentheses).
(2) This is typically a diagram with a house (or some type of building). Various illustrations represent actions associated with '*être* verbs' such as *entrer* ('to enter'), *sortir*, ('to leave/exit'), and so forth.
(3) Concept-based instruction is also known as systemic-theoretical instruction.
(4) See Negueruela-Azarola (2011) for a discussion of the terms *verbalization* and *conceptualization*.
(5) Galperin (1992) refers to the didactic/learning tool as a scheme for complete orienting basis of action (SCOBA).
(6) See http://www.chatzy.com/.
(7) Worksheet 1 included nine items, but Worksheet 2 included 10. The difference in the number of items was due to a printing error that was not noticed until the lesson had already begun. Since both worksheets did not include the same number of items, a paired-samples t-test was not able to be used.
(8) The author recognizes that not every facet of a language can be taught through concept-based instruction. Therefore, it is important to select salient features and structures that occur frequently for this type of instruction in order to impact learning in a substantial way.

References

Anderson, B., Golato, P. and Blatty, S. (2012) *En avant! Beginning French*. New York: McGraw-Hill.
Anover, V. and Antes, T. (2012) *À vous! The Global French Experience* (2nd edn). Boston, MA: Heinle/Cengage Learning.
Arievitch, I.M. and Haenen, J.P.P. (2005) Connecting sociocultural theory and educational practice: Galperin's approach. *Educational Psychologist* 40, 155–165.
Ariew, R. and Dupuy, B. (2011) *Français-Monde: Connectez-vous à la francophonie*. Upper Saddle River, NJ: Prentice Hall.
Cohen, J. (1992) A power primer. *Psychological Bulletin* 112, 155–159.
Cooper, D.E. (1983) *Authenticity and Learning: Nietzsche's Educational Philosophy*. London: Routledge.
Galperin, P. (1989) Organization of mental activity and the effectiveness of learning. *Soviet Psychology* 27, 45–65.
Galperin, P. (1992) Stage-by-stage formation as a method of psychological investigation. *Journal of Russian and East European Psychology* 30, 60–80.
Lai, W. (2012) Concept-based foreign language pedagogy: Teaching the Chinese temporal system. Doctoral dissertation, Pennsylvania State University. See https://etda.libraries.psu.edu/paper/16124/.
Lantolf, J.P. (2007) Conceptual knowledge and instructed second language learning: A sociocultural perspective. In S. Fotos and H. Nassaji (eds) *Form Focused Instruction and Teacher Education: Studies in Honour of Rod Ellis* (pp. 35–54). Oxford: Oxford University Press.
Lantolf, J. and Thorne, S. (2006) *Sociocultural Theory and the Genesis of Second Language Development*. Oxford: Oxford University Press.
MacDonald, M.N., Badger, R. and Dasli, M. (2006) Authenticity, culture and language learning. *Language and Intercultural Communication* 6, 250–261.

Manley, J.H., Smith, S., McMinn, J.T. and Prévost, M.A. (2015) *Horizons* (6th edn). Boston, MA: Cengage Learning.
Negueruela, E. (2003) A sociocultural approach to teaching and researching second languages: Systemic-theoretical instruction and second language development. Unpublished doctoral dissertation, Pennsylvania State University, University Park, PA.
Negueruela, E. and Lantolf, J.P. (2006) Concept-based instruction and the acquisition of L2 Spanish. In R.A. Salaberry and B.A. Lafford (eds) *The Art of Teaching Spanish: Second Language Acquisition from Research to Praxis* (pp. 79–102). Washington, DC: Georgetown University Press.
Negueruela-Azarola, E. (2011) Beliefs as conceptualizing activity: A dialectical approach for the second language classroom. *System* 39, 359–369.
Valdman, A., Pons, C. and Scullen, M.E. (2010) *Chez nous: Branché sur le monde francophone* (4th edn). Upper Saddle River, NJ: Prentice Hall.
van Compernolle, R.A. (2012) Developing sociopragmatic capacity in a second language through concept-based instruction. Unpublished doctoral dissertation, Pennsylvania State University, University Park, PA.
van Compernolle, R.A. (2014) *Sociocultural Theory and L2 Instructional Pragmatics*. Bristol: Multilingual Matters.
Vygotsky, L.S. (1986) *Thought and Language*. Cambridge, MA: MIT Press.
Williams, L., Abraham, L. and Negueruela, E. (2013) Using concept-based instruction in the L2 classroom: Perspectives from current and future language teachers. *Language Teaching Research* 17, 363–381.
Yáñez-Prieto, M.-d.-C. (2008) On literature and the secret art of (im)possible worlds: Teaching literature through language. Doctoral dissertation, Pennsylvania State University, University Park, PA. See https://etda.libraries.psu.edu/paper/8902/.

4 Sociolinguistic Authenticity and Classroom L2 Learners: Production, Perception and Metapragmatics

Rémi A. van Compernolle

Introduction

In a 2003 issue of the *Journal of Sociolinguistics* (Vol. 7 (3)), Penelope Eckert initiated a dialogue around the concept of authenticity in current sociolinguistics research. Focusing on the concept of the so-called 'authentic speaker', she wrote the following:

> Locally located and oriented, the Authentic Speaker produces linguistic output that emerges naturally in and from that location. The notion of the authentic speaker is based in the belief that some speakers have been more tainted by the social than others – tainted in the sense that they have wandered beyond their natural habitat to be subject to conscious, hence unnatural, social influences. (Eckert, 2003: 392–393)

This conception of the authentic speaker, according to Eckert's critique, assumes that some speakers – by virtue of their 'untaintedness' – are more authentic than others, whose linguistic output has been subject to the influences on nonlocal factors (e.g. through social or geographical mobility, dialect/style contact, media). For instance, in sociolinguistics research, speakers are often included in or excluded from studies depending on whether or not they were born and have always lived in the local of focus (e.g. a particular town or region). In other research, contact with – or desires to move to – the 'outside world' may then be used to explain why some speakers do not adhere to local speech norms (read 'authentic local linguistic identity'), a perspective that dates back at least to Labov's (1963) seminal study of Martha's Vineyard (see also Eckert, 2008, 2012; Johnstone & Kiesling, 2008, for discussion and critique). It is worth noting also that Eckert takes this perspective to task for assuming that what is conscious is unnatural and, hence, not authentic, which derives at least in part from Labov's (1972) characterization of speech styles as having to do with the degree of attention paid to speech. The goal for Labov and others who followed was to elicit a range of speech styles, favoring the style to which the least amount of attention was paid as the most authentic in terms of the speaker's natural way of using language.

In this chapter, I argue that a similar problem exists in second language (L2) research, especially with regard to sociolinguistic and pragmatic competencies and how such competencies are evaluated in terms of authenticity and L2 identity. Drawing on the case studies of two advanced (US university-level) learners of French, Thérèse and Sally (both pseudonyms), which include data from sociolinguistic interviews, oral narratives and metalinguistic tasks, I examine the ways in which the two learners lay claim to authentic identities as L2 users of French through their production, perception and metapragmatic discourse about the meaning of sociostylistic variation in French.

Conceptualizing L2 Sociolinguistic Authenticity

Can L2 users – and especially classroom language learners – ever be considered authentic speakers of the L2? The answer to this question depends, of course, on how authenticity is operationalized. If authenticity is limited to the rather conservative sociolinguistic conceptualization critiqued by Eckert (2003) – that is, the authentic speaker is from a particular geographic location, speaks its variety of language perfectly, and has escaped all external social influences that may impact upon his or her linguistic output – then, no, an L2 user is by definition not an authentic speaker of the language. (And it should be noted, as Eckert and others have argued, that this definition excludes a large swath of any population, first-language speakers included, from being considered authentic.) If, however, authenticity is seen as an ongoing process of authenticating one's linguistic identity (Bucholtz, 2003; Bucholtz & Hall, 2005) by appropriating culturally relevant and recognizable patterns of meaning and language, then, yes, L2 learners can certainly be seen as authentic speakers of the language.

Authenticities of correspondence and genesis

As sketched out in the Introduction to this volume (van Compernolle & McGregor), authenticity has been interpreted in two broad senses in the applied linguistics and L2 literature (MacDonald *et al.*, 2006). *Authenticity of correspondence* (Cooper, 1983) refers to the degree to which some use of the L2 aligns with an externally imposed, normative benchmark – typically, idealized native-speaker conventions. By contrast, *authenticity of genesis* (Cooper, 1983) refers to the origin and/or ownership of the use language – classroom language, learner language, etc. is authentic to those contexts and speakers.

L2 sociolinguistic research has typically focused on language learners' approximation of – that is, correspondence to – perceived native-speaker sociolinguistic behavior with reference to registers or styles of language described, for example, in terms of 'everyday' versus 'formal' (or a continuum of registers running from colloquial to hyper-formal or literary). Examples include Regan *et al.*'s (2009) seminal work on the acquisition of L2 French sociolinguistic competence in a study abroad context, and Mougeon *et al.*'s (2010) large-scale investigation of the sociolinguistic competence of Canadian L2 French immersion students. In such research, learners' sociolinguistic competencies are evaluated with reference to documented patterns of sociolinguistic variation among comparable native-speaker counterparts.

In other work, learners' sociolinguistic competencies have been linked more closely to the relationship between performance (e.g. use of variable forms in speech), metasociolinguistic knowledge and perceptions of desirable ways of speaking (e.g. Kinginger, 2008; van Compernolle, 2014; van Compernolle & Williams, 2012a, 2012b). In this way, authenticity of genesis is taken into account through explorations of the intentions of learners. This does not, of course, preclude reference to the degree to which learner performances correspond to normative patterns of variation, but instead simply reorients the focus of the investigation onto various forms of agency deployed by learners in their sociolinguistic choices. In this respect, van Compernolle and Williams (2012a) developed the concept of *sociolinguistic agency*, which is:

> the socioculturally mediated act of recognizing, interpreting, and using the social and symbolic meaning-making possibilities of language. It consists of an understanding of how the use of one linguistic variant or another simultaneously reflects and creates the context in which it is used, is a performance of one's social identity at the time of utterance, and affects one's environment and interlocutor(s). (van Compernolle & Williams, 2012a: 237)

In short, sociolinguistic agency entails authenticity in two ways. On the one hand, sociolinguistic agency is mediated by a learner's knowledge of recognizable patterns of meaning and language within a given community – that is, authenticity of correspondence, and, on the other, it is mediated by the learner's intent to purposefully create a particular meaning during communicative activity – that is, authenticity of genesis (see also van Compernolle & Henery, this volume). As van Compernolle and Williams (2012a) have argued, sociolinguistic agency is intimately linked to a learner's self and identity (see also van Compernolle, 2014), as discussed in the next subsection.

Authenticity, self and identity

In sociolinguistics research (e.g. Bucholtz, 2003; Bucholtz & Hall, 2005; Eckert, 2003, 2008, 2012; Johnstone & Kiesling, 2008), authenticity has often been linked to the concept of identity. Indeed, this is the crux of Eckert's (2003) critique of the traditional notion of the authentic speaker cited in the introduction of this chapter. To be an authentic speaker of a language, or a variety of a language, means having a particular identity that is, at least in part, formed through one's use of, and interaction with, that language.

Bucholtz (2003) of course reminds us that identities are not trait characteristics of individuals but are instead processes that involve *authentication*, or social practices that lay claim to particular projected identities, and are recognizable as such, in particular contexts (see also Bucholtz & Hall, 2005; Lee & Kinginger, this volume). In the sociocultural linguistics approach espoused by Bucholtz (2003), sociolinguistic practices are the primary means through which speakers engage in the authentication of identities. This is because sociolinguistic practices are indexical in nature (Silverstein, 2003): they point to macrosociological patterns (e.g. age, gender, social class, level of education), on the one hand, and, on the other, they are involved in the construction of local social meaning as well as the reification and transformation of larger, supralocal ideologies. As Eckert (2008) points out, speakers therefore have access to a rather open and malleable indexical field of meaning. Individuals and groups draw from the indexical field to create both personal and collective identities through their linguistic practices.

In L2 development, individuals are pushed to forge new and/or modify existing relationships between their sense of 'self' and the patterns of meaning available in the language they are learning. Drawing on these sociolinguistic perspectives, and reinterpreting them within Vygotskian sociocultural psychology (Vygotsky, 1978, 1986), van Compernolle and Williams (2012a) argued that L2 identities are mediational in two respects (and see van Compernolle, 2014, Chapter 3, for an expansion of the argument). First, identities mediate between a historically grounded, yet future oriented concept of self, or consciousness, and the social-material world in which individuals act. In short, identities – or roles – are somewhat ephemeral because they are particular, contextually emergent performances of aspects of one's self that mediate and are mediated by the present, and potentially dynamic, circumstances in which one is acting. Secondly, the culturally constructed artifacts that one has internalized as part of the Self mediate identities. This is to say that the identities or roles that can be performed are determined by the qualities of the psychological tools that make up consciousness. Especially important in L2 development are the patterns of L2 meaning and language that a learner has internalized or is currently in the process of internalizing. This is because the performance of aspects of the self (i.e. identity) is accomplished, at least to a large degree, through language use.

Authenticity and metapragmatics

As noted above, sociolinguistic practices are indexical in nature – they point to particular categories of social meaning. In many cases, their meanings are the object of conscious reflection among members of particular linguistic communities, or what Silverstein (2001) labels *metapragmatics*.

> From a semiotic point of view, all such [pragmatic] meanings can be described as rules linking certain culturally-constituted features of the speech situation with certain forms of speech. To give those rules, or talk about them, is to engage in 'meta-pragmatic' discourse. (Silverstein, 2001: 382–393)

Thus, we can think of metapragmatics as the often impressionistic associations people make between particular language practices and corresponding categories of social meaning. I say 'often impressionistic' since most people engage in metapragmatic discourse on the basis of their personal experiences and/or the ideologies that they have inherited from their cultural upbringing rather than from some more objective form of observation (e.g. corpus analysis) (see Silverstein, 2003, especially with regard to the construction of supralocal ideologies). Metapragmatics are therefore forms of cultural knowledge. As such, developing metapragmatics in an L2 entails coming to understand and appreciate how a new culture values (i.e. assigns meaning to) different forms of speech.

L2 metapragmatics may be authenticated in two interrelated ways. On the one hand, learners may engage in the kind of metapragmatic discourse that is recognizable among members of the communities they wish to associate with. On the other hand, learners may develop their own metapragmatic values in relation to their sense of self and the various identities they wish to authenticate through their L2 sociolinguistic practices. Of course, to follow on from the arguments laid out above, authenticity – or authentication – is really about both: that is, a kind of self-generated metapragmatics that nonetheless corresponds to some recognizable system of value judgments (i.e. indexical meanings of sociolinguistic practices). Developing and authenticating an L2 metapragmatic system is particularly important for the development of sociolinguistic agency (van Compernolle & Williams, 2012a) because it is the appropriation of such value systems that mediates learners' choices of sociolinguistic forms that can index, or authenticate, desired L2 identities.

Authentication at multiple scales

Authentication is a process that occurs along multiple dimensions (e.g. language use, metapragmatics) as well as at multiple scales. Bucholtz and Hall's (2005) work on identity has demonstrated the way in which authentication unfolds at the micro level of turns at talk, as participants position themselves through sociolinguistic practices and metapragmatic discourse from one turn to the next (see also Lee & Kinginger, this volume). In sociolinguistics (e.g. Eckert, 2012; Johnstone & Kiesling, 2008), focus has been on authenticating practices at a more macro level; for instance, general (quantitative) patterns of language use during sociolinguistic interviews and responses to metalinguistic (or metapragmatics) tasks. In the current chapter, focus is on a level somewhere between the microinteractional and the macro focus, which I will simply refer to as the meso level of authentication. By this, I mean how Thérèse and Sally engage in authenticating practices in particular tasks but without a detailed focus on how they attempt to authenticate their emerging L2 sociolinguistic identities on a turn-by-by basis.

Focus of the Chapter and Research Questions

This chapter is an initial part of a broader research program that explores advanced language learners' use and perception of sociolinguistic variants (mainly in L2 French). In some ways, the chapter is a replication of the study reported by van Compernolle and Williams (2012a), and similarities will be pointed out where relevant. However, the current focus is on advanced undergraduate learners of French (as determined by course enrolment) rather than beginning and intermediate learners. The rationale for the focus on advanced learners is that while we have learned a good deal about sociolinguistic competencies in the beginning years of language study as well as in study abroad, little attention has been paid to students who have passed through, and are nearing completion of, a full program of study, which includes numerous 'content' courses at the upper levels of study (e.g. literature, film, culture, history, linguistics) where a wider range of discourse options are available in comparison to lower-level courses.

Two well-known French sociolinguistic variables were selected as the focus of the study: the presence versus absence of the negative particle *ne*, and the alternation between the pronouns *nous* and *on* for first-person plural reference (see, for example, Mougeon *et al.*, 2010; Regan *et al.*, 2009; van Compernolle & Williams, 2012a, for previous studies of L2 learners). Verbal negation in standard, written French is typically characterized by the presence of *ne* in preverbal position and a postverbal second negative (e.g. *pas* 'not', *rien* 'nothing'), as in *je ne veux pas sortir ce soir* 'I do not want to go out tonight', whereas *ne* is omitted at high frequencies in everyday spoken

French. Thus, *ne* is described as the more formal or prestige variant, whereas its absence is associated with informal, spontaneous discourse. The *nous/on* variable is similarly patterned (e.g. *nous allons* versus *on va* 'we are going'). The pronoun *nous* is considered to be the standard, formal variant, whereas *on* is widely used in everyday discourse.

The following general research questions will be addressed in this chapter:

(1) How are the sociolinguistic variants distributed in the speech of the learners?
(2) To what extent are the learners aware of the sociolinguistic variants?
(3) How do the learners position themselves metapragmatically vis-à-vis authentic (authenticating) sociolinguistic practices?

Methods

The study employed a multidimensional approach to data collection and analysis in order to elicit variable levels of speech (i.e. interview and narrative tasks in two conditions), knowledge of variable L2 forms (i.e. a sentence versions task) and metapragmatic discourse (i.e. a language awareness interview). Participation in the study included three one-hour sessions on non-consecutive days. Participants received US$10 at each session as compensation for their time. Below, each of the instruments and procedures will be presented and elaborated, followed by a presentation of the two focal participants, Thérèse and Sally.

Interview-and-narrative tasks

In order to elicit extended samples of spontaneous speech, an interview-and-narrative task was designed, inspired in part by the classic sociolinguistic interview (see Labov, 1984; Tagliamonte, 2006). The first part of the task involved interview-style questions about learners' backgrounds, studies, hobbies, family, and so on (Appendix A). The second part of the task elicited narrative discourse. Topics were suggested by the learners on a questionnaire that prompted them to give a short title for a variety of story types (Appendix B) in advance of data collection. Participants engaged in two such tasks during Sessions 1 and 2. The first was conducted by the researcher (a professor of French) and the second was conducted between peers (i.e. participants interviewed each other and retold their stories to a peer). This procedure allows the comparison of two different registers (i.e. interview versus narrative) in two communicative conditions (i.e. speaking with a professor versus speaking with a peer/classmate). This is important as a means of observing sensitivity to topic and attention paid to speech (Labov, 1972) as well as sensitivity to one's interlocutor, or audience design (Bell, 1984, 2001), as factors relevant to the use of different sociolinguistic variants.

Sentence versions task

A sentence versions task was adapted from Johnstone and Kiesling's (2008) research on monophthongization in Pittsburghese, such that the word *downtown* is pronounced *dahntahn*. In the current study, the task included a series of sentence pairs that included the *ne/0* variants and the *nous/on* variants (in addition to several distractor items). A native French speaker from France who was an age peer of the participants recorded the sentences. In the task, which was administered during the third and final session of the study, participants heard two versions ('a' and 'b') of the same sentence, which differed only in the realization of a sociolinguistic variable, such as:

(a) Luc ne vient jamais en cours!
(b) Luc vient jamais en cours!

While both sentences mean 'Luc never comes to class!', they differ in terms of the presence (version 'a') and absence (version 'b') of the negative particle *ne* (i.e. the two possible variants). Participants were asked to respond to the following questions for each pair of sentences:

(1) Which version is more like the way a native French speaker would say the sentence?
(2) Which version is more like the way somebody would say the sentence to a friend?
(3) Which version is more like the way a younger person would say the sentence?
(4) Which version is more like the way you would say the sentence?
(5) Which version is more correct?

These questions aimed to tap into learners' awareness of native-speaker patterns, their knowledge of some of the social correlates of the sociolinguistic variants and their perceptions of correctness in language.

Language awareness interview

Following the sentence versions tasks, the researchers engaged participants in a language awareness interview following the procedures outlined in Kinginger (2008) and van Compernolle (2014). The first part of the language awareness interview involved explicit discussion of the focal sociolinguistic variables (Appendix C). The second part of the interview involved an oral appropriateness judgment task (Appendix D) in which participants were prompted to choose which sociolinguistic variants would be appropriate to use in a series of social-interactive contexts and to explain their choices. Data from the language awareness interview helped to elicit metapragmatic discourse and to ascertain metapragmatic knowledge.

Focal participants

Sally and Thérèse were advanced-level undergraduate students in the French program at a private research university (pseudonyms were chosen by the participants). Sally's primary field of study was music, and Thérèse's was chemical engineering. Both young women were pursuing French studies as a secondary major area of specialization and had enrolled in a fourth-year undergraduate course taught by the researcher, which focused on sociolinguistic and pragmatic aspects of identity and social relationships in French. Sally and Thérèse had an estimated oral proficiency level of 'advanced mid' on the ACTFL proficiency scale. Neither of them had ever lived or studied in a French-speaking country. Sally and Thérèse were recruited to participate in a pilot stage of the current research and have been chosen as focal participants for two reasons. First, they were partners for the peer–peer interview-and-narrative task. Secondly, they completed all tasks and produced sufficient usable data for analysis. It should be added that, in an attempt to engage in a partial replication of van Compernolle and Williams's (2012a) study, Sally and Thérèse also demonstrated very different, yet equally authentic, orientations to sociolinguistic variation in French. In this way, analysis and comparison of their two cases allows me to propose a version of L2 sociolinguistic authenticity that recognizes the possibility that there are multiple ways of authenticating one's L2 sociolinguistic identity and agency.

Findings and Analysis

I present the findings of the study and then discuss them in turn in each of the following subsections, beginning with Sally's and Thérèse's use of the sociolinguistic variants in the interview-and-narrative tasks, followed by their responses to the sentence versions task, and concluding with the language awareness interview, focusing specifically on their responses to the oral appropriateness judgment task.

Production of sociolinguistic variants

Overall frequencies of *ne* omission and *on* use are provided in Tables 4.1–4.4, first for Sally (Tables 4.1 and 4.2) and then for Thérèse (Tables 4.3 and 4.4). The tables are organized such that frequencies are given for each condition (i.e. professor versus peer) and each part of the task (i.e. interview versus narrative) in addition to totals.

70 Authenticity, Language and Interaction in Second Language Contexts

Table 4.1 Sally's omission of *ne*

	With prof n (%)	With peer n (%)	Total n (%)
Interview	0/2 (0%)	2/6 (33.3%)	2/8 (25%)
Narrative	1/13 (7.7%)	1/8 (12.5%)	2/21 (9.5%)
Total	1/15 (6.7%)	3/14 (21.4%)	4/29 (13.8%)

Table 4.2 Sally's use of *on*

	With prof n (%)	With peer n (%)	Total n (%)
Interview	1/5 (20%)	4/6 (66.7%)	5/11 (45.5%)
Narrative	3/16 (18.8%)	0/3 (0%)	3/19 (15.8%)
Total	4/21 (19%)	4/9 (44.4%)	8/30 (26.7%)

Table 4.3 Thérèse's omission of *ne*

	With prof n (%)	With peer n (%)	Total n (%)
Interview	29/35 (82.9%)	13/21 (61.9%)	42/56 (75%)
Narrative	31/36 (86.1%)	19/22 (86.4%)	50/58 (86.2%)
Total	60/71 (84.5%)	32/43 (74.4%)	92/114 (80.7%)

Table 4.4 Thérèse's use of *on*

	With prof n (%)	With peer n (%)	Total n (%)
Interview	15/20 (75%)	3/4 (75%)	18/24 (75%)
Narrative	26/28 (92.9%)	10/11 (90.9%)	36/39 (92.3%)
Total	41/48 (85.4%)	13/15 (86.7%)	54/63 (85.7%)

In general, both young women demonstrated variation in their speech, meaning that they produced 'everyday' variants (i.e. *ne*'s absence, *on*) at least some of the time and more standard variants (i.e. *ne*'s presence, *nous*) at other times. This is important because it shows that Sally and Thérèse had each variant in their productive repertoires and were not, therefore, monostylistic (Dewaele, 2001). However, the data also show a clear difference between Sally and Thérèse in terms of the distribution of the variants. The totals in the lower right corner of each table indicate that Sally only rarely omitted *ne* (13.8%) and rather infrequently used *on* (26.7%), whereas Thérèse omitted *ne* (80.7%) and used *on* (85.7%) in the vast majority of possible contexts.

It is interesting to note that Thérèse, but not Sally, seemed to be sensitive to discourse task (i.e. interview versus narrative). Thérèse tended to use informal variants at higher frequencies in the narrative part of the task than in the interview part. This suggests that Thérèse produced a more 'relaxed style' of discourse (van Compernolle & Williams, 2012a) when telling stories than when being interviewed, where she produced a more 'careful style,' and this finding is true for both professor and peer conditions. No such pattern is discernable in Sally's data.

A comparison of the two communicative conditions (i.e. professor versus peers) reveals an interesting finding related to the hypothesis that, in general, learners would tend to use informal variants at higher frequencies in the peer condition than in the professor condition, assuming that they had informal variants in their communicative repertoire. This hypothesis is only partially confirmed. Sally certainly increased her use of informal variants when speaking with Thérèse, but Thérèse's high frequencies of *ne* omission and *on* use are relatively stable (Figure 4.1). One interpretation of this finding is that Sally recognized Thérèse's informal style and began to converge, at least partially, with her level of discourse, whereas Sally opted to maintain a much more formal stance when interacting with her professor. Thus, while Sally's use of informal speech features remained modest in comparison to Thérèse's, she did exhibit some sensitivity to context/interlocutor.

It should be noted, however, that the expected level of discourse in the professor condition was somewhat ambiguous because he generally spoke in an informal style, including in the interview-and-narrative task as well as in the classroom (the reader will recall that both Sally and Thérèse were

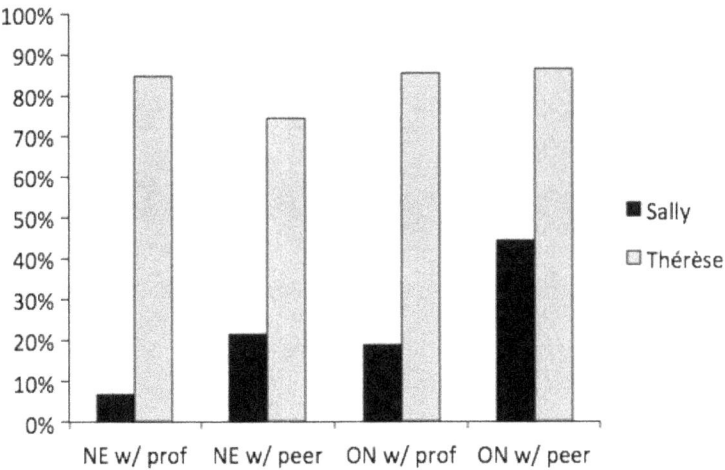

Figure 4.1 Rates of *ne* omission and *on* use by Sally and Thérèse in the two conditions

students of the researcher). Thérèse's use of informal features when speaking with her professor could therefore also be construed as an appropriate convergence with the style of her interlocutor rather than an overgeneralization of her informal style. The main point to take away here is that Thérèse and Sally used the focal sociolinguistic variants at very different frequencies, which is a starting point for discussing the two young women's sociolinguistic authenticities. To complete the picture, we will examine the sentence versions task next, and then move on to the language awareness interviews.

Responses to the sentence versions task

As noted above, the sentence versions task involved listening to a series of sentence pairs that differed only in terms of the realization of a sociolinguistic variable (i.e. *ne*'s presence versus absence or *on* versus *nous* for first-person plural reference) and then answering five questions about the sentences. Tables 4.5 and 4.6 provide a snapshot of Sally's responses to the sentence versions tasks, and Tables 4.7 and 4.8 display Thérèse's responses.

Table 4.5 Sally's responses to the sentence versions task: *ne* absence versus presence

Item	NS	Friend	Young	You	Correct
1	−ne	−ne	−ne	+ne	+ne
4	−ne	−ne	−ne	+ne	Neither
7	−ne	−ne	−ne	+ne	+ne
10	−ne	−ne	−ne	+ne	+ne
12	−ne	−ne	−ne	+ne	+ne

Table 4.6 Sally's responses to the sentence versions task: *on* versus *nous*

Item	NS	Friend	Young	You	Correct
3	On	On	On	Nous	On
6	On	On	On	Nous	On
9	On	On	On	Nous	On

Table 4.7 Thérèse's responses to the sentence versions task: *ne* absence versus presence

Item	NS	Friend	Young	You	Correct
1	−ne	−ne	−ne	−ne	+ne
4	−ne	−ne	−ne	−ne	+ne
7	−ne	−ne	−ne	−ne	+ne
10	Neither	−ne	−ne	−ne	+ne
12	−ne	−ne	−ne	−ne	+ne

Table 4.8 Thérèse's responses to the sentence versions task: *on* versus *nous*

Item	NS	Friend	Young	You	Correct
3	On	On	On	On	Neither
6	On	On	On	On	Neither
9	On	On	On	On	Neither

Column headers refer to the focus of the questions (e.g. NS = Which version is more like the way a native French speaker would say the sentence?). The labels '+*ne*' and '–*ne*' have been used in Tables 4.5 and 4.7 to refer to sentence versions in which *ne* was present and absent, respectively.

Overall, both Thérèse and Sally appeared to be aware of normative patterns of variation. Both young women identified sentence versions without *ne* and with *on* as more likely for native speakers and young persons to use, and as the versions most likely to be used among friends. In addition, both Thérèse and Sally tended to judge *ne*'s presence as more correct than *ne*'s absence. Sally also identified sentence versions with *nous* as more correct than those with *on*, whereas Thérèse appeared to be indifferent in this regard, noting that neither *nous* nor *on* was more correct. The principal difference between Thérèse and Sally was in their responses to question #4: 'Which version is more like the way you would say the sentence?' Sally indicated that she would be more likely to say sentence versions in which the more standard, or formal, variant was present. By contrast, Thérèse showed a preference for those versions in which the non-standard, or everyday, variant was realized.

These findings are important for several reasons. First, it is clear that Thérèse and Sally were both aware of, and could distinguish between, the focal variants in this study. Secondly, they were also aware of some of the important social correlates of the variation and normative judgments of correctness. Thirdly, the data provide some evidence that Thérèse and Sally were aware of their own sociolinguistic practices: the reader will note that their responses to Question 4 reflected their sociolinguistic behavior – or at least an essentialized version of that behavior[1] – in the interview-and-narrative task (see above). On the basis of these observations, it follows that the two young women were engaged to very different authentication processes: Thérèse was attempting to authenticate an informal sociolinguistic identity that aligned with young native French speaker conventions, whereas Sally was positioning herself as a more formal, sociolinguistically conservative speaker of French. This claim finds additional support in the analysis of the language awareness interview, which we turn to in the following section.

Metapragmatics in the language awareness interview

Whereas the sentence versions task dealt with awareness of the variants on a general level, the language awareness interview aimed to ascertain

74 Authenticity, Language and Interaction in Second Language Contexts

participants' cultural knowledge of the 'rules' of language use, or metapragmatics (Silverstein, 2001). Sally and Thérèse made a number of interesting comments during the interview, but in the interest of space we will focus only on their responses to the appropriateness judgment task. The task prompted the participants to indicate which variants were more appropriate in a series of social-interactive contexts in an attempt to uncover aspects of their metapragmatic knowledge (i.e. in which contexts each variant would be more acceptable to use and expected to be said in return by one's interlocutor). Sally's and Thérèse's responses are given in Tables 4.9 and 4.10, respectively.

In general, the responses to the appropriateness judgment task suggest that Sally and Thérèse were aware of some of the conventional rules or patterns of variation that would be expected in these situations. The responses are particularly interesting in light of the sentence versions task. Whereas in the sentence versions task Sally categorically selected the formal variants (i.e. +*ne, nous*) and Thérèse selected the informal variants (i.e. –*ne, on*) as the

Table 4.9 Sally's responses to the appropriateness judgment task

Situation	Ne *presence vs. absence*		On *vs.* nous	
	Use	Expect	Use	Expect
1 (friend)	–ne	–ne	On	On
2 (friend's girlfriend)	–ne	–ne	On	On
3 (favorite teacher on street)	+ne	–ne	Nous/on	On
4 (administrative assistant)	+ne	+ne	Nous	Nous
5 (friendly barman)	–ne	–ne	On	On
6 (grocery store clerk)	+ne	+ne	Nous	Nous
7 (French professor's office)	+ne	–ne	Nous	On
8 (friend of a friend)	–ne	–ne	On	On

Table 4.10 Thérèse's responses to the appropriateness judgment task

Situation	Ne *presence vs. absence*		On *vs.* nous	
	Use	Expect	Use	Expect
1 (friend)	–ne	–ne	On	On
2 (friend's girlfriend)	–ne	–ne	On	On
3 (favorite teacher on street)	+ne	+ne	Nous	Nous
4 (administrative assistant)	+ne	+ne	Nous	Nous
5 (friendly barman)	–ne	–ne	On	On
6 (grocery store clerk)	–ne	–ne	On	On
7 (French professor's office)	+ne	–ne	Nous	On
8 (friend of a friend)	–ne	–ne	On	On

forms they would be most likely to use, both young women displayed more nuanced, contextually sensitive judgments of the appropriateness of the variants in the appropriateness judgment task. This suggests that while Sally and Thérèse each had essentialized conceptions of their own sociolinguistic preferences (i.e. in sentence versions task), they also had some general, yet contextually sensitive, metapragmatic knowledge of community-wide sociolinguistic practices of French speakers.

Differences are nonetheless apparent in Sally's and Thérèse's responses to the task. For example, for situation (6), Sally opted to use and receive the more formal variants whereas Thérèse thought that the more everyday variants would be more appropriate. Their rationales were both reasonable. In the interview, Sally noted that in the workplace, the store clerk would maintain a professional stance through the use of more formal language, a stance that she would reciprocate in order to align with her interlocutor. By contrast, Thérèse assumed that because the store clerk was a peer, there would be no reason to use overly formal language. These responses are also telling in relation to the more general orientations to language variation espoused by Sally, who tended to be more sociolinguistically conservative, and Thérèse, who tended to be more ready to opt for everyday language in her interactions with others.

Discussion and Conclusions

The analysis presented above revealed two different, yet equally authentic, orientations to sociolinguistic variation. Sally was in the process of authenticating a rather academic and, therefore, formal sociolinguistic identity. Thérèse, by contrast, appeared to be forging a more informal sociolinguistic identity through her use of, and preference for, more everyday sociolinguistic forms. Both young women were aware of the possible variations and could identify at least some of the social conventions for the use of each variant. This is important because authenticating a sociolinguistic identity involves agency, which is mediated by the knowledge of what forms can vary and what such variation means. Indeed, as underscored elsewhere (van Compernolle, 2014; van Compernolle & Williams, 2012a), in order to understand L2 learners' sociolinguistic competencies in relation to agency, it is necessary to evaluate sociolinguistic performances (e.g. in speech) with reference to what learners understand about variation and how they perceive the appropriateness and desirability of linguistic variants – that is, metapragmatics (see also van Compernolle & Henery, this volume).

As noted earlier in this chapter, sociolinguistic authenticity ought to be viewed as a dialectical relationship between two opposing forces that roughly map onto MacDonald *et al.*'s (2006) concepts of correspondence and genesis (as originally described by Cooper, 1983). First, authenticating a sociolinguistic identity requires that one's use and understanding of variable L2 forms correspond to recognizable patterns of meaning and language within a particular community of speakers. This is because authenticity of correspondence provides a shared orientation to the potential sociocultural meanings of one's use of language (van Compernolle, 2011), which is necessary for the construction of locally emergent social-indexical meanings during the act of communication (Silverstein, 2003). This brings us to the second force: sociolinguistic identities are authentic to the individual because they originate with that individual. And this is why it is important to see authenticity in dialectical terms – authentication of a sociolinguistic identity cannot be an 'anything goes' affair. Rather, it is the synthesis of what originates with the individual, and how the individual performs given the various cultural tools (e.g. variable forms, metapragmatics) that mediate the construction of social meaning between people. Authenticity cannot, therefore, be achieved without correspondence to some set of available patterns of language and meanings, but neither can it be achieved without the agency of the speaker (van Compernolle & Williams, 2012a).

In development, sociolinguistic authenticities do not have an end state. Rather, authentication is an ongoing, lifelong process for all people, native and nonnative speakers alike (Bucholtz, 2003; Eckert, 2003), so one does not become once and for all times sociolinguistically authentic. Therefore, while Thérèse and Sally were, in my view at least, forging authentic sociolinguistic identities at the time of the study, I do not wish to suggest that they had reached (or surpassed) some threshold stage of authenticity in the sense that they had completed some necessary sequence of developmental stages in a linear fashion. Rather, since sociolinguistic authentication is dynamic, and it is accomplished *in situ* from moment to moment, the data analyzed here represent only a snapshot of how Thérèse and Sally were doing authenticity over a series of tasks at a particular moment in their developmental histories. Their authenticity as speakers of French, as people living in an L2 sociolinguistic world, will certainly be continually reified, modified and even challenged in the future as they live a variety of new experiences in French. For instance, Thérèse embarked on a semester-long study abroad sojourn in France following her participation in this study, which may have provided access to interactions with a wider range of interlocutors in a variety of contexts not typically available at her home institution in the United States. Indeed, study abroad experiences can be influential in developing a language learner's sense of self and identity – a notion closely related to the concept of authenticity – in relation to sociolinguistic, pragmatic and interactional competencies (e.g. Kinginger, 2013; see also several chapters in this volume: Diao; Fernández; Lee & Kinginger; McGregor; Taguchi).

This chapter is what I hope will be the opening salvo for a discussion of the nature of L2 sociolinguistic authenticity and its development. Future research would do well to expand upon the methods used to observe and evaluate authenticity and authenticating practices. Such methods might include more qualitative analysis of language awareness interviews as well as the practices in which learners and their interlocutors engage in order to authenticate their sociolinguistic identities from moment to moment. Observing sociolinguistic authenticity in L2 performance and its development might also be made possible by having learners record themselves interacting in the L2 in contexts that they deem representative or important examples of the kinds of interactions they participate in on a regular basis (see, for example, the chapters by Fernández, Lee & Kinginger, and McGregor in this volume). Such analyses – conducted in tandem with explorations of learners' metapragmatics – would certainly help to inform scholarship on L2 sociolinguistic authenticities that goes beyond the snapshot approach taken in this chapter.

Appendix A: Interview Questions

NB: This is an English version of sample questions. The interviews were conducted in French.

Part 1: Background information

(i) How old are you? Where are you from/where did you grow up?
(ii) Why do you study French? What do you like about it? Not like about it? How long have you studied? What courses have you taken?
(iii) Have you spent time in a French-speaking country? Where? When? For what purpose(s)? How long were you there? What you like/not like about it? Any other experience with French outside of the classroom?
(iv) What is/are your major(s) at [university name]? Minor?
(v) What are your future plans? Work, personal life/family, etc.?

Part 2: Narratives

Based on responses to the **narrative prompt worksheet**

Appendix B: Narrative Prompt Worksheet

To help facilitate your interview, you are being asked to consider the following categories and to provide an idea for a story. Please write down a word or short phrase that describes one or two stories for each category. If you can't think of a story for a particular category, feel free to leave it blank.

Domain	Event type	Story idea
Weekend/vacation	Memorable	
	Terrible	
	Typical	
School	Accomplishment	
	Difficulty	
	Daily routine	
Food	Dinner routine when younger	
	Funny dining experience	
	Memorable restaurant experience	
Work	First day of work	
	Funny thing that happened at work	
	Recognition at work	

Appendix C: Language Awareness Interview Questions

Part 1: Debriefing

Sample script: Thanks for being part of this study. At this point I'd like to explain what the main goal of the study is, and to ask you for some opinions about it. The study is focusing on advanced learners of French and their use and understanding of the social meaning of certain sociolinguistic features of French – namely, tu *and* vous, on *and* nous, *and the presence and absence of* ne *in negation. You may have noticed this in the sentence versions task you just completed. A secondary goal is to explore how you tell stories to different people – in the case of this study, how you tell stories to me, a professor, versus a peer or a classmate. Before moving on to some questions I have for you, do you have any questions for me? Any comments?*

Part 2: Awareness of *tu/vous*

Sample questions/topics:

(1) Can you tell me about any rules or concepts that guide *tu/vous* choice in French?
(2) How do you decide when to use *tu* and when to use *vous*?
(3) What does it mean to you when you call someone *tu*? When someone calls you *tu*?
(4) What does it mean to you when you call someone *vous*? When someone calls you *vous*?

(5) Do you have any examples or stories from your own life involving *tu/vous* choices? For example, when the choice was difficult, or maybe you made a mistake and were corrected, or when someone called you *tu* or *vous* in an unexpected way?

Part 3: Awareness of *on/nous*

(1) Can you tell me what you know about the pronouns *on* and *nous*?
(2) How do you decide when to use *on* and when to use *nous*?
(3) Is there any particular social meaning for you when you use *on* with someone? *Nous*?
(4) What about when someone uses *on* when talking to you? *Nous*?
(5) Do you have any examples or stories from your own life involving *on/nous* choices?

Part 4: Awareness of presence/absence of *ne* in negation

(1) Can you tell me what you know about negation in French – that is, using *ne* or leaving it out?
(2) How do you decide when to include *ne* and when to leave it out?
(3) Is there any particular social meaning for you when you include *ne*? Leave it out?
(4) What about when someone uses *ne* when talking to you? Leaves it out?
(5) Do you have any examples or stories from your own life involving *ne* presence or absence?

Appendix D: Oral Appropriateness Judgment Task

Script: I'm going to read a series of social situations to you, and I want you to tell me which language choices you would make, which choices you would expect the other person to make, and why. In other words, for each situation, tell me whether would you use tu or vous, on or nous, and negation with or without ne, and which of these language forms you would expect the other person to be more likely to use with you. Do you have any questions?

Situations:

You are at a local café one evening and a friend of yours, Jean, comes in. He walks over to your table and greets you.
Just before you and your friend order your drinks, your friend's girlfriend, Sophie, enters the café, sees the two of you, and comes over. You've never met her before.
You're walking down the street with some of your friends on a Saturday afternoon when you run into one of your favorite teachers, M Robinet. He's about 40 years old.

You have a question about your course schedule so you go to the main office of the department. There, the administrative assistant – a woman in her fifties – greets you. You've never talked to her before, but you know that she is relatively formal with students.
You're going to a café that you've been frequenting regularly for about three months because it's a nice place to watch soccer matches. You've got to know the owner, JF, fairly well. He's about 40 years old and very friendly to all his customers.
You're at the grocery store looking for some cheese for a small dinner party you're having with some friends. Unfortunately, you don't see the cheese you wanted. You decide to ask the clerk, a young woman who's about your age.
You are going to see your professor, Mme Triolet, during her office hours because you have a question about an up-coming French culture exam. You haven't scheduled a meeting so you don't know if she's available right now.
At a party, your friend Marc introduces you to his friend, Paul, whom you've never met. Paul is 21 years old.

Note

(1) I say 'essentialized version' here because the question prompted the learners to respond in a binary manner (e.g. *ne* absence or *ne* presence) rather than in a nuanced way that accounts for relative frequency (e.g. mostly *ne* absence but some *ne* presence).

References

Bell, A. (1984) Language style as audience design. *Language in Society* 13, 145–204.
Bell, A. (2001) Back in style: Reworking audience design. In P. Eckert and J. Rickford (eds) *Style and Sociolinguistic Variation* (pp. 139–169). Cambridge: Cambridge University Press.
Bucholtz, M. (2003) Sociolinguistic nostalgia and the authentication of identity. *Journal of Sociolinguistics* 7, 398–416.
Bucholtz, M. and Hall, K. (2005) Identity and interaction: A sociocultural linguistic approach. *Discourse Studies* 7, 585–614.
Cooper, D.E. (1983) *Authenticity and Learning: Nietzsche's Educational Philosophy*. London: Routledge and Keagan Paul.
Dewaele, J.-M. (2001) Une distinction mesurable: Corpus oraux et écrits sur le continuum de la deixis [A measurable difference: Oral and written corpora on the deixis continuum]. *Journal of French Language Studies* 11, 179–199.
Eckert, P. (2003) Elephants in the room. *Journal of Sociolinguistics* 7, 392–397.
Eckert, P. (2008) Variation and the indexical field. *Journal of Sociolinguistics* 12, 453–476.
Eckert, P. (2012) Three waves of variation study: The emergence of meaning in the study of variation. *Annual Review of Anthropology* 41, 87–100.
Johnstone, B. and Kiesling, S.F. (2008) Indexicality and experience: Exploring the meaning of /aw/-monophthongization in Pittsburg. *Journal of Sociolinguistics* 12, 5–33.
Kinginger, C. (2008) Language learning in study abroad: Case studies of Americans in France. *Modern Language Journal* 92 (1).
Kinginger, C. (2013) Identity and language learning in study abroad. *Foreign Language Annals* 46, 339–358.
Labov, W. (1963) The social motivation of a sound change. *Word* 19, 273–309.
Labov, W. (1972) *Sociolinguistic Patterns*. Philadelphia, PA: University of Pennsylvania Press.

Labov, W. (1984) Field methods of the Project on Linguistic Change and Variation. In J. Baugh and J. Sherzer (eds) *Language in Use* (pp. 28–53). Englewood Cliffs, NJ: Prentice Hall.

MacDonald, M.N., Badger, R. and Dasli, M. (2006) Authenticity, culture, and language learning. *Language and Intercultural Communication* 6 (3–4), 250–261.

Mougeon, R., Nadasdi, T. and Rehner, K. (2010) *The Sociolinguistic Competence of Immersion Students*. Bristol: Multilingual Matters.

Regan, V., Howard, M. and Lemée, I. (2009) *The Acquisition of Sociolinguistic Competence in a Study Abroad Context*. Bristol: Multilingual Matters.

Silverstein, M. (2001) The limits of awareness. In A. Duranti (ed.) *Linguistic Anthropology: A Reader* (pp. 382–401). Oxford: Blackwell.

Silverstein, M. (2003) Indexical order and the dialectics of sociolinguistic life. *Language and Communication* 23, 193–229.

Tagliamonte, S.A. (2006) *Analysing Sociolinguistic Variation*. Cambridge: Cambridge University Press.

van Compernolle, R.A. (2011) Developing a sociocultural orientation to variation in language. *Language and Communication* 31, 86–94.

van Compernolle, R.A. (2014) *Sociocultural Theory and L2 Instructional Pragmatics*. Bristol: Multilingual Matters.

van Compernolle, R.A. and Williams, L. (2012a) Reconceptualizing sociolinguistic competence as mediated action: Identity, meaning-making, agency. *Modern Language Journal* 96, 234–250.

van Compernolle, R.A. and Williams, L. (2012b) Teaching, learning, and developing L2 French sociolinguistic competence: A sociocultural perspective. *Applied Linguistics* 33, 184–205.

Vygotsky, L.S. (1978) *Mind in Society: The Development of Higher Mental Processes*. Cambridge, MA: Harvard University Press.

Vygotsky, L.S. (1986) *Thought and Language*. Cambridge, MA: MIT Press.

5 Learning Speech Style in Japanese Study Abroad: Learners' Knowledge of Normative Use and Actual Use

Naoko Taguchi

Introduction

MacDonald *et al* (2006) conceptualize authenticity as having two meanings: authenticity of correspondence and authenticity of genesis (Cooper, 1983). In the context of second language (L2) learning, authenticity of correspondence refers to the degree of match between language used by L2 learners and language used by native speakers, which is considered to reflect the norms and conventions of the target speech community. Authenticity of genesis, on the other hand, centers on the point of origin: language is considered authentic if it reflects learners' own choice and use, regardless of its correspondence to normative language use. MacDonald *et al.* claim that the field has been one-sided, focusing on the first type of authenticity, and they argue for the need to unify both notions of authenticity.

This chapter responds to this call by documenting L2 Japanese learners' pragmatic language use by presenting two types of data: data elicited from a discourse completion test (hereafter DCT) and data collected from interview data. DCT data illustrate learners' knowledge of normative pragmatic behaviors as appraised by native speakers in the target community. In contrast, interview data illustrate pragmatic choices that learners make in real-life situations, which are not always congruent with their knowledge of idealized norms and conventions. By synthesizing these two types of data, this chapter reveals authenticity of correspondence and genesis. Learners often demonstrate pragmatic knowledge that corresponds to normative conventions shared among native speakers. At the same time, they exhibit unique pragmatic behaviors that are authentic to them because of real-life constraints.

Problems of authenticity in the discourse completion test

The DCT, originally developed by Blum-Kulka (1982) to elicit speech acts, is a data collection instrument that has been used extensively in studies of interlanguage pragmatics (for a review, see Kasper, 2000; Kasper & Dahl, 1991; Kasper & Rose, 2002; Roever, 2011). A typical format of a DCT involves a brief scenario describing the setting and situation, followed by a dialogue that has at least one turn as an open slot to be completed by the participant. The description given in the scenario generally includes information on interlocutor relationships, social distance and the purpose of interaction, and it is designed to constrain the open slot in order to elicit a specific speech act. Participants are asked to imagine the situation and produce the response as if they were performing the role indicated in the description. The following example has been taken from Blum-Kulka *et al.* (1989: 14):

> A student has borrowed a book from her teacher, which she promised to return today. When meeting her teacher, however, she realizes that she forgot to bring it along.
>
> **Teacher**: Miriam, I hope you brought the book I lent you.
> **Miriam**: _____
> **Teacher**: OK, but please remember it next week.

Although DCTs have enjoyed unparalleled popularity in pragmatics research, they have come in for criticism for their lack of authenticity. Researchers have repeatedly pointed out that the situational prompts in DCTs are not authentic to the participants because they may not be familiar with the situations described in the scenarios. A classic study by Eisenstein and Bodman (1993) on expressions of gratitude presents evidence of this. Eisenstein and Bodman collected information on naturally occurring tokens of 'thank you' in American English, which resulted in 50 authentic situations involving expressions of gratitude. They chose 14 situations for the DCT administered to nonnative English speakers of different language backgrounds. A post hoc interview revealed that some nonnative participants had no previous experience with the situations in the DCT because of their limited social roles (e.g. housewives with no experience in the business world), pointing to a concern of unwarranted impact of participants' lack of familiarity on the resulting data. Other reasons why DCTs can be artificial to participants include the following: the abbreviated nature of situational descriptions; lack of real-life consequences in imagined contexts; and one-directional format of DCTs when certain speech acts (e.g. requests and promises) cannot be completed by a single person (Yamashita, 2008).

In addition to the authenticity of situations, the authenticity of language use is another area of concern that often arises with DCT-elicited data. In fact, several studies have revealed discrepancies between DCT data and naturalistic data in terms of the length of responses and number of turns, range of semantic moves, expression of emotion and number of repetitions and elaborations (e.g. Beebe & Cummings, 1996; Golato, 2003; Hartford & Bardovi-Harlig, 1992; Turnbull, 2001; Yuan, 2001). Golato (2003) gathered compliment responses from conversations among native speakers of German and compared them with those elicited via a written DCT. She found that features of DCT-elicited compliment responses did not match those found in the conversational data. For example, the archetypal complement response, *danke* (thank you), never appeared in the naturalistic data, while it occupied over 12% of the DCT responses. In addition, 12% of the naturalistic data contained a positive compliment pursuit marker in a later turn (expressions used to seek another round of compliments), but it was almost absent in the DCT data. Similar findings were obtained in Hartford and Bardovi-Harlig (1992), the only study involving L2 data. They compared data on the speech act of rejections in academic advising sessions in a US university with data collected from a written DCT. The DCT elicited a narrower range of semantic formulas: some formulas such as indefinite responses and condition statements never appeared in the DCT-based rejections. These two studies did not use the findings to discredit DCTs, but rather cautioned that the DCTs are likely to provide information about participants' pragmalinguistic knowledge of the strategies and linguistic forms by which speech acts are implemented, rather than actual performance. Kasper observed:

> Excluded from investigation (in questionnaires) are precisely those pragmatic features that are specific to oral interactive discourse – any aspect related to the dynamics of a conversation, turn-taking and the conversation mechanisms related to it, sequencing of action, speaker-listener coordination, features of speech production that may have pragmatic import, such as hesitation, and all paralinguistic and non-verbal elements. (Kasper, 2000: 325–326)

Lack of interactional features in the DCT-elicited data has become a primary source of criticisms in the current era, with the rise of discursive pragmatics that intends to examine speech acts in a situated interaction (Kasper, 2006). An increasing number of recent studies have applied conversation analysis (CA) (e.g. Heritage, 1984; Sacks *et al.*, 1974) to study action, meaning and context by collecting audio- or videotaped natural conversations and transcribing them using special conventions. Correspondingly, CA-based assessment methods have been proposed in pragmatics (e.g. Walters, 2007; Yoon, 2013). CA takes the *emic* approach to the analysis of talk-in-interaction and reveals how participants co-construct an action sequentially turn-by-turn, and design their turns to jointly accomplish the activity at hand (Mori, 2009). Thus, from the CA point of view, the primary limitation of DCTs is that they do not allow for the concept of sequential organization in data.

Rather, DCTs elicit responses relative to a predetermined, intuition-based taxonomy of behavior, which makes inferences of real-life pragmatic competence problematic.

To summarize, the brief historical sketch of DCTs and their use presented above reiterates some of the advantages and disadvantages of the DCT instrument, which have been visited in the literature time after time. The primary benefit of DCTs is that they allow for a large collection of data in one setting. Researchers can control the setting and conditions intervening in interaction, which makes it possible to quantify responses and compare data across different participant groups. DCT-elicited data can provide information about participants' knowledge of pragmalinguistic forms and sociopragmatic knowledge of contextual factors that influence choices of the forms, and reveal what participants know as opposed to what they can do under performance constraints. However, authenticity is seriously undermined in DCTs because their data may not be representative of face-to-face interaction. DCTs disregard the interactive, dynamic nature of conversation in which a communicative function is jointly constructed between the interlocutors and negotiated over multiple turns. Given these limitations, DCTs are considered to reduce the scope of analysis to discrete aspects of pragmalinguistic knowledge and do not extend to the actual language use in real-life situations.

While the limitations are noteworthy, we have to acknowledge that DCTs still remain a popular data-gathering instrument in much of the current work in speech acts and interlanguage pragmatics. Bardovi-Harlig's (2010) exhaustive literature review of pragmatics studies over the last three decades found that only 60% of the production-based studies (78 out of 129) used two-way communication data (e.g. role play and synchronous/asynchronous telecollaboration). The rest of the studies used DCTs. Bardovi-Harlig (2010: 242) argued that collecting samples of authentic, consequential language use must be the 'default design for studies of production' in order to meet the desired goals of pragmatics research involving the study of language use, interaction and speaker effects on interlocutors.

This call for alternative methods to DCTs, in my view, has not been emphasized in the literature. In my review of 58 instructional studies in L2 pragmatics published since 1990s (Taguchi, 2015), 25 studies used DCTs as a measure of learning outcome. Adding to this, a cursory examination of abstracts in the 19th International Conference on Pragmatics and Language Learning that took place at Indiana University in 2014 revealed that more than 30% of the presentations involved studies using DCTs.

Given the continuing popularity of the DCTs intersecting with unending criticisms to the instrument, it is timely to revisit the validity issues of DCTs from the point of language users. Previous validity studies examined whether or not DCT data compare to authentic data collected through real-life sampling and observation (Beebe & Cummings, 1996; Golato, 2003; Hartford & Bardovi-Harlig, 1992; Yuan, 2001). However, essentially in all of these studies, DCT and authentic data were drawn from different participant groups, making the comparability of the two data questionable. Any differences gleaned from the analysis can be attributed to differences in individual characteristics, rather than the effects of the instrument.

A more useful approach to validation, then, is to investigate what a group of individuals know in terms of the normative use of pragmatic conventions and how the same group navigates real-life instances of language use with the knowledge. Although individuals might know which forms to use under which circumstances, actual implementation of the knowledge is constrained by a number of individual and contextual factors. Cognitive factors such as memory and processing efficiency are likely to affect learners' ability to execute the knowledge while coping with the online demand of communication that involves turn-taking and negotiation. Learner agency and subjectivity are other factors to consider as learners may intentionally choose to opt out for particular pragmatic forms simply because they do not appeal to them (Davis, 2007; Ishihara & Tarone, 2009; see van Compernolle and van Compernolle & Henery, this volume). Desired identity could also come into play because of the consequentiality of real-life language use. Unlike DCTs which maintain anonymity, learners may not say what they actually think and withhold feelings that would result in a loss of face of others or themselves. Learners' perceived identities and positioning as a foreigner could also influence their participation in the target culture, consequently restricting their opportunities to practice local pragmatic norms in full (Brown, 2013; Hasall, 2013; Iwasaki, 2011; Siegal, 1996). These findings point to potential areas of discrepancies existing between learners' knowledge and their implementation of the knowledge in real-life situations.

Brown (2013) is a rare study that actually documented these discrepancies. He analyzed DCT-based data and recordings of naturalistic conversations and interviews to chart acquisition of Korean honorifics by four learners of Korean during a one-year study abroad. He found a gap between the learners' near-perfect knowledge of honorifics and the way they actually used them. The learners were found not utilizing their knowledge in the local community. One of the reasons was linguistic difficulty. One participant expressed that he could not control the full range of politeness levels, and as a result dropped certain forms of honorifics during interaction. In other cases, native-speaker patterns of honorifics were not available to the participants because their positions as foreigners resulted in the local members' belief that normative rules of honorifics (e.g. using honorifics to someone older but not the other way around) do not apply to the communication with them. One heritage learner was caught in a dilemma between his desire to establish himself as a real Korean by using honorifics fluently and his Western background which favors egalitarianism in language use.

These discrepancies between the learners' knowledge of prescriptive norms of how honorifics should be used and the way that they actually used them are highly informative for two reasons. First, they tell us what factors facilitate or constrain actual implementation of the pragmatic knowledge, thereby assisting our interpretation of the DCT-elicited data. Because factors such as linguistic difficulty, identity and positioning in the local community are not embedded in the DCT scenarios, their profound impact on actual language use tells us what considerations we should exercise when interpreting DCT data to make inferences about learners' real-life performance. At the same time, such data could contribute to our understanding of what we mean by authenticity. Close correspondence between laboratory-based performance and real-life performance can be an indicator of authenticity, but if real-life constraints indeed hinder learners from using the knowledge that they actually possess, it is debatable which data are considered as an authentic representation of learners' ability – knowledge elicited via controlled environment or skewed performance under real-life constraints. The authentic community is the place where learners' knowledge of sociocultural behaviors, norms of interaction and conventions of language use are implemented, but the correspondences and discrepancies between their knowledge and actual use can be understood only by cross-examining two sets of the data to reveal how real-life constraints may or may not impact learners' use of the knowledge in the local community.

The present study pursues this investigation, focusing on the acquisition of Japanese speech style in a study abroad setting. By cross-examining DCT-elicited data and learners' reported experience with speech style in the host community, this study intends to reveal correspondences and discrepancies between learners' knowledge of speech style and their actual use in day-to-day interaction. The study intends to contribute to the literature in the validation of DCTs by revealing learners' knowledge base of speech style, and the individual and contextual parameters that constrain their demonstration of the knowledge. The study is guided by two research questions:

(1) Do L2 learners of Japanese show development in their knowledge of speech style during a semester abroad as demonstrated in their DCT responses?
(2) What are the sources of discrepancies between their knowledge of speech style and actual use in the host community?

Before presenting the methods of the study, in the next section I will provide a brief overview of Japanese speech style, the focal pragmatic feature in this study.

Japanese speech style

The Japanese language contains two primary speech styles – the polite form and the plain form – which occur at clause-final position and index social meanings of formality, affect and attitudes (Cook, 1999, 2006, 2008; Ikuta, 2008; Okamoto, 1999). In the polite form, the copula *desu* is placed after nouns, adjectives and adjectival verbs, and the suffix *masu* is attached as a verb ending. The plain form involves the base form of verbs and adjectives, as well as *da/dearu*-ending of nouns and adverbs, which can be omitted. The examples below illustrate these two forms. Both sentences have the same meaning (i.e. It's raining.), but the copulas attached to the noun *ame* (raining) are different: the polite form *desu* in (1), and the plain form *da* in (2).

(1)   Polite form   Ame   **desu.**
                    Rain Cop
(2)   Plain form   Ame   **da.**
                    Rain Cop

Broadly speaking, the polite form is associated with formal speech used for addressing age-rank superiors, strangers and non-intimates, whereas the plain form is associated with informal speech when interacting with intimate age-rank equals, subordinates and children (Ide, 1989). This one-to-one mapping between context and speech style, however, has been challenged by the recent indexical approach (Cook, 2006, 2008; Fukushima, 2007; Ikuta, 2008; Nazkian, 2010). It is now widely understood that Japanese speakers shift between these forms in a single context by attending not only to static contextual features but also to dynamic ones, such as the addressee's attitudes, interpersonal distance and sequential turns that change in the unfolding course of interaction. For instance, shifts from the polite to the plain form can express spontaneous assertion of one's emotions and thoughts, evaluations, soliloquy-like remarks and empathy and closeness, whereas shifts from the plain to polite form can index increased psychological distance, presentation of public self and authoritative voice (Cook, 2002, 2008; Fukushima, 2007; Ikuta, 2008; Makino, 2002; Okamoto, 1999).

Methods

This study was conducted over a period of one academic semester, from April to July 2012 (13 weeks), in a study abroad setting in Tokyo, Japan. As stated earlier, one of the goals of the study was to ascertain the degree to which learners' metapragmatic knowledge of speech acts corresponded with their actual performances on a DCT. In what follows, I provide a brief overview of the participants, data collection procedures and analytic methods that are relevant to the present investigation.

Participants

The participants were 22 international students (five males and 17 females) enrolled in a Japanese language program at a private university in Tokyo (average age of 22, ranging from 19 to 29). Their nationalities were widespread, including: Chinese (6), Taiwanese (6), American (4), Singaporean (2), New Zealand (1), Brunei (1), Korean (1) and French (1). All of them were studying abroad in Japan for the first time. Fourteen students were living in an international dormitory, six had a homestay arrangement and two were living alone in an apartment.

The target participants were intermediate-level students who had received formal education on two primary speech styles in Japanese (polite and plain forms). This group was placed at Levels 3 and 4 in the Japanese language program based on the placement exams. I distributed a flyer to all Level 3 and 4 students (a total of 233) to solicit participation. From about 100 students who came forward, I excluded the students who had studied in Japan before or who were continuing on from the previous semester. Because the test instructions were in English, I excluded students who did not indicate confidence in English. As a result, 22 students remained in the study.

From the group of 22 participants, eight were recruited as informants for interviews. I first solicited interest in participating in the interviews from the 22 participants. Twelve participants indicated interest, from whom I selected eight participants who demonstrated diversity in terms of nationality, gender, length of previous Japanese study, living arrangements and purpose of study abroad. The participants were interviewed three times during the period of study (one semester). The informants represented six different nationalities. Six of them were living in an international student dormitory, one student had a homestay arrangement, and the eighth was living in a shared house owned by a Japanese couple.

Instrument

An oral discourse completion test (oral DCT) was used to measure participants' speech act production. The test contained two practice items and 10 test scenarios. Of the 10 test scenarios, five described a formal setting in which a student is talking to someone superior (larger social distance and unequal power relationship), while the other five described an informal setting between close friends or family members (smaller social distance and equal power relationship).[1] Participants read each scenario and produced the target speech act in each situation by using the appropriate speech style (polite or plain form). The DCT elicited five speech acts: compliment, compliment response, request, apology and thanking. A pair of formal and informal scenarios was prepared for each speech act. See Appendix A for the complete DCT scenarios.

The situational scenarios were adapted from Ishihara and Maeda's (2010) Japanese pragmatics textbook in which materials were validated with empirical data. Different levels of formality between the two situation types and speech styles (polite versus plain form) reflecting those situational differences were confirmed. In addition, the DCT was piloted with two native speakers: they used polite forms in formal situations of professor–student interaction and used plain forms in informal situations between two friends. The test was administered twice, at the beginning and end of the semester. To avoid practice effects, two different versions were prepared by making minor modifications in the scenarios (e.g. names of people and location).

Two native Japanese speakers evaluated speech samples using a six-point scale (see Table 5.1). The rating descriptions are attached. Raters focused on the sentence-ending form (polite or plain) and judged if the linguistic choice matched the situation type. Because Japanese speakers sometimes switch between these forms in the same context depending on the speaker's feelings and attitudes, raters took this style shifting into consideration when evaluating the samples. If a sample contained a mix of forms, they assessed whether the mixing was natural and determined a score.

Raters were female Japanese native speakers in their forties who grew up in Tokyo and taught English to adults in Japan.[2] At the norming session, we discussed the rating scales, evaluated samples, checked consistency and modified the scales when necessary. After finalizing the scales, they evaluated samples independently. Interrater reliability based on Pearson correlation was 0.89. About 7% of all the samples involved a discrepancy of two points or more. These discrepancies were resolved through discussion. Samples with a discrepancy of one point received an averaged score.

After signing the informed consent form, 22 participants completed the oral DCT individually by computer (once at the beginning and again at the end of the semester). They practiced two items and moved on to the 10 test

Table 5.1 Rating scale for DCTs

6 Excellent	Almost perfect control of speech style. Forms are used appropriately and accurately in situation.
5 Good	Good control of speech style. Forms are used appropriately in situation. Grammar and lexical errors exist but they are not so noticeable.
4 Fair	Moderate control of speech style. Forms are used appropriately in situation but grammar and lexical errors could cause misunderstanding.
3 Poor	Poor control of speech style. Unnatural mixing of forms.
2 Very poor	Almost no control of speech style. Formal form used in informal situation and vice versa. Speech is obviously unnatural.
1 Can't evaluate	Speech is incomprehensible.

items. Each item started with a scenario on the computer screen in English. When they were ready, they clicked on the 'continue' button. Then, the scenario disappeared and the message 'start speaking' appeared. After they finished, they clicked on the 'continue' button to move on to the next item. The computer recorded their speech. Participants on average took about 15 minutes to complete the test.

Interview data

In addition to the DCT data, this study collected interview data from a subset of eight participants in order to explore their study abroad experiences. The interviews took place once a month during the study period (a total of three interviews per participant). The interviews were conducted in English in a quiet office on campus for 40–60 minutes and were recorded on a Macintosh computer. The interviews were semi-structured to include certain preselected themes but allowed flexibility in incorporating themes nominated by the informants.

In the first interview, my questions focused on the informants' educational background and experiences. I asked questions about their formal Japanese study in their home country, amount of contact with native Japanese speakers before they came to Japan, and goals of their Japanese study. I asked questions related to the degree of their adjustment to the new environment. I asked what kind of expectations they had before they came to Japan and how they had changed (or had not changed) over time. I also asked what they considered to be their most valuable experience in Japan. Finally, my questions focused on their degree of social networking. I asked how much time they spent speaking Japanese every week, with whom and for what purposes.

Many of these questions were followed up on in the second interview, but the topic was extended to elicit more detailed accounts of the informants' opportunities to communicate in Japanese. I specifically asked about their perceived importance of Japanese speaking skills in establishing relationships and networks with local people. I also asked whether, and in what ways, their Japanese abilities improved as a consequence of their social contact and involvement with local Japanese interlocutors. Another addition in the second interview was about their understanding of intercultural competence. I asked about the skills and personal qualities that they thought were important in order to function and fit in with the Japanese community, and whether they thought they had made any improvement in those areas.

The last interview was conducted at the end of the semester, a few days after the last DCT administration. While revisiting the questions from the first and second interviews, I directly asked questions about speech style. I asked what they knew about the polite and plain forms, what observations they had about Japanese speakers' use of them, and what experiences they had in their own use and any difficulties related to the use.

Data analysis

DCT samples were transcribed and assessed on a six-point scale for the appropriate use of speech style in the situation. The score had an interval scale of 0–60 ($k = 10$). Gain scores were calculated by subtracting the pretest score from the posttest score. A paired-sample t-test was used to assess the degree of gains over a semester.[3]

The interviews were transcribed and analyzed using the strategy of content analysis. I first divided the interviews into semantic units – a complete thought expressed in a connected group of words separated from other utterances on the basis of content. Here, changes in content served as the criteria for segmenting units. In the interview excerpt below, the student responded to my question about difficult aspects of Japanese study. This excerpt contains two semantic units. He first said that grammar and expressions are difficult. Then he shifted to another aspect of difficulty – making jokes in Japanese.

> Yes, lack of expressions, grammar expressions. When someone says something to you and you don't have the correct words, find phone to look for vocabulary. It's difficult. (Unit 1) / And also joke, I sometimes wonder if it is appropriate to do. For example, yesterday I was with my girlfriend at the airport, she was putting her bag on the electronic balance you use when you check in, and some employee came and stood on this balance, so we saw his weight on this electronic balance. So I said *anata wa omokunai* and he didn't answer. (Unit 2)

Then individual semantic units were analyzed for the key terms relevant to the investigation: the polite form (*desu/masu* form), the plain form (casual form or *da*-form), honorifics (*keigo*), speech style and speech forms/levels. A total of 145 units were extracted and submitted to the second round of coding. I coded the data for the *indication of ambivalence* around speech style found in the participants' comments. I extracted units that involved any uncertainty, doubt, difficulty or questions that the participants voiced about their real-life experiences of speech style, mistakes they made with speech style, and contradictions or inconsistency that they expressed regarding their understanding and use of speech style. In the excerpt below, the student expresses confusion about different speech forms. She tries to use the plain form with friends, but sometimes the polite form (*masu*-form) comes out unintentionally. This unit was coded as an instance of ambivalence.

> Friends, it's OK, I don't have to be so careful. But sometimes I use *masu*-form to friends. (Why is that?) I don't know. It comes out more easily this way. I still get confused with all these forms.

In the excerpt below, the student explains that she has become familiar with the casual form (plain form) during her stay in Japan. Since she simply reports her observation about her own use of the speech style, this unit was not coded as an expression of ambivalence.

> I think maybe the first month or two *desu/masu* was more common for me, because at the beginning, when I was first learning Japanese, I learned *desu/masu* in China and Japan. So *desu/masu* was more familiar to me. And now I am talking to my friends, and they use casual all the time, so casual is more normal for me now.

This process yielded a total of 96 units of expressed ambivalence. Then I conducted the content analysis on the units for salient patterns and themes, focusing on the sources of or reasons for ambivalence. Comments that involved the same sources or reasons were grouped together and assigned the higher level label. This process was repeated twice over different days to ensure accuracy in coding. The second coder checked 10% of the excerpts for consistency.

Results

DCT findings: Knowledge of speech style

Table 5.2 displays descriptive statistics of oral DCT scores from the beginning (pretest) and end (posttest) of the semester (13 weeks). A paired-sample *t*-test showed significant gains from pretest to posttest: $t = 8.65$ ($p = 0.0001$). The effect size, based on the η^2, was large: $\eta^2 = 0.70$, indicating that the participants made a strong gain over time.

Analysis of score distribution at pretest and posttest confirmed that over 60% of the samples received a perfect score of six at posttest, whereas this score occupied only 25% at pretest. The majority of the samples at pretest fell in the score range of 1–3, indicating that the learners showed poor control of speech style (see the scoring rubric). Their choice of the speech style did not perfectly follow the situation type: they used the plain/causal form in formal situations and the polite form (*desu/masu*) in informal situations,

Table 5.2 Oral DCT speech style scores

	Mean	S.D.	Min	Max
Pretest	40.73	7.91	28.00	59.00
Posttest	49.34	6.93	36.50	60.00

Note: Maximum possible score was 60. There was no ceiling effect based on the average score.

or they used an odd mixing of the plain and polite form within a single situation. Example 5.1 illustrates the former case.

In this scenario, participants were instructed to ask their nine-year-old host sister to turn down the TV volume. In an informal situation of speaking to a child the plain form is expected, but this learner used the polite *desu/masu* form at all utterance-endings. Together with the use of the formal address term *san* (Ms), this speech addressed to a host sister sounds overly formal and distant. This participant received the score of 2. (In all excerpts below, the polite form is in bold, and the plain form is underlined. Appendix B contains the abbreviations.)

Example 5.1 Learner #22 : Pretest; Request – informal

Hiroko-san	*ano*	***sumimasen.***	*Ano*	*waruikedo*	*ano*	*terebi*	*no*
Hiroko-san	HES	excuse me	HES	sorry, but	HES	TV	Lk

koe	*wa*	*chotto*	*shizuka*	*ni*	*shite*	*mo*	*ii*	***desu***	***ka.***
voice	Top	a little	quiet	Lk	do		OK	Cop	Q

'Ms. Hiroko, well, excuse me, Well, sorry but, well, is it OK to turn down the TV volume a little?'

The same learner achieved the perfect score of six for the same DCT item at posttest. The reader will note the change in her use of the plain form at utterance-ending, along with the informal address term, *chan*, attached to the name (a diminutive suffix which expresses that the speaker finds a person endearing) (Example 5.2):

Example 5.2 Learner #22 : Posttest; Request – informal

Kenta-chan	*terebi*	*no*	*koe*	*o*	*chotto*	*chiisaku*	*nattemo*	*ii?*
Kenta-chan	TV	Lk	voice	O	a little	small	become	OK

'Kenta-chan, is it OK to turn down the TV volume a little?'

The excerpt below is an example of odd mixing of the two forms. Japanese speakers switch between the plain and polite forms occasionally by attending to dynamic contextual factors such as the addressee's attitudes and interpersonal distance (e.g. Cook, 1999; Ikuta, 2008). For instance, shifts from the polite to the plain form can express spontaneous emotion, evaluations, soliloquy-like remarks, empathy and closeness, whereas shifts from the plain to the polite form can index increased psychological distance, presentation of public self and authoritative voice. However, in many cases, the raters judged that the learners' style shift did not follow these conditions. In Example 5.3, the learner was attempting the speech act of an informal apology. The learner used the polite *desu/masu* form in three utterance-ending positions, but switched to the plain form in the last utterance when asking for permission to go home to get the book. This was a case of random mixing, not following any principles, resulting in the score of three.

Example 5.3 Learner #20 : Pretest; Apology – informal

*Tomo-chan,   hontoni gomen**nasai**.   Watashi kyo,   ano, hon   o   wasure**mashita**.*
Tomo-chan really   sorry-Aux.   I   today DM book O   forget-Pst
'Tomo-chan, I'm really sorry. Today I forgot the book.'

*Hontoni gomen**nasai**.   Watashi, ima   uchi   ni   itte, hon   o   motte, mottekitemo ii?*
really   sorry-Aux   I   now home Loc   go   book O bring   bring   OK
'Really sorry. Is it OK if I go home and bring the book?'

The same learner received the full score of six at posttest for the same item because she consistently used the plain form throughout, without shifting to the polite form (Example 5.4).

Example 5.4 Learner #20: Posttest; Apology – informal

Gomen   ne   Watashi,   noto   o   <u>wasureta.</u>
sorry   FP   I   notebook   O   forget-Pst
'Sorry, I forgot to bring the notebook.'

Mata,   mata,   ie   ni modotte   mottekuru   kara   chotto   <u>matte</u>   ne.
Again, again, home   to return   bring   CP   a little   wait   FP
'Again, again, I will return home to get it, so wait a little.'

Hontoni   gomen   ne.
really   sorry   FP
'I'm really sorry.'

Interview findings: Mismatch between knowledge and actual use

The data in the previous section revealed the students' strong knowledge regarding the contexts in which different speech styles are applied. However, interview data found that this high level of performance on the DCT did not always coincide with the patterns of speech style because of a range of factors that constrained their actual use in authentic contexts.

A total of 24 interviews (eight participants × three interviews) were transcribed and analyzed for the units that contained the key terms relating to speech style and the indication of ambivalence around speech style expressed by the participants (see the data analysis section for details). The entire process yielded a total of 96 units of expressed ambivalence.[4] Then the units were submitted for content analysis and coded for the sources or reasons for ambivalence. Comments that involved the same sources or reasons were grouped together. As a result, two unique themes emerged as sources of ambivalence: linguistic difficulty (53 comments), and complexity and dynamicity of speech style (43 comments). The next section presents the findings according to these themes.

Linguistic difficulty

Linguistic difficulty was the most common source of uncertainty that the learners experienced with their use of speech style. This confirms a shortcoming of the DCT instrument; namely, that DCTs give participants time to think and plan their speech, and they do not therefore elicit spontaneous responses to the prompts. Due to various performance-level constraints, knowledge of speech style (as demonstrated in DCTs) was not always put into use in actual interaction with local members. Short-term memory and processing demands are likely to interfere with the implementation of the knowledge, unless the knowledge is robust enough to cope with the demand. The demand is particularly high in the case of Japanese speech style since it involves complex grammatical forms and conjugations.

Participants' comments were concentrated on form-related difficulties (18 comments), but they also expressed difficulties in classifying the forms according to levels of politeness (eight comments). Although the polite and plain forms are two main categories of speech style, the polite form technically belongs to a larger category of an honorifics system that involves three levels: the respect, humble and polite forms. The polite form is placed at the lowest end of the honorifics hierarchy, which makes its association to formal register ambiguous to L2 learners. I found that some learners indeed did not know the distinction between the polite and plain form in terms of the social meaning they encode (e.g. Excerpt 5.1).

Excerpt 5.1 Learner #14

> In Singapore I learned the *desu/masu* form first, not the casual form, so that time, I didn't realize the *desu/masu* form is very formal. I thought it's the same with the casual form. Then I learned that it's actually a bit more formal than the casual form. Here, I started using these two forms but for me it's one. It's all one.

Confusion with the categorization of the forms seems to come from the order of instruction: the polite form first, and the plain form second. Although this learner considered the *desu/masu* and the plain form at the same level of linguistic politeness, other learners expressed a tendency of using the *desu/masu* as a default form in their communication (19 comments). Since they learned the polite form first, they became familiar with the form to the extent that it just slips off everywhere, even when the plain form is required. In Excerpt 5.2, the learner expressed awkwardness with the use of the plain form: she feels that something is missing at the sentence ending when she omits the long polite morphemes and produces their plain form equivalents.

Excerpt 5.2 Learner #3

> I learned the casual form in Brunei, but because I'm so used to using the *desu/masu* from the first time I studied Japanese, it stuck to me. But using *desu/masu* with friends sounds a little bit funny because it sounds formal. So I'm still adjusting to using informal. (Is it difficult to use the casual form?) No, it's not difficult, but I'm so used to using *desuka* or other *desu-* ending, so when I say like *Naniga aru?* ('What's there?'), it sounds a bit empty to me not having *desu*-ending. I feel like I'm ending my sentences awkwardly.

What is interesting with the 'default polite form' tendency is that the learners used certain expressions in the polite form as memorized chunks, retrieved as a whole without linguistic analysis (eight comments). This typically happened with discourse markers, backchannels and response forms that are short, linguistically simple and occur frequently in conversations. It seemed that the learners automatized their use with these common formulaic expressions, making the use of their plain form equivalents difficult, as Learner #14 suggested (Excerpt 5.3).

Excerpt 5.3 Learner #14

> Sometime confusing. When I was using the *futsutai* (the plain form), a phrase like *sodesune* (the polite form of 'I see.') just came out.

As illustrated above, the learners in this study experienced a great deal of linguistic difficulty when dealing with speech style in their everyday interaction. Grammatical difficulty and categorical complexity of the plain and polite forms, familiarity with one form over the other and fossilization of formulae tied to certain speech styles were found to be the primary sources of linguistic difficulty that obstruct learners' implementation of knowledge. The discrepancies between the knowledge and actual use found in this excerpt can be considered an artifact of the format of the DCT instrument. DCTs do not detect the same patterns of speech style because their format does not consider a variety of linguistic and cognitive factors, or history of learning, which inevitably influence learners' execution of their knowledge in real-time.

Complexity and dynamicity of speech style in context

Another salient source of ambivalence was found in the complexity and dynamicity of speech style (43 comments in total). As described previously, in Japanese, a structuralist approach associates the polite form with formal speech addressed to out-group members (people who are older, of higher status, and non-intimate), and the plain form with informal speech addressed to in-group members (people of lower status and age, and in intimate relationships) (e.g. Harada, 1976; Ide, 1989; Niyekawa, 1991). However, real-life situations are not that simple. The recent indexical approach refutes the static view on Japanese speech style and argues that speech style indexes a variety of social meanings (Cook, 2006, 2008; Fukushima, 2007; Ikuta, 2008; Nazkian, 2010). Notably, Cook (1996, 2006) described how Japanese speakers use the *desu/masu* form in diverse social contexts (e.g. family dinner time talk, elementary school classrooms, TV interviews and academic advising sessions) and encode different social identities and self-presentational stances. Under the indexical approach, the *desu/masu* form is not merely a marker of politeness or formality: it is an index of social meaning that one wishes to express in interaction with others.

The fact that there is no one-to-one mapping between the linguistic forms and social settings in real-life situations presents challenges to learners because they have to consider myriads of contextual information and guide their own choice of speech style. Sociocultural factors such as power and social distance are not expressed in a binary relationship of superior versus subordinate or close versus distant. Rather, they are expressed on a continuum. Learners need to weigh different factors before making a decision on what forms to use and, often, the decision has to be made case-by-case because configurations of the factors are unique to the situation. The factors also change with time – over the course of several turns within a single interaction or over a period of time as one's relationship and interaction patterns with others shift.

The learners in this study were aware of the complexity and dynamicity of the context and its relation to form. Because there is no one-size-fit-all rule, they were ambivalent when a situation presents several competing factors to consider. In the excerpt below, the learner speculated the case of style shift she observed during her tennis club activities. In the first few practice sessions, she noticed that senior members' language was different from their ordinary speech. What was confusing to her, as shown in excerpt 5.4, was their use of the respect form (the highest level of honorifics) at the end of the practice when members were invited to express their comments and reflections about their practice that day. She wondered why this extraordinary form of politeness was used in this particular moment, especially because people immediately switched back to their ordinary mode of speaking after the reflection session and started talking casually.

Excerpt 5.4 Learner #6: Time 1

> After practice, there is group gathering. There are two people in the front (usually *senpai*), summarizing today's lesson, and they ask the question, 'How does everyone feel about it?' It goes something like, *Hanashi o shitaikata irasshaimasuka?* I thought, why is she saying that? Because for me, English doesn't have *keigo*, except for 'May I go to the toilet?' So when she said, that, why? Why is there like different level of politeness needed for that?

The respect form *irrashaimasenka* ('Is there anyone …?') is a type of subject honorification. It is ranked the highest on the scale of politeness and is usually reserved for someone who is clearly superior. This rule, however, is in conflict in this situation because it is the senior who is using the respect form to juniors and age-equal peers. The use of honorifics here can be understood only when the contextual element 'setting' comes into the figure. The end-of-practice reflection session is a type of institutional talk associated with specific goals, constraints and procedures in which members assume specific roles and follow conventions (Drew & Heritage, 1992). Use of honorifics is a way of marking boundaries between the current ritualized practice and adjacent practice. Senior members are expected to use honorifics in this context because they assume the formal, on-stage presentation mode of communication. The data suggest that learners sometimes miss a complex configuration of context associated with a specific speech style. Relationship or hierarchy among people (e.g. senior versus junior) is one element of context, but other elements such as occasion, setting and rituals configure context and affect our linguistic choices.

A similar case was found in another learner in a homestay environment. This learner reported her understanding of style shifts occurring within the same relationship (i.e. the host mother and her), but she was not able to articulate the reasons behind the style shifting. She observed that the particular speech style (plain or polite) routinely practiced between the same individuals is not fixed or constant across contexts. Speech style changes when a different contextual element, such as setting, comes into the relationship (Excerpt 5.5).

Excerpt 5.5 Learner #11: Time 3

> With my host family sometimes it's hard because they talk to me in the casual form sometimes and then other times in the *desu/masu*, and also, ah … there are different relationships, like between my host father and me versus my host mother and me, so … It's like, you know, who should I use the *desu/masu* in what situation.

Like, when we went to the tea ceremony, I was like, should I use the *desu/masu* or casual here because it was a different situation, around different people. I wonder, ah, when I meet my host mother's friends, should I talk 'casual' with them or should I use the *desu/masu*, because we are with different people, and you know, I want to show some respect around them. When we go out together, I wonder which form I should use.

When the same individuals, in this case the learner and her host mother, are placed in an atypical setting outside the home, such as a tea ceremony, the learner is suddenly uncertain about the choice of speech style. Although the plain form is the norm at home between her and her host mother, the formality of the tea ceremony occasion brings a totally different contextual parameter that obscures the selection of speech style. Combined with the learner's subjectivity of wanting to express respect to her host mother in front of strangers, she is no longer sure whether the everyday use of the plain form applies to this situation.

The same learner also expressed ambivalence about the choice of speech style when the degree of imposition becomes a significant element to consider in the speech act performed. Excerpt 5.6 illustrates this. The plain form is the default style in the learner's speech to her host mother, but when she made a high-imposition request (asking for permission to use the kitchen), she switched to the polite form so she could reduce the potential face-threat of disrupting her host mother's territory (i.e. kitchen).

Excerpt 5.6 Learner #11: Time 1

It's sometimes uncomfortable using the casual form with my host father so I switch to the *desu/masu*. (Researcher: Why do you feel uncomfortable?) With *otosan* (host father), he is kind of like, the head of the household, and I feel weird speaking to him in the casual form, so I use the *desu/masu* mostly with him. For my host mom, I use the *desu/masu* when I ask her something. For example, when I asked her if I can use the kitchen to make my own *obento* (lunch box), I used the *desu/masu* because the kitchen is her domain, and I didn't want to impose, so I wanted to be more respectful.

This excerpt shows that the indexical approach to speech style is in place in L2 communication: Just like native speakers, L2 learners make their own personal choice of speech style in order to index the social meaning of respect, depending on the purpose of communication (what to ask to whom). The style shift from the plain to the polite form observed here can be considered the learner's politeness strategy. Although native speakers in this situation probably use syntactic mitigations and indirect expressions to do the face-work, the learner seemed to use style shift as a tactic to express her consideration and respect. The case of style shift across speech act types was found in other learners' comments. One learner reported that she switched to the polite form to a friend when asking for forgiveness on a serious matter.

To summarize, in addition to linguistic difficulty, this study found that the complexity and dynamicity of context was the cause of the learners' uncertainty about speech style. The data showed that the learners were exposed to a complex configuration of context in their everyday interaction and faced a situation in which they had to disentangle a range of contextual elements (e.g. setting, occasion and rituals) that are new to them. Strong metapragmatic knowledge of speech style, as evidenced by DCT performance, did not always give confidence to learners about their linguistic choice in the context that they needed to negotiate because of the complexity and ever-changing dynamics of the authentic contexts in which they participated within the community.

Conclusions and Implications

This study investigated the knowledge of speech style among 22 learners of Japanese and their actual use of speech style in a study abroad setting. The DCT administered over a semester revealed significant gains in the production of speech style with a large effect size, indicating learners' solid knowledge of speech style in a range of role-based social interaction encoded in the DCT scenarios. However, interview data from a subset of participants revealed a nuanced picture in regard to their implementation of the knowledge in the authentic community.

Linguistic difficulty was most frequently reported as a source of uncertainty and problems relating to the use of speech style. Learners were often unsuccessful with their implementation of the knowledge: they struggled to produce correct forms in spontaneous speech, to navigate different levels of politeness and to overcome the default status of the *desu/masu* style in order to use the plain form when required in a situation. These difficulties are likely a reflection of the demand of online processing at multiple levels. In contrast to the DCT, which allows time to plan responses, face-to-face interaction requires on-the-fly responses to the prompts. It also requires joint construction of discourse. Learners must align their behavior to the projection of the unfolding course of the interaction, as dictated by their interlocutor's talk-for-action, in order to shape their contributions to the talk. Hence, knowledge of pragmalinguistic forms demonstrated in the DCT is no guarantee in the real world when learners have to accomplish higher level goals such as negotiation and mutual understanding in a spontaneous manner.

These findings clearly point to the limitation of the DCT and lend support to the previous studies that found a range of discrepancies between DCT-elicited data and naturalistic data (Beebe & Cummings, 1996; Golato, 2003; Hartford & Bardovi-Harlig, 1992; Yuan, 2001). Contributing to the previous studies, the present findings revealed why such discrepancies occur in the context of Japanese speech style. Some of the reasons that emerged in the interviews include learners' use of the polite form as default style and the awkwardness they developed using the unfamiliar plain form. In other cases, several polite forms had entered learners' systems as memorized chunks and formulae, making it difficult to avoid the polite endings and replace them with their more casual counterparts.

While limitations of the DCT are real, the present findings point to several directions for future refinement of DCTs. Because the items in most DCTs are developed based on situational variables alone (interlocutors' distance and power difference, degree of imposition), researchers can introduce the concept of task difficulty and cognitive complexity into the design of the DCTs. Researchers can create situations or items of differing modality and task demands (e.g. a timed spoken task that taps into processing versus an untimed written task that targets knowledge) or different linguistic demands (e.g. chunks and formulae versus extended, creative discourse). In this way, DCTs can potentially be advanced into a tool that elicits L2 learners' ability to deal with situations of a variety of task difficulty, modality and processing demands. As a result, DCTs can more closely approximate their interaction demands in the authentic community.

In addition to linguistic difficulty, this study identified another source of a discrepancy between knowledge and actual use – complexity and dynamicity of the association between speech style and context. The learners in this study were often ambivalent about their use of speech style because of the idiosyncratic nature of authentic contexts where multiple speech forms coexist and shift according to contextual dynamics. Because one-to-one, straightforward mappings between the form and context, such as those presented in the DCT scenarios, are rare in the authentic community, the learners encountered difficulty when multiple competing elements (e.g. setting, occasion and rituals) came into the configuration of the context. In addition, the learners were found to be confused by the fact that context and speech style are not stable or fixed. They change within a single course of interaction or over a period of time corresponding to the change in interpersonal distance, attitudes, affect, formality of occasion and sequential organization of talk (Cook, 2008; Ikuta, 2008; Nazkian, 2010). Hence, in authentic situations, learners have to become sensitive to the changing contextual specifics, and adapt and align their communicative behaviors responding to a dynamic, changing context.

These abilities expected in naturalistic interaction – adaptability, flexibility and reciprocity – are difficult to measure with the current DCT format.

Yet, discrepancies between learners' knowledge and their actual use found in the present data suggest a need for introducing expanded, more complex metapragmatic information in DCT scenarios. Previous studies have typically followed Brown and Levinson (1983) and used power, social distance and degree of imposition as contextual factors to develop situational descriptions, but different dimensions such as formality, affective stance and rituals can be incorporated into the DCT scenarios. To counter for the dynamic nature of the form–context associations, different versions of a scenario can be prepared by changing one or two aspects of the situation while retaining other aspects. For example, a scenario about a conversation between a student and her host mother can take place in two different locations (e.g. at home versus outside the home) or for different occasions (e.g. chatting at home versus giving a public talk), or over two different speech acts involving different degrees of imposition. These modifications to the DCT could improve its format as an instrument that assesses learners' ability to cope with a range of contextual information and variability that are likely to represent real-world situations.

This study presented a renewed analysis of DCT data by revealing areas where discrete aspects of pragmalinguistic knowledge elicited via DCT do not extend to the actual language use in real-life situations. Study abroad settings present opportunities to practice learned knowledge, but at the same time present challenges and demands that cause difficulty in implementing the knowledge. The discrepancies between the knowledge and actual use found in this study are not meant to discredit DCTs. Rather, they are intended to reveal the causes of the discrepancies so DCTs can be improved and refined in the future to capture more realistic pragmatics abilities. DCTs have survived three decades despite persistent criticisms, which suggests that there are long-standing benefits shared among researchers regarding the instrument. I hope that the next decade finds a way to balance the practicality and validity of the DCT, and cultivates ways to improve the instrument to address criticisms about authenticity.

Previous studies attempted some refinements in the format by increasing the amount of situational descriptions (Billmyer & Varghese, 2000) and providing rejoinders (Rose, 1992). What is needed in the future is the modification of the content and construct of DCTs based on data from language users themselves. Learners' perception and experiences with pragmatics features – ambivalence and uncertainty or difficulty they experienced in understanding and using pragmatics features – can serve as a rich data source in the refinement process of DCTs. The present study is a modest contribution in this direction.

Finally, the present findings problematize the traditional concept of authenticity in research instruments. Mainstream practice in the language assessment literature draws on concept of the target language use (TLU) domain to elicit an adequate representative sample of the kind of language to be evaluated. A type of evidence needed to establish construct validity is the degree of correspondence between test tasks and the TLU domain, where learners' abilities can be generalized beyond the test situation to the real-life situation. This concept is also noted in MacDonald *et al.*'s (2006; and see also Cooper, 1983) argument that authenticity is in part a correspondence between the performance of learners and that of idealized native speakers. However, MacDonald *et al.* emphasize another dimension of authenticity – authenticity of genesis or authenticity of language use in terms of its origins – and argue for the importance of synthesizing the two accounts of authenticity.

Although my study was not designed to test this dual approach to authenticity, findings that emerged from the DCT and interview data combined lend support to these two dimensions of authenticity. Participants demonstrated a large gain in their use of speech styles on the DCT, indicating their understanding and adaptation of target language conventions (authenticity of correspondence). However, interview data revealed learners' uncertainty about the normative use of speech styles. Learners exercised their own understanding and perception of speech styles (authenticity of genesis), which were different from normative use. For example, Learner #11 in Excerpt 5.6 was able to interpret and negotiate the complex, dynamic nature of the polite and plain forms and use those forms to express her own stance of politeness and respect to people with whom she routinely interacted. She did not blindly follow normative patterns or adopt L2 conventions; rather, she took ownership of the speech styles and used them in a way that made most sense to her, which is a direct indication of authenticity within the learner. The findings suggest that the two types of authenticity introduced by MacDonald *et al.* (2006; in their adaptation of Cooper's, 1983 work) can be conceived as a unified in interpreting learners' performance.

These findings reiterate the importance of using multiple data sources to make inferences about learners' pragmatic knowledge and authenticity. This study clearly showed that DCT data alone were insufficient to reveal learners' knowledge of pragmatic linguistic forms and sociopragmatic notions associated with the forms. Interview data were critical in illuminating learners' engagement with real-life pragmatics as they constantly adapted their knowledge to complex, changing contexts of use. Hence, data triangulation helps us gain multiple insights about pragmatic competence – what learners know about pragmatics, how they apply their knowledge in real-life interactions, and how they confirm or revise their understanding corresponding with their experiences. Although this study used only two data sources – DCT and interview – future research could expand the scope of data collection by incorporating researcher observation, introspection (e.g. think-aloud, diary-keeping), and narrative and life-story methods.

Appendix A: Oral DCT Scenarios

Compliment	Informal	You are a student at a Japanese university. A good friend of yours, Takako, has just made an excellent presentation in class today. After class, you want to compliment her on her performance. What do you say to Takako?
	Formal	The class you take with Professor Sato was really good today, as always. He is an experienced senior professor about 30 years older than you. Today's lecture was particularly interesting. You decide to tell him this after class. What do you say to Prof Sato?
Compliment response	Informal	You are wearing a new T-shirt you just brought back from your trip to Kyoto during the summer vacation. A close friend of yours, Naoko, has noticed the T-shirt. She says it is beautiful and it fits you well. What do you say to Naoko?
	Formal	It is about half way in the semester. You are talking with Professor Ito, the instructor of your Japanese conversation class. She tells you that your Japanese has improved dramatically since the beginning of the semester. What do you say to Prof Ito?
Request	Informal	You are doing homework in your host family's house. Your host sister, Hiroko, is nine years old, and you get along with her very well. She is watching TV loud, and you can't concentrate. You want Hiroko to turn down the volume. What do you say to her?
	Formal	Your father is visiting you next week. Narita airport is a three-hour drive from your host family's house. There is no easy public transportation from the airport, so you want to ask your host father to drive you out to the airport to pick up your father. What do you say?
Apology	Informal	You and your friend, Tomo, are in the same class and are working on a project together. You and Tomo meet in the library to talk about the project. You forgot to bring a book that you promised to bring to the meeting. What do you say?
	Formal	You are living in an apartment in Tokyo. It's midnight, and you have just returned to the apartment. You realize that you have left your keys in your room and are locked out. You go to your landlord, Ms Ohta who lives across the street to borrow keys. What do you say?
Thanking	Informal	You and your close friend, Mari, are taking the same history class. You were absent from class last week due to illness, so you borrowed some notes from her. As you return them, what do you say to her?
	Formal	You are talking with Professor Suzuki, a senior professor at your university. You are working on a big project with her. Today, she has given you very helpful advice. As you leave her office, you thank her for her time. What do you say?

Source: Adapted from Ishihara and Maeda (2010).

Appendix B: Abbreviations in the Oral DCT Excerpts

kimasu	desu/masu form
<u>kuru</u>	plain form
Cop	various forms of copula verb *be*
Prog	Progressive
Lk	linking nominal
Neg	negative morpheme
Nom	Nominalizer
Loc	locative particles (*ni, de*)
M	particles for means
O	object marker
S	subject marker
Q	question marker
QT	quotative marker
IF	conditional if-clause
FP	sentence final particle
CP	conjunctive particle
Top	topic marker
DM	discourse marker (*nanka*)
HES	hesitation marker (*etto, ano*)
Aux	auxiliary

Notes

(1) These two distinct situation types were used purposefully in order to gain a clearer understanding about participants' use of complex pragmalinguistic resources because these two situation types clearly require different linguistic forms.
(2) Although pragmatic variation is an important factor to consider when evaluating L2 samples, I acknowledge that these rating guidelines did not reflect age or regional variation in Japan. Raters were born and grew up in Tokyo and they were much older than the participants.
(3) Normality of data distribution was confirmed by using the Shapiro–Wilk test (for sample size under 50).
(4) Remaining comments were mostly about their observations of DCT speech style or how they learned speech style.

References

Bachman, L.F. and Palmer, A.S. (2010) *Language Testing in Practice: Developing Language Assessments and Justifying their Use in the Real World.* Oxford: Oxford University Press.

Bardovi-Harlig, K. (2010) Exploring the pragmatics of imterlanguage pragmatics: Definition by design. In A. Trosborg (ed.) *Handbook of Pragmatics* (pp. 219–260). Berlin: Mouton de Gruyter.

Beebe, L.M. and Cummings, M.C. (1996) Natural speech act data and written questionnaire data: How data collection method affects speech act performance. In J. Neu and S.M. Gass (eds) *Speech Acts Across Cultures* (pp. 65–86). Berlin: Mouton de Gruyter.

Billmyer, K. and Varghese, M. (2000) Investigating instrument-based pragmatic variability: Effects of enhancing discourse completion tests. *Applied Linguistics* 21, 517–552.

Blum-Kulka, S. (1982) Learning to say what you mean in a second language. *Applied Linguistics* 3, 29–59.

Blum-Kulka, S., House, K. and Kasper, G. (1989) *Cross-cultural Pragmatics: Requests and Apologies*. Norwood, NJ: Ablex.

Brown, L. (2013) Identity and honorifics use in Korean study abroad. In C. Kinginger (ed.) *Social and Cultural Dimensions of Language Learning in Study Abroad* (pp. 269–298). Amsterdam: John Benjamins.

Brown, P. and Levinson, S. (1983) *Politeness: Some Universals in Language Usage*. Cambridge: Cambridge University Press.

Cook, H.M. (1996) The use of addressee honorifics in Japanese elementary school classrooms. In N. Akatsuka, S. Iwasaki and S. Strauss (eds) *Japanese/Korean Linguistics* 5. (pp. 67–81). CSLI Publication: Stanford.

Cook, H.M. (1999) Situational meanings of Japanese social deixis: The mixed use of the masu and plain forms. *Journal of Linguistic Anthropology*, 8, 87–110.

Cook, H.M. (2002) The social meanings of the Japanese plain form. In N. Akatsuka and S. Strauss (eds) *Japanese/Korean Linguistics* (Vol. 10; pp. 150–163). Stanford, CA: CSLI Publications.

Cook, H. (2006) Japanese politeness as an interactional achievement: Academic consultation sessions in Japanese universities. *Multilingua* 25, 269–292.

Cook, H. (2008) *Socializing Identities Through Speech Style*. Bristol: Multilingual Matters.

Cooper, D.E. (1983) *Authenticity and Learning: Nietzsche's Educational Philosophy*. London: Routledge and Keagan Paul.

Davis, J. (2007) Resistance to L2 pragmatics in the Australian ESL context. *Language Learning* 57, 611–649.

Drew, P. and Heritage, J. (1992) *Talk at Work: Interaction in Institutional Settings*. New York: Cambridge University Press.

Eisenstein, M. and Bodman, J. (1993) Expressing gratitude in American English. In G. Kasper and S. Blum-Kulka (eds) *Interlanguage Pragmatics* (pp. 64–81). New York: Oxford University Press.

Fukushima, E. (2007) On the topic of mixed style of *desu/masu* form and non-*desu/masu* form: Taigu communication among Japanese business people. *Waseda daigaku Nihongo kyoikugaku [Waseda University Study of Japanese Language Education]*, 138, 24–32.

Golato, A. (2003) Studying complement responses: A comparison of DCTs and recordings of naturally occurring talk. *Applied Linguistics* 24, 90–121.

Harada, S.-I. (1976) Honorifics. In M. Shibatani (ed.) *Syntax and Semantics, Vol. 5: Japanese Generative Grammar* (pp. 499–561). New York: Academic Press.

Hartford, B. and Bardovi-Harlig, K. (1992) Experimental and observational data in the study of interlanguage pragmatics. In L. Bouton and Y. Kachru (eds) *Pragmatics and Language Learning* (Vol. 3; pp. 33–52). Urbana-Champaign, IL: University of Illinois.

Hassall, T. (2013) Pragmatic development during short-term study abroad: The case of address terms in Indonesian. *Journal of Pragmatics* 55, 1–17.

Heritage, J. (1984) Conversation analysis. In J. Heritage (ed.) *Garfinkel and Ethnomethodology* (pp. 233–292). Cambridge: Polity Press.

Ide, S. (1989) Formal forms and discernment: Two neglected aspects of universals of linguistic politeness. *Multilingua* 8, 223–248.

Ikuta, S. (2008) Speech style shift as an interactional discourse strategy: The use and non-use of desu/masu in Japanese conversational interviews. In K. Jones and T. Ono (eds) *Style Shifting in Japanese* (pp. 71–89). Amsterdam: John Benjamins.

Ishihara, N. and Maeda, M. (2010) *Advanced Japanese: Communication in Context*. London: Routledge.
Ishihara, N. and Tarone, E. (2009) Emulating and resisting pragmatic norms: Learner subjectivity and pragmatic choice in L2 Japanese. In N. Taguchi (ed.) *Pragmatic Competence* (pp. 101–128). Berlin/New York: Mouton de Gruyter.
Iwasaki, N. (2011) Learning L2 Japanese 'politeness' and 'impoliteness': Young American men's dilemmas during study abroad. *Japanese Language and Literature* 45, 67–106.
Kasper, G. (2000) Data collection in pragmatics research. In H. Spencer-Catey (ed.) *Culturally Speaking* (pp. 316–341). London: Continuum.
Kasper, G. (2006) Politeness in interaction. Introduction. Special Issue. *Multilingua* 25, 243–248.
Kasper, G. and Dahl, M. (1991) Research methods in interlanguage pragmatics. *Studies in Second Language Acquisition* 13, 215–247.
Kasper, G. and Rose, K. (2002) *Pragmatic Development in a Second Language*. Oxford: Blackwell.
MacDonald, M.N., Badger, R. and Dasli, M. (2006) Authenticity, culture and language learning. *Language and Intercultural Communication* 6, 250–261.
Makino, S. (2002) When does communication turn mentally inward: A case study of Japanese formal-to-informal switching. In N. Akatsuka and S. Strauss (eds) *Japanese/Korean Linguistics* (Vol. 10; pp. 121–135). Stanford, CA: CSLI Publications.
Mori, J. (2009) The social turn in second language acquisition and Japanese pragmatics research: Reflection on ideologies, methodologies and instructional implications. In N. Taguchi (ed.) *Pragmatic Competence* (pp. 335–358). New York/Berlin: Mouton de Gruyter.
Nazkian, F. (2010) Interviewdanwaniokeru jyotaino kino [Functions of plain form in interview]. In M. Minami (ed.) *Gengogakuto nihongokyoiku [Linguistics and Japanese Education]* (Vol. V; pp. 141–173). Tokyo: Kuroshio.
Niyekawa, A. (1991) *Minimum Essential Politeness: A Guide to the Japanese Honorific Language*. Tokyo: University of Tokyo Press.
Okamoto, S. (1999) Situated politeness: Manipulating honorific and non-honorific expressions in Japanese conversation. *Pragmatics* 9, 51–74.
Roever, C. (2011) Testing of second language pragmatics: Past and future. *Language Testing* 28, 463–481.
Rose, K. (1992) Speech acts and questionnaires: The effect of hearer response. *Journal of Pragmatics* 17, 49–62.
Sacks, H., Schegloff, E. and Jefferson, G. (1974) A simplest systematics for the organization of turn-taking for conversation. *Language* 50, 696–735.
Siegal, M. (1996) The role of learner subjectivity in second language sociolinguistic competency: Western women learning Japanese. *Applied Linguistics* 17, 356–382.
Taguchi, N. (2015) Instructed pragmatics at a glance: Where instructional studies were, are, and should be going in interlanguage pragmatics. *Language Teaching* 48, 1–5.
Turnbull, W. (2001) An appraisal of pragmatic elicitation techniques for the social psychological study of talk: The case of request refusals. *Pragmatics* 11, 31–61.
Walters, S. (2007) A conversation-analytic hermeneutic rating protocol to assess L2 oral pragmatic competence. *Language Testing* 24, 155–183.
Yamashita, S. (2008) Investigating interlanguage pragmatic ability: What are we testing? In E. Alcon-Soler and A. Martínez-Flor (eds) *Investigating Pragmatics in Foreign Language Learning, Teaching, and Testing* (pp. 201–223). Bristol: Multilingual Matters.
Yoon, S-J. (2013) Validating task-based assessment of L2 pragmatics in interaction using mixed methods. Unpublished doctoral dissertation. University of Hawai'i at Manoa.
Yuan, Y. (2001) An inquiry into empirical pragmatics data-gathering methods: Written DCTs, oral DCTs, field notes, and natural conversations. *Journal of Pragmatics* 33, 271–292.

6 Gender, Youth and Authenticity: Peer Mandarin Socialization Among American Students in a Chinese College Dorm

Wenhao Diao

Introduction

Authenticity concerns itself with what is 'real'. In language learning and teaching, what is real often is associated with ideas about the 'real language' or 'real communication'. However, the danger of doing so lies in the assumption that there is *one* real language and/or *one* real type of communication. In the search for authentic discourse, language educators and learners seek the 'real' language or the 'real' context of communication, which leads to two common ways of conceptualizing what is authentic. In the first case, real language is believed to be normative and stable, and the stable norms are the object of learning for second language (L2) learners. Meanwhile, there is the other popular view that real language is what takes place in a specific context, regardless of the history of the form. To understand how the two views may apply to foreign language education, we may take a common situation we teach – for example, ordering food at a restaurant. According to the conceptualization of 'real language', a learner's language cannot be considered authentic unless it corresponds to what a native speaker would say in the same situation. According to the latter conceptualization of 'real language', however, anything the learner says in the classroom could be considered authentic, because language is actually being used.

As coined by MacDonald and associates (2006), in their extension of Cooper's (1983) work, these two views represent the 'Hippy' and 'Punk' versions of authenticity. Both versions are ideologically associated with a prescriptive view of language and communication. However, each utterance is situated within utterances (Bakhtin, 1986); in other words, language and context mutually shape each other. Thus, the fundamental problem with both Hippy and Punk authenticity is that the dialogic relationship between language and context is overlooked. If we search for the one real context or the one real speaker, we are then viewing both language and context as static. Language and context also becomes dichotomous from this perspective.

In this chapter, I provide a further critique of these two views of authenticity by examining language used among American study abroad students in China. Beliefs about study abroad often manifest the Hippy and/or Punk views of authenticity. As opposed to the classroom setting, study abroad is often believed to be an opportunity for immersion in an authentic context. These days, study abroad is an even more curious case in the discussion of authenticity. Ongoing globalization processes continue to transform the goals and conditions of our L2 learners (Block & Cameron, 2002), and therefore more and more language learners have the opportunity to participate in L2 use in contexts beyond the classroom. Meanwhile, study abroad is also increasingly being outsourced to for-profit institutions, which capitalize on the rhetoric about study abroad as an authentic linguistic and cultural experience and further circulate the ideological link between study abroad and authenticity. Study abroad is now of particular relevance to the discussion of authenticity in applied linguistics.

What I intend to do in this chapter is to problematize the widely assumed link between study abroad and authenticity – either in the Hippy or Punk form. In what follows, I begin by analyzing the two versions of authenticity in more detail and their manifestations in discourses about study abroad and L2 learning. I then introduce the concept of 'entextualization' as my framework and describe my study which was conducted in a study abroad program taking place in Shanghai, China. As my findings illustrate how these American students appropriate linguistic practices to enact their gender and sexual identities in conversations with their Chinese peers, I conclude that linguistic forms are always discursively linked with previous text and yet gain new meanings in the present context. Both historicity and multiplicity are crucial for our understanding of meaning making in authentic discourse.

Background

'Hippy' authenticity: Native speakers and study abroad

The Hippy version of authenticity can be characterized by 'the search for the "real self"' (MacDonald *et al.*, 2006: 256). It is the attempt to identify a singular true self from a multitude of selves that can '"shine through" a panoply of distractions' (MacDonald et al., 2006: 256). A common example of Hippy authenticity in language education can be found in the idealization of a native speaker as the real speaker. Although native speakers of a certain language may have varying individual histories and backgrounds, from the perspective of the Hippy authenticity their language is viewed as stable, homogenous and normative. An L2 learner's language, moreover, can never be considered authentic unless it corresponds to what the idealized native speaker produces and is recognized by the native speaker as acceptable. Therefore, the Hippy version of authenticity can also be viewed as one that emphasizes correspondence.

The Hippy version of authenticity is prevalent in both study abroad research and pedagogical practices. Because study abroad is often rhetorically made equivalent to having opportunities to interact with native speakers, idealized native speakers' linguistic behaviors are routinely used as the norm to prescribe to L2 learners in teaching materials and practices. The idealization of the native speaker can be found in research as well. For example, it is not uncommon for researchers to recruit native speakers to evaluate students' linguistic gains over their time abroad (Dubiner et al., 2006; Freed, 1995b). In other cases, native speakers' performance is presented as the baseline against which L2 learners are compared (e.g. Li, 2012). Findings from these studies certainly provide us with insights into how L2 learners' language may be received locally and in what ways it may deviate from the norms. But, because academic research constitutes an institutionally sanctioned discourse of expertise (Johnstone, 2010), the experts (i.e. researchers) in these cases also contribute to the Hippy version of authenticity by endorsing the idealization of the native speaker.

The Hippy version of authenticity has been criticized widely in recent years for its assumption of a homogeneous, static, normative speech community (e.g. Firth & Wagner, 1997; Leung et al., 1997; Mori, 2007). Within the subfield of study abroad research, more and more scholars are also departing from the idealization of the native speaker and switching their attention to examine the complexity of the study abroad experience, illuminating a range of issues related to identity (Block, 2007; Kinginger, 2009). Yet, with only a small (although increasing) number of exceptions, these investigations often focus on learners' perspectives without sufficient attention being paid to existing cultural discourses in locality about these identity categories (Kinginger, 2010b). Thus, the other version of authenticity – the Punk version of authenticity – is still present in the literature.

'Punk' authenticity: Study abroad as one context

As its name suggests, the Punk version of authenticity refers to the '"total overthrow of previous conventions and standards", which can sometimes go as far as the rejection of the existing social order' (MacDonald et al., 2006: 257).

In applied linguistics, this version of authenticity is represented by the view that any type of context in which language is used should be considered to be authentic, despite the roles of the participants in the speech event and the ways the forms are being used. MacDonald *et al.* (2006) illustrate the Punk version of authenticity by citing Breen's (1985) study, which claimed that the classroom is a context for authentic language to take place because learners and instructors actually engage in linguistic practices. The problem with Punk authenticity is that it overlooks the historicity of language forms, and therefore it fails to recognize the genesis of language and the dialectic nature between language and context (MacDonald *et al.*, 2006). Linguistic forms can gain multiple layers of social meanings through everyday use, and these meanings are connected with each other in a complex manner (Mendoza-Denton, 2008). If we view the classroom as the point of origin of linguistic forms, we are erroneously separating these forms from their history. The result is that we overlook the social meanings that have emerged from prior use of the forms and the links with their meanings, however they shift or are maintained.

To summarize, if the Hippy version of authenticity can be characterized by its emphasis on the correspondence between classroom practices and the idealized native speaker, then the Punk version is the rejection of the correspondence by treating the classroom as the genesis of language. Now, let us return to L2 learning in the study abroad setting. It seems intuitive that people interested in study abroad would not typically claim the classroom as a context where authentic language takes place. However, recent research and pedagogical practices still demonstrate a tendency to both prescribe one context as inherently more authentic and to ignore the historicity of language.

One example is the popular assumption that study abroad is one homogenous context of L2 learning. Since the publication of Freed's (1995a) seminal volume on L2 acquisition in a study abroad context, researchers have continued for two decades to label study abroad as one context. In numerous articles, study abroad is termed as a context and is used to compare with other contexts (e.g. the classroom) to discuss its impact on a learner's linguistic and cultural development. Even among studies that undertook a qualitative approach to examine the experience in depth, the tendency to ignore the genesis of language remains. A notable example is the research of gender in the study abroad literature. A number of studies have explored the issue of gender and its relationship with L2 learning (Bacon, 2002; Isabelli-Garcia, 2006; Kinginger, 2008; Pellegrino Aveni, 2005; Polanyi, 1995; Talburt & Stewart, 1999; Twombly, 1995), illuminating the gendered study abroad experience. However, only a few studies in this line of inquiry (Diao, 2014; Iwasaki, 2011; Siegal, 1995) have examined learners' linguistic construction of gender in interactions with the local speakers when abroad. Because the majority of the studies on this topic focus only on the students' perspective without sufficient consideration being paid to prior discourse about gender in the locality, the historicity of language is still overlooked. Therefore, by thinking of study abroad as a stable context and focusing only on the learners, this way of conceptualizing also reflects the Punk version of authenticity.

Language is always linked with both its previous discourse and the new meanings that emerge in the current context (Silverstein, 1976, 2003). Unfortunately, this dialectic nature has not yet been adequately addressed in the study abroad research. What underlines the Hippy and the Punk versions of authenticity is a structuralist view that assumes that authenticity is a product of either the idealized speaker or the context of use. However, in L2 use situations, learners do not simply imitate linguistic practices (as the Hippy authenticity claims); nor do they create forms out of nowhere (as the Punk authenticity claims). Rather, they engage in the appropriation of linguistic and other social practices – a process that involves both adopting and adapting (Kramsch, 1993). Furthermore, as study abroad students encounter local cultural discourses through language use, they also evoke their own linguistic and cultural histories. Therefore, language and context are a unified whole because they mutually shape each other.

Rethinking text, context and study abroad

To further conceptualize meaning as emergent in interaction, I draw on the theory of entextualization as my framework of analysis to show that meaning in authentic interaction is a process instead of a product.

Influenced by the work of Bakhtin (1981), one philosophy of language is to conceptualize context as fluid and meaning as situated and yet ever emerging (Briggs & Bauman, 1992; Goodwin & Duranti, 1992; Hopper, 1987). This theoretical stance allows us to view the relationship between form, meaning and context as no longer that of one-to-one correspondence. Using evidence from sociolinguistic and anthropological research, linguists have demonstrated how one form can index multiple layers of social information and these meanings emerge from repeated use of language in context (Eckert, 2012; Johnstone, 2013; Ochs, 1992). This point reveals the inadequacy of Hippy authenticity, because the idealization of native speakers' language assumes that meaning is normative and static. Moreover, context and language mutually shape each other instead of one shaping the other. In other words, there is no one and exclusive 'real' meaning of a certain form. Forms are not only shaped by context; they are also recontextualized and shape context in return (Goodwin & Duranti, 1992). As language users, L2 speakers' ability to use a form to construct meaning is also constantly emerging through language use in context (Larsen-Freeman & Ellis, 2002).

The notion of entextualization introduced by Bauman and Briggs (Bauman & Briggs, 1990; Briggs & Bauman, 1992) can help us to further understand the historicity and multiplicity of meaning in authentic discourse. Entextualization, as defined by Bauman and Briggs (1990: 73), constitutes two processes. First, they speak of 'the process of rendering discourse extractable', that is, a linguistic unit (what the authors call 'a text') can be 'lifted out of its interactional setting'. Bauman and Briggs (1990) call this step 'decontextualization'. Entextualization is completed through recontextualization, which takes place when the text that has been 'rendered decontextualizable' now incorporates aspects of the present context. From the perspective of entextualization, we can see how language (or 'the resultant text') always carries 'its history of use within it' and yet contains new meaning due to the present context (Bauman & Briggs, 1990: 73).

This view is of particular relevance to the critique of the 'one-sided' view of authenticity (MacDonald *et al.*, 2006), because it highlights the dialogic nature of language and context. As Baughman and Briggs stress, language in one context must come from some kind of existing discourse and thus always contain 'its history of use'. This historical aspect renders the Punk version of authenticity insufficient for our understanding of language and context. Meanwhile, because language also often incorporates aspects of the current context, which includes many factors such as speakers' histories and their current relationship (Goodwin & Duranti, 1992), it also renders the model of the ideal native speaker as over-simplistic and unrealistic.

Although entextualization encompasses the notion of multiplicity and historicity, we have not seen much research that examines L2 learning and use from this perspective. Thus, in my critique of the Hippy and Punk versions of authenticity, I use the notion of 'entextualization' as a framework to analyze my data that came from a longitudinal study on American students learning of Mandarin in China. As I have shown elsewhere (Diao, 2014), these American students frequently engaged in emerging Mandarin practices in their dorm conversations to construct gender and youth identities. Here, as I continue to highlight their engagement in the linguistic and discursive construction of gender, my focus is how prior discourses become relevant in these dorm conversations and yet how new meanings emerge in the current context. In so doing, I illustrate how the conceptualization of authenticity needs to address both the historicity and the multiplicity of meaning.

The Study

The data came from a 15-week project conducted in the spring semester of 2012 in a study abroad program in Shanghai, China. They were collected from multiple sources, including: (1) background and linguistic surveys; (2) semi-structured interviews; (3) field observations; and (4) audio recordings made by the students of their routine conversations. During my site visits, I also informally interviewed the students, their roommates, tutors, instructors and other associates. After the interviews and recordings were transcribed, I used NVivo to organize and code the qualitative data (see Baralt, 2012 for a description of using NVivo in qualitative applied linguistic research).

The focal students presented here, Ellen and Tuzi (both pseudonyms), were selected from 20 students who participated in the study. Both of them were living with a Chinese roommate and agreed to routinely record their conversations in the dorm rooms. The dorm was co-ed but only students of the same sex could share a room. Their Chinese roommates (pseudonyms 'Helen' and 'Li', respectively) also agreed to participate in the study.

Tuzi came to Shanghai with only one semester of formal instruction. He had taught English in southern China for six months, during which he 'picked up' some Mandarin and Cantonese (Tuzi, interview). As someone who tends to be critical of mainstream culture, Tuzi was drawn to Shanghai because it linguistically represented an alternative to Beijing Mandarin, the base of standard Mandarin in China. His roommate Li was a college senior student in the hosting institution. He was applying for graduate schools in the United States and was accepted by a university in New York during this time.

Ellen had studied Mandarin for four semesters at her college and another at a different study abroad program in China before her arrival in Shanghai. She was placed into the most advanced class in the program in Shanghai. She chose to go to Shanghai and live with a roommate in the dorm not simply because she wanted to learn more about the language; she was also interested in learning more about gender and sexuality in China. She came from a conservative family and came under a great deal of pressure when she was mistaken for a lesbian in high school. Shanghai's reputation for being one of the most liberal places in Mainland China (Farrer, 2002) and the opportunity to interact with a Chinese peer of her own age allowed her to combine her interests in the language and in gender. Helen was Ellen's roommate. She was in her senior year of college studying applied Chinese linguistics. She came from Jiangsu and spoke eastern Mandarin as her native tongue. She had spent one semester in the United States and was applying for graduate programs outside Mainland China at the time.

Findings

The most frequently recurring theme in the recorded dorm conversations was gender and sexuality. This finding is probably unsurprising, because the dorm rooms constitute an important space for college students to construct homosociality, which refers to friendship between people of the same sex. Homosociality is a key dimension for young adults to manage social relationships and organize their social world (Kiesling, 2005). It is of particular importance to the college students in this study who came from very different backgrounds. The homosociality that they constructed allowed them to move beyond the prevalent Chinese cultural discourse of *laowai* ('foreigners', literally 'big-outsiders') – a discourse that effectively excludes people of non-Chinese heritage from local communities (McDonald, 2011; Zhu & Li, 2014).

Homosociality often involves linguistic and discursive construction about gender and sexuality (Kiesling, 2004, 2005). As they discussed gender, linguistic forms were also frequently decontextualized and then recontextualized to construct gender and organize their gender relationships. In what follows, I show instances from their recorded authentic discursive practice to demonstrate the dialectic nature of language and meaning. My findings presented below are organized by themes that emerged from the analysis.

Homosociality through entextualization in the dorm

In their dorm conversations, the young adults engaged in entextualization to construct homosociality. By taking forms from previous discourse and assigning new meanings to the linguistic forms, they established codes that were only shared between them as a means to organize their gender and sexual relationships.

Excerpt 6.1 is an example of such entextualization from Helen and Ellen, The two of them frequently engaged in an event they identify as 'gossiping'. During these gossiping events, entextualization of linguistic forms took place routinely. In this episode of interaction, Helen recalls her conversation with a female student and becomes concerned about what she might have accidentally revealed about a male student's romantic interest. In the excerpt, they entextualize the expression *nǐ dǒng de* ('you know') for their purpose of 'gossiping':

Excerpt 6.1 Conversation in the dorm between Helen and Ellen: 'You know.' *(HL = Helen, EL = Ellen, WD = Researcher; 17 May 2012)*

```
1  HL:  wo jiu jiang le (.) ta- >haoxiang< gen biede nvhaizi a- ((in English)) blah blah blah=
        I   conj say PRT  he   seems    with other girl   PRT
        'I just said he seems to be with another girl.'
2  EL:  =dui. hh. dui. hhh. ((in English)) blah blah.
        right      right
        'Right.   Right.'
3  HL:  hhh. blah blah.
4  EL:  heh heh heh heh.
5  HL:  dajia dong    jiu   keyi le.
        all understand CONJ allow PRT
        'It's fine as long as everyone knows.'
6  EL:  ((laughs)) wo hui kaishi yong zhe ju hua. dajia dong jiu keyi le. blah blah.
                   I  will begin use this MSR speech. all understand CONJ allow PRT
        'I will begin to use this sentence. "It's good as long as everyone knows".'
7        nimen dong     jiu   keyi le.
         you understand CONJ allow PRT
         'It's good as long as you all know.'
8  HL:  dui. women jingchang hui shuo (.) ah (.) ni  dong    de. ranhou jiu   bu shuo le.
        right we    usually    will say            you understand PRT then  CONJ NEG say PRT
        'Right. We usually say, "you know", and then just don't say anything more.'
```

Here, when Helen says *dàjiā dǒng* ('everyone knows') in line 5, she provides no more information about what she has revealed. Yet it is clearly understood by Ellen, who shows great interest in using the form as a way to say something without actually saying anything (lines 6–7). The phrase Helen then teaches Ellen, *nǐ dǒng de* ('you know'), was initially used among young people to make comments that would be otherwise censored on the internet (*Hudong*, n.d.). Its ambiguity allows people to say the 'unsayable' without actually saying it and achieves a humorous effect (Liu, 2010). But here the phrase has clearly become detached from its original context which is associated with political censorship and China's rebellious youth in the virtual space. Yet its ambiguity and unseriousness remains in the present context, as the two women recontextualized form in their event of gossiping. By entextualizing this form, they become able to exchange information without saying anything to construct a space for homosociality.

Similar instances of entextualization for solidarity also took place in interactions between Tuzi and Li. The two heterosexual men frequently engaged in conversations about women. In Excerpt 6.2, for example, they are chatting in a café when Li notices a girl and tries to direct Tuzi's attention to her. Yet the café is a public space where paying attention to a stranger may be seen as inappropriate and even intrusive. Thus, he entextualizes the angle system in Mandarin to construct a secret code for locating people in the space.

Excerpt 6.2 'The girl at 45 degrees is looking at you.' (LI = Li, TZ = Tuzi, WD = Researcher; 9 May 2012)

```
1   LI:   nabian you ren  zai kan ni. sishiwu du   jiao.s
          there have people PRT look you forty-five MSR angle
          'Over there someone is looking at you. [At] forty-five degrees.'
2   TZ:   heh heh heh heh
3   LI:   nabian you ren zai kan ni
          there have people PRT look you
          'Over there someone is looking at you.'
4   TZ:   heh heh heh mei shi heh heh
                      NEG matter
          'Nothing.'
5         (3.8)
6   LI:   sishiwu du jiao jiu shi-
          forty-five MSR angle just cop
          'Forty-five degrees just is-,'
7         (2.1)
8   LI:   jiu  shi- ((in English)) ninety degree right? jiu shi s- jiu shi=
          just COP                                     just COP    just COP
                                                         'just is- just is, just is'
9   TZ:   =ah=
```

10 LI: =jiu shi ((in English) ninety
           just COP
           'Just is'
11 TZ: ah=
12 LI: =sishiwu du jiao shi- sishiwu=
           forty-five MSR angle COP forty-five
           'Forty-five degrees is just- forty-five'
13 TZ: =dui. you shenme yisi.
           right have what meaning
           'Okay. What does it mean?'
14 LI: sishiwu du jiao jiushi- ((in English)) forty five degree
           forty-five MSR angle just
           'Forty-five degrees is just'
15 TZ: ah (0.8)
16 LI: jiushi-
           just
           'Just'
17 WD: jiu zai yingwen limian nimen bushi shuo xian[zai-]
           just LOC English LOC you NEG say now
           'Just in English don't you say now-'
18 LI: ((in English)) [ten] o'clock=

As shown in the excerpt, Tuzi is initially unaware of how to respond to Li's angle system, evidenced by his laughter (lines 2 and 4) and silence (lines 5 and 7). Then Li explains its referential meaning in Chinese and then in English ('forty-five degrees') (lines 8, 10, and 12). But Tuzi remains confused, because the angle system in this context has shifted from its original function of describing spatial distribution to become a pragmatic request between two heterosexual young men for a social purpose (locating young women in a public space). This layer of social meaning is not made transparent to Tuzi yet. Eventually, Li uses the temporal reference in English to explain the situation ('ten o'clock') (line 18), which is understood by Tuzi as a spatial reference in the situation.

What we see in Excerpt 6.2 is an instance of entextualization of the angle system. The angle system becomes decontextualized from its original use, and yet some of its meaning related to spatial location remains in the new context. Possibly because of this very complex decontextualization process, its social meaning in the new context is not transparent to Tuzi until it becomes sufficiently recontextualized and then the new meaning emerges (although anecdotally similar usage can also be found in the United States).

I have illustrated thus far how these young adults construct solidarity among themselves by entextualizing linguistic forms and constructing codes whose meanings are no longer as literal or transparent (such as using the angle system to locate girls). In their recordings, entextualization serves more than solidarity construction in the data. It is also an effective way for them to organize social relationships such as gender and sexuality among these young adults in the homosocial space of the dorm rooms.

Policing sexuality through entextualization

Another theme of entextualization in their recordings is the policing of sexuality. It took place not only among the two heterosexual young men (Diao, 2014), but also the women. Excerpt 6.3 is an example of such policing. Here, Ellen recalls her childhood experience of violating conventional gender norms:

Excerpt 6.3 'Becoming a man' or 'being like a boy' (EL = Ellen, HL = Helen; 19 April 2012)

```
1   EL:   danshi wo chuan de hen nanxinghua. wo shi zheyang de.
          but    I  wear  PRT very masculine    I  COP such PRT
          'But I dressed in a masculine way. I was like that.'
2         suoyi wo changchang gen nansheng chaojia.
          so    I  often      with boy      quarrel
          'So I often fought with       boys.'
3         changchang hui da tamen.
          often      will hit they
          '[I] often would hit them.'
4         zai zhe ge- zhong (.) zhongxue de shihou.
          LOC this MSR middle   middle-school PRT time
          'When [I] was in the- middle, middle school'
5         changchang shi wo de laoshi shuo. ((smacking lips))
          often     COP I  PRT teacher say
          '[it] often was my teacher saying'
6         ((changing to a low voice)) aiyi. qing bie da na ge nansheng.
                                            please NEG hit that MSR boy
                                      'Aiyi, please do not hit that boy.'
7   HL:   hhh. [heh heh heh heh.]
8   EL:   jiushi (.) changchang hui zheyang zuo. hhh.
          just       often      will such    do
          '[I] just would often do such things.'
9   HL:   shuoming ni xiao shihou hen- nanhaizi qi.
          show     you little time very boy     feeling
          '[It] shows you were very much like a boy when you were little'
```

In Excerpt 6.3, Ellen begins by using *nánxìnghuà* ('masculine', literally 'becoming a man') (line 1) to categorize her childhood behaviors. Helen rephrases it using the term *nánháizi qì* ('like a boy') (line 9). The two phrases overlap in terms of their referential meaning, but in the popular cultural discourse about gender, they have come to index divergent social information. In mass media, *nánxìnghuà* is frequently used to indicate women's transgender mentality/performances, with the implication that they are unattractive to heterosexual men (a popular wiki site, Baike, n.d.). *Nánháizi qì*, by comparison, is considered a description of unfeminine but yet 'cute' performances by women (e.g. a fashion magazine, *Chic! Exchange*, 2011). The divergence is unsurprising, because unlike *nánxìnghuà* ('becoming a man'), *nánháizi qì* ('like a boy') infantilizes women by linking them with young boys. Infantilization is a key process for women to be considered 'cute' in Chinese popular culture (Chuang, 2005). Here in the excerpt, when Helen helps her American peer describe her own behaviors, they also engage themselves in policing (hetero)sexuality by continuing to assign new meanings to these linguistic forms and organizing their sexual relationship accordingly.

Policing sexuality was more salient in the interaction between the two heterosexual young men. This is probably because for young men, homosociality has become a 'small zone of "safe" solidarity between camaraderie and intimacy' (Kiesling, 2004: 291). Numerous incidences were found in the recordings between Tuzi and Li, in which they meticulously scrutinized linguistic forms to index masculine solidarity but not homosexual intimacy. Excerpt 6.4 is an example of such an entextualization process. During their tutorial, Tuzi encountered a word in his textbook, *tèbié* ('special'). When he used it in a sentence to Li, the word 'special' soon becomes entextualized to index homosexuality and thus is deemed inappropriate between the two heterosexual men:

Excerpt 6.4 'You are very "special".' (TZ = Tuzi, LI = Li)

1   TZ: > ((in English)) so< ni hen tebie
                you very special
                'So you are very special?'

2   LI: ni hen tebie=
                you very special
                'You are very special.'

3   TZ: =((laughs))=

4   LI: =dui.
                right
                'Right.'

5   TZ: ((in English)) you are special. feichang tebie=
                                      extremely special
                'You are special. EXTREMELY special.'

6   LI: =ni hen tebie.
                you very special
                'You are very special.'

7   TZ: ((laughs))

8   LI: ((laughs)) ni buyao gen <u>wo</u> shuo. hhh.
                you NEG with me speak.
                'Don't say that to ME.'

9		((both laugh))
10	TZ:	**jiushi- women zhi gen nage nvren shuo shi ba=**
		just we only with FLR women speak right PRT
		'We just only say it with women, right?'
11	LI:	=**dui. zhi gen nvren >ni hen< tebie.**
		right only with women you very special
		'Right. Only tell women "you are very special".'
12		**ni shi- ni shi zui tebie de.**
		you COP you COP most special PRT
		'You are- You are the most special'
13	TZ:	((laughs)) Hm.

Here in the excerpt, Tuzi laughs immediately after Li utters the sentence, repeats it in English and utters the word in an exaggerated tone. Both men then find the sentence laughable. Li then prohibits Tuzi from using it in conversations with a heterosexual man ('Don't say that to me' in line 8). The two men continue to confirm each other's interpretation in the following turns and continue to assign the meaning associated with sexuality (lines 12–13). Here, as they carefully select what forms can be used between themselves to manage men's homosociality, we see here a case of policing heterosexual masculinity that resonates with Kiesling's (2004, 2005) work but between college-age men in the L2 use situation.

Excerpt 6.4 is also a curious case in which entextualization is initiated by an L2 speaker (Tuzi) and is completed jointly between the two men. This observation shows that nonnative speakers also participate in meaning-making processes instead of taking the passive role in conversations (Mori, 2007). In the specific case of Excerpt 6.4, it may be due to more widespread ideologies about the safe zone between solidarity and intimacy among young men in North America. Unfortunately I was unable to find research on young men's talk in Chinese; however, despite the extent to which the safe zone ideology is shared among men in China, Li's immediate response is clear evidence of his understanding of the cultural meaning. As both men assign the new layer of social meaning to the word, it becomes decontextualized from the textbook scenario and recontextualized to police heterosexuality and manage homosociality in the dorm.

Two ways of becoming through one linguistic feature

Linguistic features with the potential to index gender are natural candidates to show the historical and multiple sides of meaning in authentic communication, because they often contain multiple social meanings which are often linked with one another through prior discourse in complex ways (Ochs, 1992). Thus, I focus on what follows with one such linguistic feature in Mandarin – the sentence-final particles. The particles are often believed to contain no referential meaning (Luke, 1990), but recent research has

122 Authenticity, Language and Interaction in Second Language Contexts

shown that these particles can express complex emotions and construct stance (Wu, 2004). What is of particular interest here is a subset of these particles called 'affective sentence-final particles' (ASPs). ASPs can index a multitude of social identities, including region (Callier, 2007; Starr, 2011), maturity (Starr, 2011) and gender (a cute girl) (Chan, 1998; Diao, 2014; Farris, 1988). The central concern of my following analysis is which meaning becomes relevant in context and how it in return shapes the context.

As we have already seen, Tuzi and Li engaged in this linguistic practice to manage between solidarity and intimacy and do complex identity work. Because ASPs can express affect and index a 'cute girl' identity, policing of sexuality was also present in their use of these particles. Excerpt 6.5 shows how they become decontextualized from indexing region and recontextualized to enact gender (and sexuality) in the interaction between Tuzi and Li. Because Tuzi previously lived in Guangdong where more frequent ASP use can be found, through implicit socialization he also started to use them regularly in his own speech. Here, his roommate Li notices this pattern and engages himself in the entextualization of these ASPs:

Excerpt 6.5 'Men don't use ya.' (TZ = Tuzi, LI = Li; 14 March 2012)

1 LI: nan- nande buyao yong ya.
        male man NEG should use ASP
        'Men shouldn't use "ya".'

2 TZ: zai Guangdong yong a.
        LOC Guangdong use ASP
        'In Guangdong they use.'

3 LI: bu- buyao
        NEG NEG should.
        'No, don't.'

4 TZ: shi de.
        COP PRT.
        'Yes.'

5 LI: nande yong ya ting qilai xiang yi ge (.) ((in English)) girl
        man use ASP sound COMP like a MSR
        'Men using "ya" sound like a girl.'

6 TZ: danshi Guangdong-
        but Guangdong-
        'But Guangdong-'

7 LI: bu yao yong a.
        NEG should use ASP
        'Don't use "a".'

8 TZ: Guangdong ren yong baihua- yong nage Guangdong hua de shihou (.) a- you yisi.
        Guangdong people use colloquial use that Guangdong speech PRT time asp have meaning
        'When the Guangdong people use colloquial- use Cantonese, "a" has meaning.'

9 LI: ((Correcting TZ)) ya.
                          ASP
        'Ya.'

10 TZ: ya- ta ye you a.
        ASP he also have ASP
        'Ya. They also have "a".'

11	LI:	bu yao yong. hhh. nan- <u>nan</u>de bu yao yong=
		NEG should use male man NEG should use
		'Don't use it. Men shouldn't use-'
12	TZ:	=wo- >wo juede< [yinwei]
		I I feel because
		'I, I think, because'
13	LI:	[yong <u>a</u>]
		use ASP
		'Use "a".'
14		**nande buyao yong.**
		man NEG should use.
		'Men shouldn't use [it].'
15	TZ:	gaosu ni <u>a</u> (.)>yinwei-< hhh.
		tell you ASP because
		'I tell you "a". Because-'
16	LI:	<u>zhe-</u> hhh. ting qilai <u>xiang yi ge- xiang yi ge-</u> xiang yi ge- hhhh
		this sound off like one MSR like one MSR like one MSR
		'This sounds like a, like a, like a…'
17	TZ:	zai zhe'r keneng a (.) danshi wo zai Guangdong de shiyou ta changchang shuo a.
		LOC here maybe ASP but I LOC Guangdong PRT time he often say ASP.
		'Here maybe "a". But when I was in Guangdong, they often say "a".'
18	LI:	wo zhidao.
		I know.
		'I know.'
19	TZ:	yinwei wo juede yinwei tamen yong Guangdonghua de shihou you a (.)
		because I feel because they use Guangdong-speech PRT time have ASP
		'Because I think because when they use Cantonese, they have "a".'
20		you <u>a- a- a-</u> tamen changchang shuo.
		have ASP ASP ASP they often say
		'They have "a" "a" "a". They often say it.'
21		suoyi tamen shuo Putonghua (.) tamen shizhe- xiguan yong <u>a</u>.
		so they speak Putonghua they try accustomed use ASP
		'So when they speak Putonghua, they try- they are used to using "a".'
22		((in English)) they want to sound like the same rhythm.
23	LI:	danshi zai zheli <u>nüsheng-</u> keyi yong <u>ya</u>! <u>a</u>!
		but LOC here girls may use ASP ASP
		'But in here GIRLS may use "ya"! "A"!'

This excerpt is an excellent example of the complex appropriation (rather than simply imitation) of native speakers' linguistic practice among adult L2 learners. In Excerpt 6.5, Li entextualizes the ASPs as indexical of sexuality and prohibits the use of ASPs between heterosexual men, repeatedly stating that 'men shouldn't use them' in lines 1, 11 and 14. But, because of his prior socialization experience in Guangzhou, Tuzi insists that ASPs are simply a regional feature in southern China (lines 2, 4, 6, 8). Although Li continues to assign gendered meaning to these particles and describes them explicitly as features used by young women ('sounds like a girl' with the word 'girl' uttered in English in line 5), Tuzi still argues that ASPs do not index gender but may have locally embedded social meanings (lines 17 and 19–21). Indeed, frequent use of ASPs indexes place (southern region) in China (Callier, 2007), but the ASPs used in Excerpt 6.5 have been decontextualized from the regional use to become mainly indexical of gender/sexuality in this dorm setting. However, their potential to express affect, which the ASPs carry from their history, is still present in this context. It is this potential that links them with the ideological gender stereotype of a 'cute girl'. As Li and Tuzi jointly negotiate and entextualize ASPs in the dorm space, we see a case in which meaning is not stable in what is considered to be 'authentic' discourse.

Excerpt 6.6 is another example of how ASPs become entextualized to index gender in the dorm conversations. The excerpt was taken from a recording of Ellen and Helen discussing how girls act 'cute' by using different resources (linguistic resources included). Here, as Ellen describes to Helen her interaction with another female student ('Wendy'), they also engage in a metapragmatic conversation about how to be a young woman:

Excerpt 6.6 'I like your dress a.' (EL = Ellen, HL = Helen; 17 May 2012)

```
1   EL:  jiushi qishi hhh zuotian  wanshang jiushi Wendy Wendy gaosu wo (.)
         just   actually   yesterday evening  just   Wendy Wendy tell   me
         'Just actually, yesterday evening Wendy Wendy just told me, "Ah, I like your-"'
2        ah wo xihuan ni de (.) tamen shuo shi yi ge chenshan (.) bu shi chenshan. T xushan
            I  like   you POS   they  say  COP one MSR shirt       NEG COP shirt    T-shirt
         'They said [it] was a shirt. [It] was not a shirt. A T-shirt.'
3   HL:  hm
4   EL:  zheyang de qishi shi qunzi. danshi tamen shuo shi T xushan. danshi buguan.
         this way PRT actually COP dress  but    they  say  COP T-shirt    but    regardless
         'Like this. Actually [it] was a dress. But they said [it] was a T-shirt.  But regardless.'
5        tamen jiu  shuo (.) ah wo xihuan ni  de qunzi a.
         they  just say         I  like   you POS dress ASP
         'They just said, "Ah, I like your dress 'a'."'
6        wo shuo (.) ah xiexie.
         I  say        thank
         'I said, "ah, thank you".'
7        ta shuo ni yinggai shuo ni ye xihuan wo de qunzi.
         she say you should say you also like I POS dress
         'She said, "you should say you also like my dress".'
8        ((both laugh))
9   EL:  wo jiu  shuo (.) ah duibuqi. wo ye  xihuan ni de qunzi.
         I  just say         sorry    I  also like   you POS dress
         'I just said, "ah sorry. I also like your dress."'
```

By describing her initial response to Wendy's compliment as pragmatically inappropriate, Ellen's description in the excerpt (lines 7 and 9) is a reported socialization experience of her own regarding how to behave as a young woman. She positions herself as someone less experienced – at least less than 'Wendy' – in performing her gender identity in such social settings. Although her description of Wendy is brief, she uses ASPs to stylize Wendy in her reported experience ('I like your dress a!'). Her Chinese roommate Helen responded by laughing, sanctioning this usage (line 8).

In both Excerpts 6.5 and 6.6, these ASPs become almost exclusively indexical of gender/sexuality, despite the many other social meanings they contain. They are entextualized to stylize young women as expressions of affect (Eckert & McConnell-Ginet, 2013). These entextualization processes serve for these college-age language learners/users to organize their gender relationship and do identity work. What, then, do these entextualization processes mean for applied linguists and language educators? Let us now return to the discussion of authenticity.

Discussion

These dorm conversations show that the young adult learners do not simply learn how to speak as gendered beings; instead, they learn to gender through language and to police sexuality. As my analysis illustrates how the Mandarin forms became entextualized in the dorm conversations, the findings demonstrate the need to conceive authenticity as a dialectic of both correspondence and genesis.

First, linguistic forms are often assigned new meanings to evoke social identity, construct relationship and organize the social world in the present context. The word *special* presented in Tuzi's textbook became taboo in his dorm conversations with Li. The phrase for commenting on censored topics online was used for gossiping between Ellen and Helen. In these instances, the new layers of social information that emerge from the conversations are not completely unrelated to the previous context in which these forms were used, but they have been entextualized in ways in which the history of the forms has become less transparent. If we were to think of authenticity as that of correspondence, we would have to judge one meaning as more authentic than the other. But these new meanings are equally as real (if not more relevant in the present context), and the link between form and meaning is not static. For this reason, the Hippy approach to authenticity is doomed to fail. If we continue to idealize the native speaker and search for *the* way of using language that would correspond to the native speakers, our L2 learners will never be able to understand how forms can be used in creative ways and gain new meanings in different contexts.

Moreover, the new layers of meaning that emerge in the present context are jointly constructed and negotiated, as evidenced in the discussion of the word 'special' between Tuzi and Li. Thus, even if we were to incorporate sociolinguistic variations in our foreign language curricula and prescribe how learners could/should speak in correspondence to their identity categories, we would still fail to recognize learners as subjective beings in their appropriation of L2 practices (Kramsch, 2009). Instead of simply imitating, the L2 learners in this study also engaged in the discursive construction of gender/sexuality and the entextualization of forms.

Secondly, the instances of their dorm talk also show the inadequacy of the Punk approach to conceptualizing authenticity. Through the analysis of the dorm conversations, we can see how linguistic forms carry a historical aspect within them. The prior discourse also includes L2 learners' previous exposure to the form through formal instruction or other socialization experiences. As shown in Tuzi's negotiation with Li about the ASPs, learners' history of L2 use can also be evoked in the present context. Therefore, neither the classroom nor study abroad should be considered as a context that is inherently 'authentic'.

In other words, historicity and multiplicity are essentially a unified whole, because the multiple layers of meaning a linguistic form can index are often connected with each other in intricate ways and through the history of language use (Johnstone, 2013; Ochs, 1992). As shown in instances such as the phrase that used to be associated with political censorship but which now is used for gossiping, the history of the form intersects with culture and cultural changes in society (Garrett & Baquedano-López, 2002). Thus, the discussion about authenticity in language teaching is ultimately a discussion on the relationship between language, cultural context and the individual speaker. Rejecting the Punk version of authenticity not only helps us better understand authenticity; it can allow us to develop a 'multilingual ability to operate between languages' and the 'transcultural circulation of values across borders' (Kramsch, 2009: 193).

One may wonder, then, how foreign language pedagogical practices can possibly address the multiplicity and the historicity to better connect students' L2 learning process with their authentic language experience. Let us return to the point of entextualization. Through entextualization, a form carries both elements of its history of use and its emergent meaning in the current context (Bauman & Briggs, 1990; Briggs & Bauman, 1992). The connection between history and its current meaning may not always be transparent, but it is possible to reveal historicity and multiplicity through an emphasis on discourse analysis. Kramsch (1993) has illustrated ways through which foreign language education can benefit from using a discourse approach to analyze authentic texts (e.g. films and literature). Today, we are seeing more potential for the incorporation of a discourse analytic approach in L2 learning contexts. Because we now have a more mobile student population living in a more multilingual linguistic landscape such as those studying abroad as well as learners of many different kinds (e.g. heritage learners, learners living in multilingual neighborhoods and/or on multilingual campuses), our students no longer have to rely solely on texts such as films in order to expose themselves to authentic discursive practices.

In classroom practice, we can begin by emphasizing the multiplicity of meaning and encouraging our learners to document their language experience both within and outside the classroom. The next step can include using a discourse analysis approach to incorporate different discursive practices and compare the similarities and differences in the ways language is used. When we guide our students to discover the sociolinguistic and stylistic variations from their own language experience both within and beyond the classroom, students will become more aware of the multiplicity of meaning in context. Meanwhile, as we ask them to document and compare the different meanings and usage of one linguistic form they have encountered, the historical aspect of language is also being incorporated into the pedagogical practice. For example, in the case of Mandarin sentence-final particles, our pedagogical practice should include not only the instruction of the form and its function; we can also engage the learners in reflective discussions about the ideological link between expressions of emotion, gender and sexuality (Eckert & McConell-Ginet, 2013). By engaging learners in the analysis of the oral and written discourse they have experienced, we may become able to depart from both the Hippy and the Punk versions of authenticity at last and help students understand their multilingual experience in today's world (Kramsch, 2009).

Finally, the dialectic between language and context also highlights the need for scholars and language teachers to promote study abroad opportunities as 'activists' (Kinginger, 2010a). As I have attempted to show throughout this chapter, learners do not simply observe and imitate what native speakers do; nor do they create forms that have no history of use in the language. They adopt L2 forms and adapt them in various contexts – in the case of this study, with their Chinese roommates in the dorm. Settings like study abroad are where many different contexts of interaction may emerge, and where language can become entextualized in complex ways. Thus, study abroad researchers need to actively engage in a conversation that promotes study abroad as a space where local cultural discourses can and will be evoked and linguistic forms may be assigned new meanings. In this way, scholars and teachers can promote study abroad and language learning not only as an 'opportunity space' (Cook, 2008), but also as a 'problem space' where the link between form and meaning can become contested.

Appendix A: Transcription Conventions

(0.5)	elapsed time in 10ths of seconds
(.)	dot in parenthesis marks pauses shorter than 0.4 second
underline	underline marks increased volume of voice
¿	raised intonation
!	animated voice
.	full stop marks falling intonation
(())	double parentheses contain transcriber's comments
-	prolongation of immediately prior sound
[]	bracket marks overlapping turns

>faster<   inward arrows show faster speech
=   equal signs indicate no discernable pause between turns
hhh   out-breath
(¿¿¿)   unclear talk

Appendix B: Grammar Glossary

ASP   affective sentence-final particle ('a/ya', 'me', 'ou', 'eh', 'la')
COP   copula be
PRT   all other particles
POS   possessive marker
LOC   locative marker
MSR   measure word
CONJ   conjunctive adverb
NEG   negation
COMP   verb complement

References

Bacon, S. (2002) Learning the rules: Language development and cultural adjustment during study abroad. *Foreign Language Annals* 35 (6), 637–646.
Baike (n.d.) 'Nvzi liuxing shuaiqi mei: Jiedu nvxing nanxinghua' [Masculinity is in for women: Understanding masculine women]. See http://w.baike.com/a544f74c077c43539325caa726266394.html.
Bakhtin, M. (1981) *The Dialogic Imagination: Four Essays* (trans. M. Holquist). Austin, TX: University of Texas Press.
Bakhtin, M. (1986) *Speech Genres and Other Late Essays* (trans. M. Holquist). Austin, TX: University of Texas Press.
Baralt, M. (2012) Coding qualitative data. In A. Mackey and S.M. Gass (eds) *Research Methods in Second Language Acquisition: A Practical Guide* (pp. 222–244). Oxford: Blackwell.
Bauman, R. and Briggs, C.L. (1990) Poetics and performance as critical perspectives on language and social life. *Annual Review of Anthropology* 19, 59–88.
Block, D. (2007) The rise of identity in SLA research, post Firth and Wagner (1997). *Modern Language Journal* 91 (Focus Issue), 863–876.
Block, D. and Cameron, D. (2002) Introduction. In D. Block and D. Cameron (eds) *Globalization and Language Teaching*. London: Routledge.
Breen, M. P. (1985) Authenticity in the language classroom. *Applied Linguistics* 6 (1), 60–70.
Briggs, C.L. and Bauman, R. (1992) Genre, intertextuality, and social power. *Journal of Linguistic Anthropology* 2 (2), 131–172.
Callier, P. (2007) Not so obvious: The sociolinguistic distribution of *me* in Mandarin Chinese. Poster presented at *New Ways of Analyzing Variation* (NWAV) 36, Philadelphia, PA.
Chan, M.K.M. (1998) Gender differences in the Chinese language: A preliminary report. In H. Lin (ed.) *Proceedings of the Ninth North American Conference on Chinese Linguistics, Vol. 2* (pp. 35–52). Los Angeles, CA: University of Southern California.
Chic! Elegance (2011) Nvrenmen suowei de nanhaizi qi [The so-called boyish by women]. See http://xazi.qikan.com/ArticleView.aspx?titleid=xazi20112224/.
Chuang, T-I. (2005) The power of cuteness: Female infantilization in urban Taiwan. *Stanford Journal of East Asian Affairs* 5 (2), 21–28.

Cook, H. (2008) *Socializing Identities through Speech Style: Learners of Japanese as a Foreign Language*. Bristol: Multilingual Matters.
Cooper, D.E. (1983) *Authenticity and Learning: Nietzsche's Educational Philosophy*. London: Routledge and Keagan Paul.
Diao, W. (2014) Peer socialization into gendered L2 Mandarin language practices in a study abroad context: Talk in the dorm. *Applied Linguistics*; doi: 10.1093/applin/amu053.
Dubiner, D., Freed, B.F. and Segalowitz, N. (2006) Native speaker's perception of fluency acquired by study-abroad students and their implications for the classroom at home. In S. Wilkinson (ed.) *Insights from Study Abroad for Language Programs* (pp. 2–21). Boston, MA: AAUSC, Heinle & Heinle.
Eckert, P. (2012) Three waves of variation study: The emergence of meaning in the study of sociolinguistic variation. *Annual Review of Anthropology* 41, 81–100.
Eckert, P. and McConnell-Ginet, S. (2013) *Language and Gender* (2nd edn). Cambridge: Cambridge University Press.
Farrer, J. (2002) *Opening Up: Youth Sex Culture and Market Reform in Shanghai*. Chicago, IL: University of Chicago Press.
Farris, C.S. (1988) Gender and grammar in Chinese: With implications for language universals. *Modern China* 14 (3), 277–308.
Firth, A. and Wagner, J. (1997) On discourse, communication, and (some) fundamental concepts in SLA research. *Modern Language Journal* 81 (3), 285–300.
Freed, B.F. (1995a) *Second Language Acquisition in a Study Abroad Context*. Amsterdam/Philadelphia, PA: John Benjamins.
Freed, B.F. (1995b) What makes us think that students who study abroad become fluent? In B.F. Freed (ed.) *Second Language Acquisition in a Study Abroad Context* (pp. 123–148). Amsterdam/Philadelphia, PA: John Benjamins.
Garrett, P. and Baquedano-López, P. (2002) Language socialization: Reproduction and continuity, transformation and change. *Annual Review of Anthropology* 31, 339–361.
Goodwin, C. and Duranti, A. (1992) Rethinking context: An introduction. In A. Duranti and C. Goodwin (eds) *Rethinking Context: Language as an Interactive Phenomenon* (pp. 1–42). Cambridge: Cambridge University Press.
Hopper, P. (1987) Emergent grammar. *Berkeley Linguistic Society* 13, 139–57.
Hudong. (n.d.). *In ci [In Words]*. See http://top.baike.com/.
Isabelli-García, C. (2006) Study abroad social networks, motivation and attitudes: Implications for second language acquisition. In M.A. Dufon and E. Churchill (eds) *Language Learners in Study Abroad Contexts* (pp. 231–258). Clevedon: Multilingual Matters.
Iwasaki, N. (2011) Learning L2 Japanese 'politeness' and 'impoliteness': Young American men's dilemmas during study abroad. *Japanese Language and Literature* 45, 67–106.
Johnstone, B. (2010) Making Pittsburghese: Communication technology, expertise, and the discursive construction of a regional dialect. *Language & Communication* 31, 3–15.
Johnstone, B. (2013) Speaking Pittsburghese: *The Story of a Dialect*. New York: Oxford University Press.
Kiesling, S. (2005) Homosocial desire in men's talk: Balancing and recreating cultural discourses of masculinity. *Language in Society* 34 (5), 695–727.
Kiesling, S. F. (2004) Dude. *American Speech* 79 (3), 281–305.
Kinginger, C. (2008) Language learning in study abroad: Case histories of Americans in France (Monograph). *Modern Language Journal* 92, 1–124.
Kinginger, C. (2009) *Language Learning and Study Abroad: A Critical Reading of Research*. New York: Palgrave Macmillan.
Kinginger, C. (2010a) *Contemporary Study Abroad and Foreign Language Learning: An Activist's Guidebook*. University Park, PA: Center for Advanced Language Proficiency Education and Research (CALPER) Publications.

Kinginger, C. (2010b) American students abroad: Negotiation of difference? *Language Teaching* 43 (2), 216–227.
Kramsch, C. (1993) *Context and Culture in Language Teaching.* Oxford: Oxford University Press.
Kramsch, C. (2009) *The Multilingual Subject.* Oxford: Oxford University Press.
Larsen-Freeman, D. and Ellis, N. (2002) Language emergence: Implications for applied linguistics. Introduction to the Special issue. *Applied Linguistics* 27 (4), 558–589.
Leung, C., Harris, R. and Rampton, B. (1997) The idealized native speaker: Reified ethnicities and classroom realities. *TESOL Quarterly* 31 (3), 543–560.
Li, S. (2012), The effects of input-based practice on pragmatic development of requests in L2 Chinese. *Language Learning* 62, 403–438.
Liu, J. (2010) Deviant writing and youth identity: Representation of dialects with Chinese characters on the internet. *Chinese Language and Discourse* 1 (2), 183–219.
Luke, K.K. (1990) *Utterance Particles in Cantonese Conversation.* Philadelphia, PA: John Benjamins.
MacDonald, M.N., Badger, R. and Dasli, M. (2006) Authenticity, culture, and language learning. *Language and Intercultural Communication* 6 (3–4), 250–261.
McDonald, E. (2011) *Learning Chinese, Turning Chinese: Challenges to Becoming Sinophone in a Globalised World.* London/New York: Routledge.
Mendoza-Denton, N. (2008) *Homegirls: Language and Cultural Practice Among Latina Youth Gangs.* Malden, MA: Wiley-Blackwell.
Mori, J. (2007) Border crossings? Exploring the intersection of second language acquisition, conversation analysis, and foreign language pedagogy. *Modern Language Journal* 91 (5), 847–860.
Ochs, E. (1992) Indexing gender. In A. Duranti and C. Goodwin (eds) *Rethinking Context: Language as an Interactive Phenomenon* (pp. 335–358). Cambridge: Cambridge University Press.
Pellegrino Aveni, V. (2005) *Study Abroad and Second Language Use: Constructing the Self.* Cambridge: Cambridge University Press.
Polanyi, L. (1995) Language learning and living abroad: Stories from the field. In B. Freed (ed.) *Second Language Acquisition in a Study Abroad Context* (pp. 271–292). Philadelphia, PA: John Benjamins.
Siegal, M. (1995) Individual differences and study abroad: Women learning Japanese in Japan. In B.F. Freed (ed.) *Second Language Acquisition in a Study Abroad Context* (pp. 225–244). Philadelphia, PA: John Benjamins.
Silverstein, M. (1976) Shifters, linguistic categories, and cultural description. In K.H. Basso and H.A. Selby (eds) *Meaning in Anthropology* (pp. 11–55). Albuquerque, NM: University of New Mexico Press.
Silverstein, M. (2003) Indexical order and the dialectics of sociolinguistic life. *Language and Communication* 23, 193–229.
Starr, R. (2011) Variation in affective sentence-final particle use and transcription on Taiwanese Mandarin TV dramas. Paper presented at *Symposium about Language and Society (SALSA) XIX*, Austin, TX.
Talburt, S. and Stewart, M.A. (1999) What's the subject of study abroad? Race, gender and 'living culture'. *Modern Language Journal* 83 (2), 163–175.
Twombly, S.B. (1995) Piropos and friendship: Gender and culture clash in study abroad. *Frontiers: The Interdisciplinary Journal of Study Abroad* 1, 1–27.
Wu, R.J. (2004) *Stance in Talk: A Conversation Analysis of Mandarin Final Particles.* Philadelphia, PA: John Benjamins.
Zhu, H. and Li., W. (2014) Geopolitics and the changing hierarchies of the Chinese language: Implications for policy and practice of Chinese language teaching in Britain. *Modern Language Journal* 98, 326–339.

7 Authenticating Language Choices: Out-of-Class Interactions in Study Abroad

Julieta Fernández

Introduction

Before embarking on study abroad (SA), many students (as well as language professionals and college administrators) believe that living in a foreign country will effortlessly lead to improved second-language proficiency thanks to countless 'opportunities to participate in language use that is genuine, natural, and reflective of the host community's norms' (Kinginger, 2009: 159). Understandably, their most common assumption is that the SA environment's principal advantage over at-home language study is the authenticity it affords within, but crucially outside, the language classroom. A stay abroad surely offers them plenty of opportunities to engage in meaningful and consequential out-of-class interactions with host community speakers, thus providing unique access to authentic language use. These interactions are believed to provide ample opportunities to learn pragmatically salient formal and informal language features, making it superior to the at-home classroom environment. The research to date, however, seems to indicate that the cultural and linguistic authenticity traditionally ascribed to the SA context under this assumption is problematic and in need of critical exploration.

The SA literature indicates that exchanges with expert speakers do not necessarily or automatically result in the authenticity that symbolizes the idyllic SA experience. Calling this assumption into question are studies showing that during their sojourn, students do not always gain legitimacy as group members (Lave & Wenger, 1991) of the L2 culture. Brown (2013) and Siegal (1996), for example, argue that on some occasions SA students can negotiate only a limited range of subject positions (i.e. they are often positioned as 'foreigners' or 'outsiders'), preventing them from being exposed to and developing situationally appropriate language resources. Further research shows that, even when able to establish social networks with locals, some students may 'limit their own interactive repertoires' (Kinginger, 2009: 166). One of the most fertile environments in which to establish relationships with locals and participate in authentic interactions during a stay abroad is the host family. Some studies have shown (e.g. Wilkinson, 2002), however, that some students extend and/or over-rely on classroom discourse and student roles in their interactions with their expert-speaker host families. Also, many SA students report that their interactions are mostly restricted to the dinner table (Fernández, 2013; Rivers, 1998), and often co-opted by the television, or plagued by rather unsophisticated and repetitive topics (Kinginger, 2009; Rivers, 1998). Miller and Ginsburg (1995: 312) argue that students tend to 'carry a duplicate of their pedagogical world into interactions with native speakers, implicitly recreating the classroom in other, diverse cultural settings', including the host family environment. As Kinginger (2009) points out, in a later study, Ginsburg and Miller (2000: 141) 'cited evidence in the ethnographic data to suggest that their participants' experiences with foreigner register might lead to questions about the extent to which the language that students encounter in SA is always as authentic as it is believed to be'.

This chapter explores authenticity in out-of-class interactions between students and their conversation partners in light of MacDonald *et al.*'s (2006) criticism of the binary conceptualization of authenticity in the applied linguistic literature – i.e. authenticity of correspondence and authenticity of genesis (Cooper, 1983). MacDonald *et al.* establish authenticity 'within the [intercultural] experience of being and becoming' and make a case for authenticity as the *process* by which L2 learners act as and become 'authentic' and 'intercultural beings' (MacDonald *et al.*, 2006: 260, emphasis mine). This process involves the dialectic interaction between a set of 'situational' and 'projective' self-concerns, thereby establishing an inextricable link between the present and the future. For example, an L2 learner's situational self-concerns may involve the present desire to approximate 'real' language use, that is, language that *corresponds* to what is considered native like in a particular situational context without considering her own development. Situational self-concerns lead a language user to evaluate the context in which she finds herself. This context is always embedded in a culture that comes with its own set of values and beliefs (MacDonald *et al.*, 2006: 259) and results in the language user (re)appraising her own cultural beliefs and values. Projective self-concerns, on the other hand, refer to the idea that language users assess 'the goals to pursue in [their] life; considering the value to put on [their] activities' (MacDonald *et al.*, 2006: 259). The learner's projective self-concerns may involve a desire to stay true to her own long-term trajectory (or *genesis*) without considering the need to coordinate or adjust to the immediate situational or local context. Macdonald *et al.*'s (2006) conceptualization of authenticity is thus better suited for acknowledging students' agency (van

Lier, 2008) in their language use in SA settings, focusing on 'a dialogic exchange between two versions of being and becoming, which continually interact and reflect, one upon the other' (MacDonald *et al.*, 2006: 260).

The Study

This study aims to gain better insight into the often-taken-for-granted authenticity of out-of-class interactions in the SA context. Drawing from Macdonald *et al.*'s (2006) reconceptualization of authenticity, it examines the dialectic relationship between two authenticities (i.e. authenticity of correspondence and genesis; Cooper, 1983) of out-of-class interactions in an SA context. The current study also analyzes the out-of-class face-to-face spoken and online written interactions between an English L1 undergraduate student (Kaelyn) and her Argentine undergraduate conversation partner (Analía) during a four-month sojourn in Buenos Aires, Argentina.

The analysis focuses on the use of two linguistic affordances crucial in the construction of identity (Norton, 2013) for the speaker and her interlocutors, i.e. the use of address terms (DuFon, 2010) and youngspeak features[1] (Stenström *et al.*, 2002). Attested instances of Kaelyn's and Analía's language use are triangulated with insights into their understanding of the social meanings of address terms and informal lexical features, and their reflections on their use in Argentine spoken Spanish.

The conversation partnerships

Data for the case study presented here were selected from a larger investigation of language learning in SA (Fernández, 2013). Participants (American undergraduates) were each paired with one or two conversation partners for the duration of their four-month stay in Argentina to afford more opportunities for them to meet locals and build social networks. Whenever possible, they were matched with conversation partners (all 18–25 years old) who shared similar general or academic interests, and were attending the same or a nearby university. Participants met their assigned conversation partners face-to-face at least once a month (four meetings in total) for a minimum of 30 minutes each time. They also held a minimum of one weekly text chat session (about 15 in total of a minimum of 20 minutes) on any internet-mediated platform of their choosing. Most participants chatted over Facebook, although a few used Gmail chat or Skype text chat.

The participants and their conversation partners were free to discuss topics of their choice, and to meet at a time, date and location of their choice. During the initial interview that the researcher had with the participants (at the beginning of their sojourn, and prior to the establishment of the conversation partnerships), she made it clear that the partnerships were not being established as a means to gain a language tutor (which participants could sign up for through their program of study in Buenos Aires). Instead, the partnerships were introduced as a way to get to know and interact with Argentine undergraduates with similar interests.

The data

Participants submitted audio-recordings of their face-to-face interactions, which were transcribed orthographically and compiled into a corpus. They also submitted their text chats with their respective conversation partners, which were compiled into a separate corpus.[2] All interactions were assembled into a longitudinal language database, henceforth referred to as the learner language database (LLD). The LLD resulted from the transcription of 27 hours of face-to-face interactions and the collection of a total of 75 chat interactions between the 12 participants and their corresponding conversation partners for the duration of four months (Fernández, 2013). All names and identifying references were changed to protect the privacy of the participants.

The participants also completed: (1) three semi-structured interviews with the researcher; (2) a modified language contact profile (Freed *et al.*, 2004); and (3) a series of language awareness measures that included a modified vocabulary knowledge scale (henceforth VKS) (Paribakht & Wesche, 1993). The researcher also conducted on-site observations in the classroom and informal contexts, and collected field notes.

For the present study, data from the LLD have been selected for a case study. The analysis focuses on two participants – Kaelyn and her Argentine conversation partner, Analía. The American participant reported on, Kaelyn, was the highest language producer in the LLD (i.e. she produced a total of 52,179 tokens). She was also one of the two most advanced students in the cohort in terms of her L2 Spanish proficiency, and one of the two students whose major was related to Spanish.

Case study participants: Kaelyn and Analía

At the time of the study, Kaelyn was a 20-year-old world languages education major at a US university. From the moment she started taking Spanish classes at the age of 13, Kaelyn developed a passion for the culture of Hispanic countries (Kaelyn & Analía, CMC 1). This passion led her to continue to learn Spanish, and ultimately to want to become a teacher of Spanish. After her semester abroad she was scheduled to start student teaching (Spanish AP) at her local high school. This was Kaelyn's first SA experience. She had never been to a Spanish-speaking country before. More information about Kaelyn is provided in Table 7.1.

Kaelyn's Spanish language proficiency upon arrival was characterized as advanced. As the Spanish teachers at her SA institution noted in their

Table 7.1 Kaelyn

Age	20
GPA	4.0
L2 Spanish proficiency	Advanced
Major	World Languages Education (Spanish instructor)
Formal learning in Spanish	1 year elementary school and middle school; 4 years high school; 5 semesters in college
Prior experience abroad	None
Living arrangements	Host parents (mom and dad; retired)
Courses in Buenos Aires	Language institute: • Spanish 400 (highest level offered); • Argentine Politics (instruction in Spanish); • Argentine Literature (instruction in Spanish); • Argentine Poetry (instruction in Spanish) Partner university: English–Spanish Translation (instruction in Spanish and English)
Learner language database	A total of 4:25:50 hours of face-to-face interactions and 15 text chats, resulting in a total of 52,179 tokens

evaluation of her performance in the oral placement exam, Kaelyn displayed a quite advanced use of past, present and future tenses, the subjunctive mood, and rather ample vocabulary. Overall, she was deemed to have a solid foundation of Spanish upon arrival.

Mid-semester (June 2012), Kaelyn took the *Certificado de Español Lengua y Uso* (CELU) (Certificate of Spanish Language and Use).[3] She was rated Intermediate, which is equated to a score of Advanced Low on the oral proficiency interview (OPI) offered by the American Council on the Teaching of Foreign Languages (ACTFL). Upon her return to the United States, Kaelyn took the OPI, and this time received a score of Advanced High in L2 Spanish speaking – Level 9 on a 10-level rating system ranging from Novice Low to Superior.

Kaelyn's conversation partner, Analía, was an ESL and Spanish teacher, as well as a certified tango instructor from Buenos Aires (for further information about Analía, see Table 7.2). Because hers was a family of modest means, Analía had only been abroad once – she briefly visited Florida when she was a child. At the time of the study, she had a few American acquaintances she had met mostly at pubs in Buenos Aires, with whom she kept in touch only sporadically. As a result, until the time of the study, Analía had learned about the United States at second hand. She had studied English at a private language institute in her neighborhood for seven years. She then enrolled in the teacher training program at her university. The teaching profession, according to Analía, 'ran in the family' – her grandmother, grandfather, mother and aunt were all teachers (Kaelyn & Analía, CMC 1).

Table 7.2 Analía

Age	24
L2 English Proficiency	High Advanced
Major	English as a Second Language
Formal learning in English	7 years private language institute
Other languages	Basic knowledge of French
Prior experience abroad	Short family trip to Florida at 10 years of age

Analía was particularly interested in learning more about American culture in general and academic culture in particular because she had applied, and been accepted during her semester as a conversation partner, to do an academic exchange in the United States in Fall 2012. She was hired to teach Spanish at a US university. Analía had one year of experience teaching Spanish in Buenos Aires, although she did not have formal training in L2 Spanish language teaching and/or pedagogy.

Analía and Kaelyn shared an interest in language teaching. During their interactions they not only shared ideas for classroom activities but also discussed their beliefs about good pedagogy and its importance. They were also going through similar experiences given that Analía was getting ready to embark on a work and SA experience of her own. But the fact that Analía lived quite far from Kaelyn and had a busy schedule precluded them from spending more time together. Consequently, their incipient friendship did not consolidate until later in the semester. When Analía's schedule became more open towards the end of the academic semester, they spent more time together and were able to bond.

In the interactions between Kaelyn and Analía there were no apparent instances of miscommunication. Rather, their exchanges appeared to flow smoothly. Kaelyn seemed to gather the meaning of new words and expressions from the interaction (for example, *dando clases ... o sea enseñando, verdad¿*, literally 'giving classes ... you mean teaching, right¿'). Their contributions aligned with one another's and to the topic at hand, and on occasion they finished each other's turns, showing a fairly high level of intersubjectivity.

Findings

Address terms: Accommodation strategies

The use of Spanish address terms is nuanced in Argentina. While *tú* is practically not present at all in Argentine Spanish (Lipski, 1994), the use of *vos* is stable (i.e. it does not compete with *tú* as in other Spanish-speaking countries) and is considered as one of the most distinguishing morphological characteristics of Argentine Spanish (Gassó, 2009; Weyers, 2009). In Argentina, the use of *tú* seems non-Argentine and is generally used only by foreigners (Fontanella de Weinberg, 1999; Gassó, 2009; Weyers, 2009). The *voseo* 'is accepted at all social levels and in all contexts' in Argentina, and 'the universal use of *vos*' represents part of the local identity (Lipski, 1994: 172). While researchers disagree as to how frequent it is in formal contexts (e.g. Fontanella de Weinberg, 2000; Gassó, 2009), it has been identified as a marker of informality and closeness, both in spoken and written language, and across socio-economic and stylistic variations (Gassó, 2009).

Prior to studying abroad, Kaelyn seemed to 'have simple representations of the address system' in Argentine Spanish, 'often perceiving it as straightforward' (DuFon, 2010: 321). According to her (Excerpt 7.1), the rules of politeness in the use of '*tú/vos*' versus '*usted*' were more relaxed compared to those she had learned from her Mexican (line 5) and Venezuelan (line 7) friends. She explained that she used *vos* most of the time (line 12) because her Venezuelan friend had told her always to use it in Argentina (lines 16–19) until she learned (when and how) to use it (line 21). When unsure, her friend had suggested she use *usted*. Kaelyn also seemed to have considered age (over intimacy) as the overriding factor that determined pronoun choice. For example, seeing as they were pensioners (lines 32 and 34), Kaelyn first addressed her host parents using *usted* '(formal) you' but they explicitly asked her to address them using *vos* '(informal) you' (lines 27 and 29). Thus, in terms of contextual variables, it appeared that Kaelyn would rely on the rules of thumb she had been given by her native Spanish-speaking friends in the United States.

Excerpt 7.1 Kaelyn on Argentine Spanish (Kaelyn & Analía, F2F 1)

1	**K**:	*Es verdad, y también no sé las*	it is true, and also I don't know the rules
2		*reglas de:, no sé, por ejemplo es*	of, I don't know, for example the different
3		*diferente el uso de **usted** acá*	uses of *usted* [formal you] here
4	**A**:	*sí.*	yes
5	**K**:	*y en comparación con Méjico*	and in comparison with Mexico
6	**A**:	*sí*	yes
7	**K**:	*Venezuela mucho más (.) estricto*	Venezuela is much more (.) strict
8	**A**:	*sí*	yes
9	**K**:	*no sé, este, y yo, de lo que yo no*	I don't know, hmm, and I, from what no I
10		*he notado acá*	have noticed here
11	**A**:	*sí.*	yes
12	**K**:	*uso **vos** casi todo el tiempo.*	I use *vos* [informal you] all the time
13	**A**:	*sí, sí, aquí no se usa mucho*	yes, yes, here it is not used much
14	**K**:	*y entonces*	and then
15	**A**:	*el **usted***	*usted* [formal you]

16	K:	*pero sí, yo hablaba con mi amiga*	but yes, I was talking with my friend (.)
17		*(.) y le preguntaba muchas cosas*	and I asked her many things about when
18		*sobre*	to use it and she told me that there, you
19		*cuando usarlo y me dijo que ahí, tenés que usarlo todo el tiempo*	have to use it all the time
20	A:	*claro*	right
21	K:	*hasta que sepas, y yo le dije, no*	until you know and I told her I don't think
22		*creo que es así y, en, en Argentina (…)*	that this is so and in in Argentina
23	K:	*porque yo, yo intente hablar en*	because I, I tried to speak in u:hm *usted*
24		*a:hm, usted con mis padres o:, con la*	[formal you] with my host parents o:r
25		*familia con quien*	with the family with whom
26	A:	*sí*	yes
27	K:	*me quedo acá y me dijo no no no*	I'm staying here and (she/he) told me no no no
28	A:	*[laughter]*	[laughter]
29	K:	**vos** *por favor [laughter]*	*vos* [informal you] please [laughter]
30	A:	*sí, aquí se utiliza mucho este el, el*	yes, here it is widely use u:hm the the
31		*ya* **tutearse**	already use *vos* [informal you]
32	K:	*y son mayores así que*	and they are old so
33	A:	*sí*	yes
34	K:	*no sabía, no. y, son jubilados*	I didn't know, no. and they are retired

In her classes at the language institute during her stay abroad, Kaelyn did not receive instruction about the use of forms of address in Argentine Spanish. Presumably, it could be expected that as her 'access to *authentic* use of the language' grew, she would 'observe the sociolinguistic and interactional complexities of the system and judge address form use increasingly difficult' (Kinginger, 2009: 94, emphasis mine). For Kaelyn, this process was further complicated by Analía's linguistic adjustments. From their first interaction, Analía displayed a range of accommodation strategies when communicating with Kaelyn. While accommodation strategies are not an altogether uncommon phenomenon in SA (Kinginger, 2009), in some aspects Analía's modifications resembled what has been labeled 'teacher talk', especially in grammar and vocabulary (van Lier, 1996).

Most notably, Analía used the second-person singular pronoun *tú* rather than the second-person singular pronoun preferred by speakers of Argentine Spanish, namely *vos* 'you'. Consequently, she also used the verbal inflections associated with *tú*, which in the indicative and imperative are distinctly different from those associated with *vos*.[4] For example, during their first chat, Analía opened with the question, *quieres hablar ahora¿* rather than *querés hablar ahora¿* 'do you want to talk now?' (Excerpt 7.2, lines 4–5).

In their interactions, Analía also used *tú* in contexts where in conversational Spanish the subject would probably be omitted (resultantly being redundant, given that in Spanish the information about the person and number is encoded in the verbal inflection). For example, in the excerpt below, Analía uses *tú* in her opening questions (lines 4–5), resulting in a rather formal construction.

Excerpt 7.2 Language accommodation (Kaelyn and Analía, CMC 2[5])

1	**K**:	*hola ana, solo queria saber si hay*	hello ana, I just wanted to know if there is
2		*algun momento que te conviene para*	a time that is best for you to chat this
3		*escribirnos esta semana*	week
4	**A**:	*hola Kaelyn, como estas¿* **quieres**	hello Kaelyn, how are you¿ Do you want
5		*hablar ahora¿ o cuando puedes* **tú**¿	to talk now¿ or when can **you**¿
6	**K**:	*si! esto está bien, tengo tiempo*	yes! this is okay, I have free time now, is
7		*libre ahora, está bien para* **vos**¿	it okay for **you**¿

Analía continued to rely on *tú* even though during their first interaction Kaelyn demonstrated several attempts to use *vos*, initially as part of largely formulaic expressions (*bien y vos* 'good and you', *bien para vos* 'okay/good for you'). In fact, during their very first interaction Kaelyn opened the conversation with *vos* (line 7), as shown in Excerpt 7.3.

Excerpt 7.3 Kaelyn's use of vos (Kaelyn and Analía, CMC 1)

| 1 | **A**: | *Cómo estás¿* | How are you [=vos or tu]¿ |
| 2 | **K**: | *estoy bien, y* **vos**¿ | I'm good, and you [=vos]¿ |

However, Kaelyn shuttled between *vos* to *tú* throughout her first chats with Analía. When they first met for coffee, Kaelyn explained that because she had friends from Mexico and Venezuela, she was aware of (at least some of) the differences in the use of *vos* in other Spanish-speaking countries (Excerpt 7.4).

Excerpt 7.4 Kaelyn's language awareness (Kaelyn & Analía, F2F 1)

1	**K**:	*bueno estoy bueno mi amiga de*	well I'm well my friend from Venezuela
2		*Venezuela habla de* **vos** *pero es un poco*	speaks using **vos** but it's a little different
3		*diferente como el* **voceo** *de ahí*	like the use of **vos** from there
4	**A**:	*sí*	yes
5	**K**:	*como (..) ¿cómo* **estáis**¿	like (..) how are **you**¿
6	**A**:	*sí*	yes
7	**K**:	*en vez de ¿cómo* **estás**¿ *No sé*	instead of how are **you**¿ I don't know
8	**A**:	*sí, eso sí*	Yes, that yes
9	**K**:	**contáis** *y no* **contás**, *no, no sé*	**tell** and not **tell**, I don't, I don't know

It was only in their third CMC interaction that Analía used *vos* twice, but overwhelmingly continued to use *tú*. It could be argued that Analía's use of *tú*, especially in contexts where it would be omitted in spoken interactions, was influenced by or attributed to the hybrid nature of text chat. However, Analía also used it in their face-to-face (F2F) interactions, although in a more inconsistent manner (perhaps indicating that she was swerving from the form that would be more natural). In their F2F meetings, Analía would shift between forms even in contiguous turns, as illustrated in Excerpt 7.5, or even within the same turn. In this example, she first uses *vos* (lines 1 and 2), and almost immediately switches to *tú* (line 4).

Excerpt 7.5 Analía's language accommodation (Kaelyn & Analía, F2F 2 p. 4)

1	**A**:	*claro sí bueno sí* **tenés** *que*
2		*aprovechar si te* **levantás** *temprano*
3	**K**:	*sí sí*
4	**A**:	**empiezas** *bien temprano*
5	**K**:	*y vos tenés planes¿*

right yes well yes **you** [= *vos*] have to make the most [of the day] if **you** [= *vos*] wake up early
yes yes
you [= *tú*] start very early
and do **you** [= *vos*] have plans¿

Analía's use of *tú* was striking to Kaelyn, especially because, according to her (third interview, Excerpt 7.6), among the experienced speakers Kaelyn interacted with in Argentina (although not as much as she interacted with her conversation partner), Analía was the only one who used *tú* to address her:

Excerpt 7.6 On Analía's language accommodation strategies (Kaelyn, interview #3)

```
 1  R⁶:  did you feel that people talk to you differently¿ Because I can tell that Analía
 2       talked to you very differently so she would use 'tú' and
 3  K:   yeah and she would and (.) I think she she doesn't do that anymore 'cause we
 4       talked about it once I was like why do you use tú and she was like I'm used to
 5       doing
         it with my students
 6  R:   okay
 7  K:   she kinda had that same (.3) issue in her class right¿ because she had a lot of
 8       students from a lot of different places and so she was like well a lot of the time
         I'll
 9       use tienes 'cause they don't know tenés and I don't know [laughs] that's a
10       problem
         that people try to shy away from using it
```

According to van Lier (1996), in an *authentic* context, 'both a teacher's foreigner talk or teacher talk and demonstrations (or samples reproduced in one way or another of language use from extra-mural settings) can, in appropriate circumstances, be authenticated by the participants' (van Lier, 1996: 131). This conceptualization of authenticity allows us to avoid getting entangled in the dualism 'classroom language' versus 'real language' (or 'classroom' versus 'outside world') (van Lier, 1996: 131). Kaelyn found an explanation for Analía's marked use of *tú* in her experience teaching Spanish to foreigners at that time (lines 4–5). As a Spanish teacher, Analía was used to switching to a variety of Spanish that would more likely be understood by greater numbers of Spanish speakers. After Kaelyn brought this to her attention (Excerpt 7.6, lines 3–4) and towards the end of the semester, Analía moved completely to the use of *vos*. This appears to be a trajectory whereby Kaelyn gradually authenticated her partner's use of the address form culminating in a rich point (Agar, 1994) whereby Kaelyn validated her authentication of Analía's use of *tú*, simultaneously serving as a developmental advance in their relationship.

Ironically, during their first F2F interaction, Kaelyn and Analía had a rather long exchange (Excerpt 7.7) about how important it is to learn and use *lenguaje callejero* 'street language' as opposed to the 'formal' language typically taught in many classrooms (Excerpt 7.7, lines 7 and 8). While she continued to use *tú* elsewhere, Analía makes her point regarding what she sees as the differences between classroom language and the language spoken by expert speakers (in 'reality', line 11) by contrasting the use of *usted* '(formal) you' and *vos* '(informal) you' (lines 14 and 17). This would indicate that through her linguistic choices Analía, at least initially, regarded her meetings with Kaelyn as an extension of the classroom. For Kaelyn, Analía's 'classroom' language choices marked the beginning of a trajectory of authenticating Analía's and her own language use through the lenses of her Spanish history and professional goals in life – a dialectic between situational self-concern and projective self-concern (MacDonald *et al.*, 2006).

Excerpt 7.7 Kaelyn on Argentine Spanish (Kaelyn & Analía, F2F 1)

```
 1  A:  sí, sí. sí, no eso eso, es e:h, muy          yes, yes. yes, no that that, is u:h, very
 2      divertido porque [laughs] por lo menos       funny because [laughs] at least for me I
 3      para mí me parece que o sea todos los        think that I mean [in] all the languages it
 4      idiomas está bueno aprender (.) un           is great to learn (.) a bit of, you know, of
 5      poco de, viste, del lenguaje callejero       the street language that is spoken
 6      digamos que se habla porque m:, no           because
 7      sé, lo que te enseñan muchas veces en        m:, I don't know, what they teach you
 8      las academias o en los institutos es         many times in the academies or in the
 9      como lenguaje formal digamos                 institutes is like formal language, let's say
10  K:  sí                                           yes
11  A:  y después vos vas a la realidad y            and then you go to the reality and (it) is
12      no es, no te hablan así, no te hablan        not, they don't talk to you like that, they
                                                     don't talk to you
```

13	**K**: *sí, pero*	yes, but
14	**A**: ***usted*** *quiere tomar (.) no![laughter]*	do **you** (formal) drink (.) no! [laughter]
15		
16	**K**: *no*	no
17	**A**: *te dicen ¿che* ***querés****¿ [laughter]*	they tell you che [informal vocative] do **you** (informal) want¿
18	**K**: *[laughter]*	[laughter]
19	**A**: *sí*	yes

Notably, Analía's teacher-talk orientation also surfaced in other lexical choices, such as the use of *aquí* 'here' and *allí* 'there' (for example, *hace mucho calor **aquí** adentro* 'it's too hot in here') rather than *acá* and *allá*, the corresponding two lexical features in Argentine Spanish used by all other conversation partners in the LLD. Analía also used the synthetic future rather than the periphrastic future (e.g. *estaré conectada* rather than *voy a estar conectada* 'I will be online'), which was very frequent in the spoken interactions by the other conversation partners in the LLD. Furthermore, Analía initially accommodated her language by recycling some of the non-Argentine youngspeak terms Kaelyn would use in their interactions. That is, Kaelyn would first use an item more frequent in another Spanish dialect, and Analía would use the same item in the immediate and subsequent interactions. For example, during their first chat, Analía recycled *la uni* (abbreviation for *la universidad* 'the university'), which Kaelyn had used a few turns earlier. Only in their fourth chat (and onward) did she use *la facu* (abbreviation for *la facultad* 'the university'), which was the Argentine youngspeak chosen by all other conversation partners. While Analía's use of colloquialisms increased as they continued to interact, it remained rather sparse, especially in their computer-mediated interactions.

Youngspeak: Kaelyn's imagined L2 Spanish identity

Kaelyn's language use shows that although she used a few 'argentinisms' (such as *colectivo* for 'bus') she did not use much Argentine youngspeak. She barely used any of the selected youngspeak lexical features (for selection criteria, see Fernández, 2013) in her interactions with her conversation partner or the researcher. Based on her language performance, one could assume that she did not know these lexical features. However, in her VKS responses she demonstrated that she knew the meaning, could provide appropriate examples and could identify appropriate context of use (i.e. matching those identified by the conversation partners) for almost all features (see Figure 7.1).

Kaelyn then seemed to be unconcerned about using language that corresponded to the *authentic* language of similarly aged local speakers of Argentine Spanish. In fact, she appeared to be more preoccupied with making interactional choices that would best align with and support the larger

14. WORD/EXPRESSION: boludo/boluda

I. I don't remember seeing/hearing this word. _____

II. I have seen/heard this word before, but I don't know what it means. _____

III. I have seen/heard this word before, and I think it means _____
(provide an English translation or Spanish synonym.)

IV. I know this word. It means *buddy, dude, idiot*
(provide an English translation or synonym.)

V. I can use this word in a sentence (If you answer this item, you MUST also answer item IV)
Che, boludo, y ¿Cómo estás? / ¡Sos un boludo!

VI. I know in which contexts I can use/would use this word *really informal settings*
(describe contexts: e.g. with friends; with teacher(s); in academic papers; with older people; with peers you don't know well; with acquaintances; with conversation partners)

VII. I know the functions this word has in conversation: *to sound casual, to get someone's attention, to insult someone*
(e.g. to sound casual: to sound more fluent; to change the topic; etc)

VIII. I would rate the politeness of this word as *depends → neutral — impolite depending on situation*
(choose from: very impolite rude/vulgar; impolite; slightly impolite; neutral; polite; very polite)

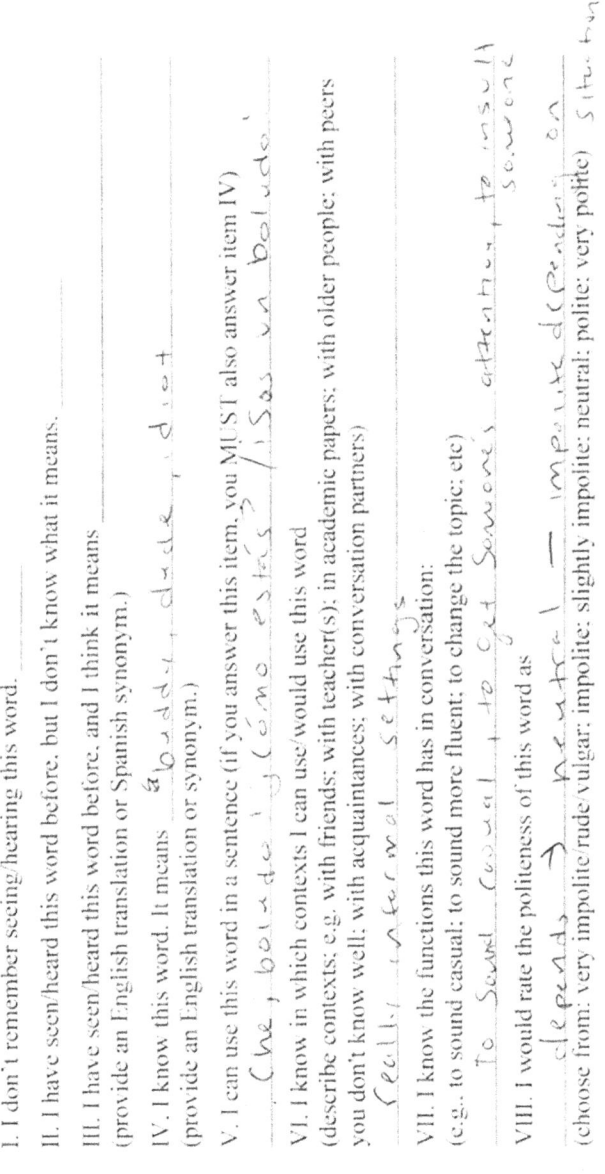

Figure 7.1 Sample VKS response, Kaelyn

developmental trajectory behind the 'public self' she was portraying. When reflecting on her semester in Buenos Aires (Interview 3, Excerpt 7.8), Kaelyn admitted to taking a 'neutral route' in her language choices (line 4) while interacting with Argentines. She argued that, if she ever drew on slang from Argentine Spanish, it would be intentional in order to 'get, like, a reaction out of people' (line 6), often to create a humorous effect (line 5).

Excerpt 7.8 On using Argentine Spanish (Kaelyn, Interview 3)

1 **K**: I was overly aware of like what words came from different places because I'd
2 already had a lot of experiences with natives¿
3 **R**: okay
4 **K**: so I feel like I kinda just took a neutral route (.2) like underst- if I used
5 Argentinian slang or if I do later I do more in a joking way because I know how to
6 use it but it's more to get like a reaction out of the people I'm talking to just because
7 like (.4) I know I can't really I mean I can but I can't really use those words when
8 talking to like Mexican friends or Venezuelan friends 'cause they're going to be like what are you (..) what are you saying
9 **R**: right
10 **K**: so I learned to sort of (.5) navigate between them
11 **R**: while in Argentina then why did you choose the neutral route then¿
12 **K**: u:hm (.4) I don't know maybe because I was still in touch with some of those
13 other speakers¿
14 **R**: okay
15 **K**: maybe it was a comfort thing too I don't know (.6) or it didn't feel like genuine to me
16 **R**: it didn't feel genuine¿
17 **K**: yeah, like to use those words because I felt like I I was struggling a lot of the time
18 like trying to decide well how do I want my Spanish to be¿
19 **R**: huh
20 **K**: because like I like I didn't know especially when coming back and like teaching and
21 **R**: right
22 **K**: not being sure of like okay should I have sort of a clear (.10) sort of type of
23 Spanish that is reflected in one sort of (.3) dialect or should I try to be more able to
24 like distinguish between and teach between the different kinds
25 **R**: and so what do you think would be a more useful dialect [in the US] (.2) Mexican¿
26 **K**: u:hm maybe yeah maybe like a Mexican variety or central American (...)

In the United States, Kaelyn had friends and acquaintances from different Spanish-speaking countries (i.e. Colombia, Mexico, Venezuela) and was aware of the dialectal differences between them, especially in terms of vocabulary (Excerpt 7.8, lines 1–2). Kaelyn explained that while in Argentina she still considered her Spanish-speaking friends from the United States as her primary audience, which she 'lumped' into a somewhat homogeneous dialect group (i.e. she did not address having to navigate the Mexican, Colombian and Venezuelan dialects, for example, perhaps because the differences among them seemed less marked to her in comparison to Argentine Spanish), leading her to keep to her choice of being 'neutral' in Argentine Spanish. Faced with a constant choice between dialects, Kaelyn argued that she learned to 'navigate' among them (line 10), but her newly acquired Argentine dialect did not feel 'genuine' (or *authentic*) to her (line 15).

Kaelyn also gave plenty of thought to her language choices based on the fact that in the following academic year she would start teaching L2 Spanish in the United States (Excerpt 7.8, lines 20, 22–24). She argued that the differences between Spanish dialects are worth explaining to L2 Spanish students in the United States in more advanced courses; only then would she be more willing to let those different aspects of grammar, vocabulary and pronunciation come out. She was very worried that students who are still mastering the basic conjugations might be negatively affected if she started 'twisting it a little bit' (Kaelyn, Interview #3). She believed that beginning students would have trouble doing the present tense on their own even if they were doing so in just the 'standard kind of speak' (Kaelyn, Interview #3).

In fact, prior to choosing Argentina as her SA destination and during her time in Buenos Aires, Kaelyn discussed how the different dialects of Spanish would factor in her choices in the classroom (Excerpt 7.9, lines 2–5). Even though she was not fully sure what dialect she wanted to teach her students (line 6), she strongly believed that she should focus on the dialect that would have more use value and be more instrumental for her students. She defined instrumentality based on the speakers that her students would most likely be interacting with on a regular basis (i.e. Mexican Spanish users).

Excerpt 7.9 On using Argentine Spanish (Kaelyn, Interview 3)

1 **R**: Did you think about all this before going to Argentina?
2 **K**: yeah yeah I did actually I had talked to my professor about it before. We talked a
3   lot about variety in language and like how to accommodate for that in the
4   classroom
5   (.4) and I remember having discussions because I was doing the online blog class I
6   think I told you about? Having discussions with Michelle (.2) uhm about oh I don't
      know I still haven't decided like [laughs] how I wanna teach in Spanish in my class or
7 **R**: right
8 **K**: like what would I mean it's not really an answer it's sort of just based on your
9   experiences but (.6) like I've noticed based on like how people will react to me
10   sometimes if I say something that's (.3) more influenced based on what I learned in
11   Argentina just like native speakers in the US and they don't understand me? I think
12   well maybe that's not as useful for my students if those are the speakers that they're
      gonna be interacting with

It appears that, when it came to Argentine youngspeak, Kaelyn's conscious decision was not to perfunctorily approximate the perceived 'real' Argentine 'norms' of communication but instead 'authenticating her intercultural being and becoming' (MacDonald *et al.*, 2006: 256) along her own long-term trajectory as a Spanish language teacher. It is important to note, however, that not all participants in the context share the same beliefs and values, or in this case understand the dialectic relationship between a learner's situational and projective self-concerns. Even after extensive interactions, Kaelyn's decision to remain 'neutral' had an unwanted social consequence. Comparing her interactions with Kaelyn in English and in Spanish, Analía argued that in Spanish Kaelyn always tried to maintain a level of formality evident in the fact that she did not know 'how to get close' (lines 35–37), thus creating a 'space' between her interlocutors and herself (lines 39–40). Kaelyn's reflections (during the interviews) seem to suggest this usage pattern was motivated by projective self-concerns. The unintended effect, however, was that she was considered detached.

Excerpt 7.10 Analía's opinion of Kaelyn's formality (Analía, Interview 3)

```
12  A:  m: o sea sí trataba de integrarse           m:, I mean yes she always tried to
13      siempre a la (.) a todo digamos pero era    integrate with the (.) with everything
14      como que siempre tenía eso (.) como que     let's say but it was like she always had
15      vos te dabas cuenta del, le preguntaban     that (.) like you could tell, everyone
16      todos ¿de dónde sos¿ o                      asked her, where are you from↗ or
17  R:  creés que era por el acento, por la, las    do you think it was because of the
18      palabras que usaba (.) por¿                 accent or for the (sing) the (plural)
                                                    words that she was using (.) for↗
19  A:  por, por las palabras (.4) como es          because of (.) because of the words (.4)
20      muy formal Kaelyn acá.                      it is like she is very formal Kaelyn here
21  R:  okay. creés que es una diferencia           okay. do you think that it is a difference
22      entre inglés y español que es la, la        between English and Spanish that it is
23      formalidad o                                the formality or
24  A:  m:, no, no, no creo. bah, no sé, pero       m: no no I don't think so, well I don't
                                                    know but
25  R:  no sabés.                                   you don't know
26  A:  vos sabés más que yo pero                   you know more than me but
27  R:  no, no sé                                   no, I don't know
28  A:  pero                                        but
29  R:  cuando te hablaba en inglés pensaste        when she spoke to you in English did
30      que era menos formal en inglés que en       you think that she was less formal in
31      castellano o¿                               English than in Spanish or↗
32  A:  sí, me parece que sí, en inglés era         yes, I believe so, in English she was like
33      como menos formal que en castellano. en     less formal than in Spanish. in Spanish
34      castellano como que trataba de mantener     like she tried to maintain always a a
```

35		*siempre la, la formalidad, no sabía*	formality she didn't know maybe like
36		*quizás como si, si acercarse demasiado o no*	yeah yeah to get too close or not
37	**R**:	*este, ¿acercarse de espacio decís?*	u:hm you mean to get closer in space?
38	**A**:	*de espacio exacto, sí, creaba un espacio*	in space exactly, yes, she created a space

Interestingly, as discussed earlier, Analía herself relied on formal features heavily, particularly at the outset of her interactions with Kaelyn. Kaelyn's level of formality in her interactions with Analía may therefore be explained in part as an effort to show 'attunement to the attunement of the other' (Rommetveit, 1992: 10). Kaelyn's preference to be largely 'neutral' in interactions with her conversation partners did not necessarily undermine her desire to know youngspeak features and dialectal differences associated with informal language choices. Kaelyn ultimately developed an awareness of a wide range of dialectal differences, albeit without a strong intention to regularly put them to interactional use. A related aspect of this issue was the contextual need to use those items in interaction. Kaelyn chose not to spend time in bars and similar settings, so the contextual need to use features that mark youngspeak on a semi-regular basis did not emerge. Given Kaelyn's tendency to think of Spanish use through the lens of a future Spanish instructor, she appeared to distance herself from thinking like a 'teenager' interested in engaging in various 'teenage' acts. This is not to say that typical teenage acts would necessarily comprise going to bars and frequently using expressions such as *boludo* 'stupid'/'dude'; it is quite clear, however, that Kaelyn very rarely found herself in situations where she may have found the use of Argentine youngspeak categorically necessary.

Discussion and Conclusions

The analysis presented in this chapter suggests that naturally occurring interactions with experienced age-peer speakers in an SA context do not necessarily expose students to discourses distinctly different from those of the classroom variety. In fact, such interactions do not always involve the mutually constructed interactive 'authenticity' typically taken for granted in out-of-class SA interactions. It is argued that the authenticity of correspondence of out-of-class interactions to perceived conventions and their dispositions toward the L2 language and culture (synchronicity, or being) is inextricably connected with the subject positions that the SA students desire and are able to negotiate and the relevant goals they would like to pursue (diachronicity, or becoming).

The analysis of the interactions between the participants showed that Kaelyn's conversation partner relied extensively on formal features in their interactions. From their first meeting, Analía employed the same language accommodations with Kaelyn as she would with her L2 Spanish students. The fact that Kaelyn had a very advanced general proficiency and pragmatic competence in L2 Spanish did not seem to influence Analía's language choices. Kaelyn also contributed to the perceived 'inauthenticity' of their interactions with her desire to use 'neutral' Spanish. While they discussed the differences between classroom or textbook language and 'real' language, much of their (early) communication bore resemblance to classroom discourse between an instructor and a student. It follows that even at advanced levels of L2 proficiency, more interactions with expert speakers do not necessarily result in more use of informal features – more clues are found when the quality of the interactions is scrutinized, and the (desired and imagined) identities (Norton, 2013) of the interlocutors are carefully considered.

Although Kaelyn was quite invested (Norton, 2013) in learning Spanish and picked up some Argentine youngspeak during her SA, she chose to take what she considered a 'neutral route' in almost all her language choices. Kaelyn exercised her agency based on her long-term professional investment in learning Spanish, and this mediated the significance she assigned to various semiotic resources and the way she chose to learn them based on her individual social history (Lantolf & Pavlenko, 2001). Kaelyn's investment in Spanish was structured around her identity as an L2 Spanish teacher. It was therefore important for her to reproduce and maintain the type of neutral dialect that her students would probably benefit most from. Argentine Spanish did not feel as genuine or 'authentic' to her because she had originally developed a way of speaking based on her interactions with Mexican and Venezuelan friends before coming to Argentina.

Kaelyn had given plenty of thought as to who she wanted to be and how she would want to position herself as an L2 Spanish teacher upon her return – did she want to teach a 'neutral' dialect, to teach the language variety she thought would hold more use value to her students (e.g. Mexican), or give them a good grounding in various dialects of Spanish? She decided to pick the reasonably neutral path, which involved adhering to what in her opinion was a 'neutral' Spanish dialect while being in Argentina. This decision, in turn, meant not using much youngspeak. Throughout her daily engagements in Argentina, she decided to remain authentic to the imagined community she felt affiliated with through her imagined identity as a high school Spanish teacher and authenticate the language choices in her interactions with Analía through these lenses.

The interactions between the focal participant and her conversation partner suggest the need for a rounded interpretation of what it means for an intercultural exchange to be authentic or authenticated. The language choices made by the two participants described and analyzed above can be more appropriately explained in terms of a trajectory of authenticating. Kaelyn's language use and her discussion of her choices reveal not a 'stable, essential self; rather, ... different emphases of [Kaelyn's] preoccupation with a self which is always a work in progress' (MacDonald *et al.*, 2006: 259). The interaction between two self-concerns as Kaelyn takes stock of her knowledge of Spanish address forms and reflects upon her goal to become a Spanish language teacher mediates how she authenticates Analía's discreet language choices and, in turn, authenticates her own choices. This reflects the trajectory marked by the rich point at which they discuss their address choices. In addition to being distinguished by the ever-present address terms, the trajectory of authenticating is importantly distinguished by the items that are not used – but that Kaelyn is keenly aware of and attentive to – youngspeak. Language choices – both veiled and conspicuous – along with the participants' insights into their selves supply sufficiently rich descriptive information to gain insight into authenticity as a developmental process – a process of subjectification (MacDonald *et al.*, 2006).

Notes

(1) Following Stenström *et al.* (2002), the definition of *youngspeak* colloquial vocabulary adopted in this study includes: (1) words that are often associated with slang; (2) words that can have taboo meanings; (3) vague single and multi-word expressions; and (4) smallwords (Hasselgren, 2002).
(2) The interactions that the participants maintained using Facebook (or other text chat platforms, such as Skype) are undoubtedly shaped by the lack of complete synchronicity of communication (as opposed to face-to-face interactions), thus allowing both participants more introspection as to their language choices. Face-to-face and internet-mediated interactions were thus analyzed separately.
(3) Administered by the *Consorcio Interuniversitario para la Evaluación del Conocimiento y Uso del Español como Lengua Extranjera* (Inter-university Consortium for the Evaluation of the Knowledge and Use of Spanish as a Foreign Language) in Buenos Aires.
(4) Although, as the reader may see in the excerpts, for the objective, dative and possessive pronouns (i.e. *te, tu, tuyo*), the conjugations of the verb are the same (Gassó, 2009).
(5) The interactions that the participants maintained online are reproduced as they were produced – that is, maintaining all typos, punctuation conventions, etc.
(6) 'R' stands for researcher.

References

Agar, M. (1994) *Language Shock: Understanding the Culture of Conversation*. New York: William Morrow.
Brown, L. (2013) Identity and honorifics use in Korean study abroad. In C. Kinginger (ed.) *Social and Cultural Aspects of Cross-border Language Learning in Study Abroad* (pp. 269–298). Amsterdam: John Benjamins.
Cooper, D.E. (1983) *Authenticity and Learning: Nietzsche's Educational Philosophy*. London: Routledge and Keagan Paul.
DuFon, M.A. (2010) The acquisition of terms of address in a second language. In A. Trosborg (ed.) *Handbook of Pragmatics, Vol. 7: Pragmatics Across Languages and Cultures* (pp. 287–308). New York/Berlin: Mouton de Gruyter.
Fernández, J. (2013) Social networks and youngspeak in study abroad. Unpublished doctoral dissertation, Pennsylvania State University, University Park, PA.

Fontanella de Weinberg, M.B. (1999) Sistemas pronominales de tratamiento usados en el mundo hispánico. In I. Bosque and V. Demonte (eds) *Gramática descriptiva de la lengua española. 1. Sintaxis básica de las clases de palabras* (pp. 1400–1425). Madrid: Espasa Calpe.

Fontanella de Weinberg, M.B. (2000) *El español de la Argentina y sus variedades regionales.* Buenos Aires: Edicial.

Freed, B.F., Dewey, D., Segalowitz, N. and Halter, F. (2004) The language contact profile. *Studies in Second Language Acquisition* 26 (2), 349–356.

Gasso, M.J. (2009) El voseo rioplatense en la clase de español. In V Encuentro brasileño de profesores de español. Suplementos marco ELE. *Revista de didáctica español lengua extranjera* (pp. 1–26) (online).

Ginsburg, R.B. and Miller, L. (2000) What do they do? Activities of students during study abroad. In R.D. Lambert and E. Shohamy (eds) *Language Policy and Pedagogy: Essays in Honor of A. Ronald Walton* (pp. 237–261). Philadelphia, PA: John Benjamins.

Hasselgren, A. (2002) Learner corpora and language testing: Smallwords as markers of learner fluency. In S. Granger, J. Hung and S. Petch Tyson (eds) *Computer Learner Corpora, Second Language Acquisition, and Foreign Language Teaching* (pp. 143–173). Amsterdam/Philadelphia, PA: John Benjamins.

Kinginger, C. (2009) *Language Learning and Study Abroad: A Critical Reading of Research.* Basingstoke: Palgrave/Macmillan.

Lantolf, J.P. and Pavlenko, A. (2001) (S)econd (L)anguage (A)ctivity: Understanding learners as people. In M. Breen (ed.) *Learner Contributions to Language Learning: New Directions in Research* (pp. 141–158). London: Pearson.

Lave, J. and Wenger, E. (1991) *Situated Learning: Legitimate Peripheral Participation.* Cambridge: Cambridge University Press.

Lipski, J.M. (1994) *Latin American Spanish.* London: Longman.

MacDonald, M.N., Badger, R. and Dasli, M. (2006) Authenticity, culture, and language learning. *Language and Intercultural Communication* 6 (3–4), 250–261.

Miller, L. and Ginsburg, R. (1995) Folklinguistic theories of language learning. In B. Freed (ed.) *Second Language Acquisition in a Study Abroad Context* (pp. 293–315). Philadelphia, PA: John Benjamins.

Norton, B. (2013) *Identity and Language Learning. Extending the Conversation* (2nd edn). Bristol: Multilingual Matters.

Paribakht, T.S. and Wesche, M.B. (1993) Reading comprehension and second language development in a comprehension-based ESL program. *TESL Canada Journal* 11, 9–29.

Rivers, W.P. (1998) Is being there enough? The effects of homestay placements on language gain during study abroad. *Foreign Language Annals* 31, 492–500.

Rommetveit, R. (1992) Outlines of a dialogically based social-cognitive approach to human cognition and communication. In A. Heen Wold (ed.) *The Dialogical Alternative. Towards a Theory of Language and Mind* (pp. 19–44). Oslo: Scandinavian University Press.

Siegal, M. (1996) The role of learner subjectivity in second language sociolinguistic competency: Western women learning Japanese. *Applied Linguistics* 17, 356–382.

Stenström, A., Andersen, G. and Hasund, I.K. (2002) *Trends in Teenage Talk. Corpus Compilation, Analysis and Findings.* Amsterdam: John Benjamins.

van Lier, L. (1996) *Interaction in the Language Curriculum: Awareness, Autonomy, and Authenticity.* New York: Longman.

van Lier, L. (2008) Agency in the classroom. In J.P. Lantolf and M.E. Poehner (eds) *Sociocultural Theory and the Teaching of Second Languages.* London: Equinox.

Weyers, J.R. (2009) The impending demise of *tu* in Montevideo, Uruguay. *Hispania* 92 (4), 829–839.

Wilkinson, S. (2002) The omnipresent classroom during summer study abroad: American students in conversation with their French hosts. *Modern Language Journal* 86, 157–173.

8 Authenticating Practices in Chinese Homestay Interactions

Sheng-Hsun Lee and Celeste Kinginger

> **David**: *uhm, wait I I sort of knew, already knew they don't say, like when they take the phone, they don't say* níhǎo *but just* wéi.

Introduction

As a 16-year-old rising junior, David joined the Landon-in-China program to embark on an immersion learning experience in China for four weeks. Although he arrived in China with an estimated Chinese proficiency between Novice High and Intermediate Low, he was highly praised by his teacher and host family in Beijing for assiduous study throughout his stay. During a post study abroad interview, he stressed that homestay interactions had been the highlight of his overall experience. Through interacting with his host family he claimed that he had experienced different lifestyles and the traditions of another society, and that this experience was in sharp contrast with his classroom efforts to understand a foreign country through pedagogical materials. In recalling words and structures he had learned in China, David shared that when answering a phone call, people in China do not use *níhǎo* which is often taught in Chinese class as the equivalent of 'hello' in English. Instead, he learned that Chinese people say *wéi* – marking acceptance of the call. These and many other vivid descriptions of interaction with his host family were referenced by David to illustrate his claims that study abroad had changed his 'way of thinking' and 'way of acting'.

David's example resonates with the widespread representation of study abroad as a time when students are provided with the opportunity to notice spontaneous, authentic language use, in contrast to the neutralized, preselected forms characteristic of textbooks and educational settings. Nevertheless, Wilkinson's (2002) study reminds us that this belief does not correspond to reality in every case. Her study revealed that classroom roles and discourse structures continue to influence the interaction between student sojourners and their native-speaking host families. She concluded that study abroad, and particularly homestay interaction, do not necessarily liberate students from classroom restrictions. In the same vein, Iino (2006) and Siegal (1996) argued that genuine, natural interactions may be relatively rare in Japanese homestays. In these studies, some Japanese hosts tended to oversimplify their language use with students, using 'foreigner talk' (Ellis, 1997) rather than genuine, naturalistic language. The results of these studies challenge the assumption and expectation of overseas students' sociolinguistic gains during study abroad.

In this chapter, we examine authentication, defined as interactional sequences where homestay hosts provide ideologically driven comments on their student guests' performance. We focus on homestays because they are widely assumed to be particularly beneficial to students' development of communicative repertoires. We first summarize the way authenticity is hypothesized, attested and challenged by study abroad scholarship. We then draw upon ideas from Bucholtz (2003) to distinguish *authentication* as an interactional practice from the concept of *authenticity* as form of ideology. Subsequently, we present illustrative authenticating acts from daily family interactions involving two American learners of Chinese at Intermediate High and Advanced levels. Throughout, we argue that authenticity in study abroad is a socially malleable ideology, but authenticating acts may be one aspect of interactional practice in the day-to-day lives of students abroad. In conclusion, we reflect on the implications of the study for language learning abroad, discuss its limitations, and suggest directions for future research.

Literature

Authenticity in study abroad research

Among students, language educators and researchers, study abroad environments are believed to nurture students' communicative repertoires through exposure to, and engagement with, authentic language. A broad overview of this research (Kinginger, 2009) indeed revealed that a sojourn abroad has the potential to enhance language learning in every domain, whether it is defined as a holistic construct, such as proficiency or fluency, or as a more specific domain of communicative ability. The research further suggests that study abroad is particularly useful for the development of capacities related to everyday social interaction, such as discourse, interactional or sociolinguistic abilities. Beyond these generalizations, however, if there is one consistent finding of research in this domain, it is that of inconsistency. The findings of most studies reveal considerable, and often significant, individual differences in achievement. Some students make notable progress whereas the achievements of others can be quite modest. In much of this research, a baseline assumption is that overseas environments are rich in authentic language that is readily available to willing language learners. If there are individual differences, or if gaps continue to exist between native-speaker norms and students' usage (e.g. Marriott, 1993, 1995; Regan *et al.*, 2009), these must be due to deficits in quantity, for example of time spent speaking the target language (Freed *et al.*, 2004), or of opportunities for practice afforded within students' personal social networks (e.g. Dewey *et al.*, 2012).

Qualitative, interaction-based studies problematizing the availability of authentic language offer explanations as to why some students become more engaged and successful in language learning than do others. These studies consider both the ways in which students are received by host communities and the students' own attempts to communicate within these communities using structurally familiar but marginally appropriate classroom-based discourse norms. In the context of study abroad in Japan, Iino (2006), Cook (2006) and Siegal (1996) investigated the ideology of *nihonjinron* (Japanologies) – a set of beliefs about how the Japanese are unique and different from the Western world. According to their studies, *nihonjinron* permeated the ways in which some Japanese hosts interacted with their foreign guests, such that certain foods were considered too uniquely Japanese for foreigners, certain aspects of Japanese culture too different to be learned and appreciated by foreigners, and the Japanese language itself too difficult for foreigners to master at advanced levels.

Iino (2006) studied the impact of this ideology by examining how it shaped the norms of interaction in Japanese homestays. Two interactional models were identified: one-way cultural deficiency and two-way cultural exchange. On the basis of *nihonjinron*, the one-way model considered learners to be deficient participants, requiring massive assistance from the family to survive everyday life in Japan. Some students displayed their frustration with this asymmetrical power relationship. One student commented:

> I was a pet in the home. As long as I appreciated whatever they did, everyone was happy even though I didn't speak well. (Iino, 2006: 162)

The two-way model, in contrast, involved dynamic negotiations of power relationships, as both learners and hosts were actively engaged in cultural exchange activities. Iino reported that when the two-way model is adopted, the homestay experience can provide a meaningful opportunity for all parties to exchange linguistic and cultural meanings. Regardless of the approach adopted, the ideology of *nihonjinron* continued to influence interactional patterns in Japanese homestays as the host families tended to avoid correcting errors, whether they involved grammatical infelicities or sociolinguistic inappropriateness. Much of the time, the families practiced over-accommodation, adjusting their language use through foreigner talk. In this light, Iino condemned the assumption that homestay language is always and everywhere authentic. He argued that 'language use in these situations is indeed dynamic and colorful', and it is full of variations and simplified forms (Iino, 2006: 170–171).

Cook's (2006) study of Japanese homestay mealtime settings centered on the dynamic processes of constructing folk beliefs and socializing students into the discourse of *nihonjinron*. Taking into account the student sojourners' active participation, Cook showed that folk beliefs related to *nihonjinron* were brought into consciousness and were sometimes challenged by learners. There were also moments when folk beliefs were collaboratively constructed by the host family members and the learners, contributing to their closer relationships. This study confirmed the existence of Iino's two-way enrichment approach. Here, socialization into cultural belief systems is reciprocal in that all participants became aware of hidden assumptions and different perceptions involved in narrating an event or expressing an idea. In other words, through talking about *nihonjinron*, the students became familiar with, and critical of, stereotypical judgments that may have an impact on authentic language use in homestays.

Siegal (1996) conducted a case study within institutional settings, focusing on the acquisition of sociolinguistic competence by Mary, an Australian woman learning Japanese. The study provided evidence to show that even a learner with a long-term commitment to second-language learning was not well accepted as a member of the host community but instead was constantly positioned as an outsider. In analyzing Mary's interaction with her Japanese professor, Siegal noted that Mary's pragmatic failure included face-threatening acts but did not incur any irritation or offense from the professor; rarely did the professor offer to point out problems with Mary's inept use of pragmatics. The explanation Siegal offered echoed the notion of *nihonjinron*, according to which foreigners are not expected to obtain and display high levels of Japanese ability, especially the use of the honorific language which is considered to be above their inherent capabilities.

The studies summarized above indicate that the ways in which students are received by their hosts influence the extent to which their linguistic environment can be construed as authentic. Another important consideration is the extent to which interactional norms are transferred from one setting to another, particularly when these norms become obstacles to authentic, natural language use. In the context of French homestay interactions, Wilkinson (2002) lamented the lack of authentic interactional patterns. Her study revealed that even in the non-instructional setting (i.e. homestays), classroom roles and discourse structures (i.e. initiation-response-evaluation[1]) continued to dominate interactions between intermediate-level students and their native-speaking host families. For the overall quality of learning experiences, the consequences of this situation were serious, as in the end all parties were considered to be undesirable conversational partners. One of the focal students, Amelia, was frustrated by being addressed 'like ... a little kid' (Wilkinson, 2002: 168), and she accused her hosts of treating her in a condescending manner. However, the hosts' perspectives were absent in this study, which makes it difficult to understand whether, or to what extent, miscommunication of French cultural norms had a role to play in this case. Nevertheless, Wilkinson pointed out that as a result Amelia distanced herself from her hosts and turned to her American peers for company. Wilkinson concluded that study abroad and particularly homestay interaction may not liberate students from the restrictions of classroom discourse.

Piecing together the above studies, it becomes evident that authenticity in study abroad is constrained by students' awareness of interactional settings and hosts' willingness to accept students as legitimate conversational partners. Hosts may or may not intend to offer authentic input or 'natural' learning contexts, and students, especially at lower levels of proficiency, may or may not be prepared to appreciate opportunities to move beyond the comfort of classroom-style interactions. In the meantime, an important question is overlooked: what is authenticity, exactly, according to the participants involved in homestay interactions? Among language educators, authenticity has long been celebrated both as a pedagogical desideratum and as a rationale for study abroad, usually on the increasingly uneasy assumption that it can be discovered, somehow, among the practices of the generic, and idealized, native speaker.[2] In this chapter we will avoid pronouncements on the selection of appropriate models for learners, and we will not attempt to articulate what authenticity means for applied linguistics or language education in a general sense. Instead, we adopt an approach from sociolinguistics to examine how the question of authenticity plays out during interactions among Chinese host families and their student guests, thus revealing some aspects of the 'folk' (Niedzielski & Preston, 2000) or 'everyday' beliefs of the participants involved, and illustrating one way in which homestay interactions can function as learning environments. Our specific aim is to examine 'authenticating practices', when Chinese host families draw on local knowledge to evaluate their student guests' linguistic and cultural acts as more or less authentically Chinese.

Authenticity and authentication

In sociolinguistics, Eckert (2003) argued that researchers intentionally leave the notion of the authentic speaker unquestioned and tacitly accept authenticity as a characteristic of spontaneous speakers who produce pure vernacular language in relation to their natural habitat (see also van Compernolle, this volume). As a result, some speakers are considered more natural or authentic than others, in that their language is 'untainted by the interference of reflection or social agency' (Eckert, 2003: 392). In response to these unjustifiable assumptions, Eckert argued that authenticity is constructed by ideology that is central to the practices of speakers and analysts of language.

Aligning with Eckert's position, Bucholtz (2003) contended that sociolinguists need to separate *authenticity* as an ideology from *authentication* as a social practice. Authenticity, according to Bucholtz, is created out of authentication, instead of the reverse. In discussing the notion of *real language* in sociolinguistic paradigms, Bucholtz noted that, despite different analytical approaches, what is meant by *real language* remains consistent across the approaches: 'real language – that is, authentic language – is language produced in authentic contexts by authentic speakers' (Bucholtz, 2003: 398). Therefore, authenticity resides in, and is composed of, language, context and speaker. For Bucholtz, sociolinguistic research is driven by a set of language ideologies concerning authenticity. These ideologies produce the construct of authentic languages, contexts and speakers, including how researchers develop theories and collect, select and analyze their own data, as well as how they themselves discuss the performance of language users and researchers. Bucholtz argued that sociolinguists need to become aware of these underpinning ideologies about authenticity that at times limit the scope of questions they ask and answers they provide, and she asked for more attention to linguistic practices through which languages, contexts and speakers come to be viewed as authentic. Authenticity, as she emphasized, is not an object to be discovered. Rather, it is the outcome of social actors' linguistic practices and sociolinguists' metalinguistic practices. To better construe authenticity, she proposed the concept of *authentication* in reference to agentive processes in which a genuine or credible identity is asserted. On the basis of Bucholtz's notion of authentication, several studies have been generated to address the relation between authenticating practices and social identification, such as a Korean American comedian's use of Mock Asian (Chun, 2004), Asian American teenagers' appropriation of African American slang (Reyes, 2005), and bilingual Mexican Americans' construction of ethnic identities (Shenk, 2007).

As van Compernolle (this volume) pointed out, authentication has been studied on multiple scales. Adopting a macro approach, sociolinguists (e.g. Eckert, 2012; Johnstone & Kiesling, 2008) studied authenticating practices through quantifying patterns of language use during sociolinguistic interviews and from participants' responses to metapragmatic interviews. van Compernolle (this volume) approached authentication at a meso level through a multidimensional approach which entails interview-and-narrative tasks, a sentence versions task and language awareness interviews. At a more micro level of analysis, Bucholtz and Hall (2005, 2008) argued that authenticating practices unfold turn by turn in interaction during which identities emerge, are positioned as well as indexed, and become partially related. In this chapter, we adopt this micro approach to exploring how sociolinguistic and sociocultural practices are drawn upon to authenticate identities, index social categories and construct supralocal ideologies (Silverstein, 2003).

In our homestay interaction data, authenticating practices are often initiated by the homestay hosts when they notice similarities or marked difference between their own and their students' linguistic or cultural performances. For example, American study abroad students' utterances trigger their Chinese homestay hosts' comments that the students are talking and acting like Chinese or Americans. These assertions contribute to shaping learners' identity, in that an imagined national unity (Chineseness) or binary (Chinese versus American) are constituted as an ideological frame for interpreting the semiotic behavior of the students. Such practices of authentication inevitably involve essentializing particular identities and their corresponding sociolinguistic and sociocultural practices; therefore, the term *authentication*, as we will be using it throughout this chapter, also 'refers to how speakers activate these essentialist readings in the articulation of identity' (Bucholtz & Hall, 2004: 386).

The Current Project

Inspired by Bucholtz's (2003) call for understanding authentication, in this chapter we focus on one particular type of authentication in homestays: the junctures at which students' linguistic and cultural performances are publicly appraised by their hosts. We explored these acts of authentication in the homestay interactions of two American students, Sam and John (both pseudonyms), in Beijing, with two goals in mind. First, we hoped to uncover communication patterns illustrating how these authenticating acts are practiced. Secondly, we sought to understand features of language and daily practices that are valorized and negotiated by participants at homestay settings, and how these practices are the offspring of ideologies reflecting the social values of the local community. On the basis of the findings, we aimed to derive implications for study abroad research.

Study Design

Setting

The two focal participants in this study, Sam and John, each participated in different study abroad programs according to their ages, interests and length of sojourn abroad. Each program promotes different types and degrees of engagement in interaction with local Chinese people.

Sam participated in the Landon-in-China program in the summer of 2012. This program was designed for students who would be attending grades nine through 12 in the subsequent fall semester. Sam joined the program's three-week optional internship program in which he was individually placed in a homestay and worked as an intern at a company where his host father was employed. The study abroad program functioned in *loco parentis* for its teenaged students. Responsibility for the students' wellbeing was jointly shouldered by the program director, chaperones and faculty from the United States, and local instructors, as well as the Chinese host parents and siblings. Participants in Sam's homestay included a host father, a host mother and a host brother who was approximately Sam's age. All of them were capable of communicating in basic English. Therefore, their interchanges with Sam were mostly in Chinese but they also involved a complex mix of English and Chinese from time to time.

John's college-level study abroad program took place in Beijing in the spring semester of 2013. In addition to attending daily language courses, John enrolled in culture and history courses offered to foreign language students by the program. Unlike the high school program described above, John's program recruited experienced foreign students as near-peer mentors for incoming participants. The student mentors were important in constructing and negotiating the relationship between the new foreign students and their host families. John stayed with a retired couple, both in their sixties, with an adult daughter who lived outside the home. The couple did not speak or understand English at all; therefore, they only communicated with John in Mandarin Chinese. In an interview, John explained that his previous experience of living with a young couple and their toddler was not conducive to language learning because the couple sometimes talked to him in English and expressed satisfaction with John teaching their toddler English. John had therefore requested to avoid staying with young couples with children this time. He enjoyed much attention from the retired couple who spoke only Chinese to him, which he believed to be the best way to learn Chinese language and culture.

Data

This study is part of a larger research project (sponsored by the Center for Advanced Language Proficiency Education and Research at Pennsylvania State University) on language socialization in homestays, approved by the Institutional Review Board of the authors' university. The high school participant's materials come from the Landon-in-China program discussed above. A portion of the high school students in the study abroad program voluntarily joined the project in summer 2012, and submitted their assent and their parents' consent. Before leaving for China, the students were informed that every week they should make three recordings of any social events that they considered helpful in their acquisition of Chinese language and culture. Students were also interviewed at the end of their sojourns in China and six months later, after they returned to the United States.

Students' Chinese host families were also provided with the same information and were interviewed at the same intervals. The college student's data in this chapter were also collected through the above-described process, with the exception that the student consented as an adult.

Unlike some students who recorded short daily interviews with their host families, Sam's and John's recordings are of naturally occurring interactions. Their recordings were transcribed according to an adapted version of the Du Bois *et al.* (1993) discourse transcription system (Appendix A). Micro features, including terminal pitch contours and accent, were not transcribed. In order to increase the readability of the excerpts in this chapter, some features such as special voice quality, pauses and overlapping were removed from the transcripts, except when they are relevant features to be discussed. Each utterance is first presented in Romanized spelling of Chinese (Pinyin), followed by a word-by-word gloss, and then finally a free translation. A list of grammatical features referenced in the excerpts is also provided (Appendix B).

Upon transcribing and listening to all the recordings, it become clear that both students made almost all of their recordings during homestay mealtime conversations, suggesting the meal table as a potentially important venue for students to experience Chinese language and culture (see Kinginger *et al.*, 2014). Table 8.1 summarizes their estimated proficiency according to their study abroad program course placement and the program director's informal assessment (based on the ACTFL proficiency scale), years and duration of study abroad and educational levels, as well as overall numbers and time (in minutes) of recorded interactions.

Participants

Sam

As a rising senior in high school, Sam was 17 years old when he studied abroad in China during the summer of 2012. His parents had emigrated from Ethiopia as teenagers and raised their children to be bilingual in Amharic and English. When Sam joined the summer study abroad program, he had been studying Chinese for 11 years, starting with a math, science and social

Table 8.1 Participant information

Participants	Estimated proficiency	Semester/year abroad	Duration	Education	Number of recorded interactions	Total time
Sam	Advanced	Summer/2012	3 weeks	High school	9	262 minutes
John	Intermediate High	Spring/2013	15 weeks	College	64	1265 minutes

studies Chinese immersion program in elementary school. In addition to the remarkable amount of time he had devoted to Chinese, his prior experience with the language also included taking an advanced placement course as a high school junior and spending the summer of 2009 enrolled in a Chinese immersion summer camp program in the United States. Despite the richness of his prior experiences, Sam joined the Landon-in-China internship program with several expectations:

> I have been studying Chinese for a long time, and I want to solidify my ability. And I also want to, be able to, to try them out in like the *real world* and see if I could use them in a *real context*. I also want to explore that culture a little bit more than I had been able to. (Sam, post-study-abroad interview; emphasis added)

John

John participated in his college study abroad program when he was a sophomore at the authors' university. As immigrants originally from Chicago, his family had lived in Amsterdam where John received his primary and secondary education in an English–Dutch bilingual school. Later, his family moved to Singapore where John completed his secondary education at an international school before returning to the United States to begin his tertiary education. Already fluent in English and Dutch, John was motivated to study Chinese at the time when he took the first author's Chinese 001 class in the spring of 2012. He considered that part of his motivation for learning Chinese and studying in China was related to his previous immersion experience in Singapore where he did not take up the opportunity to learn Chinese. Following the completion of a Chinese course at the beginning level at his US university, he went to China for his first study abroad in Beijing in summer 2012. After returning to the United States, he was promoted to the Intermediate High level of Chinese offered in the fall of 2012 at his university. Completing the course with an A, he then went back to Beijing in the spring of 2013, where he recorded the interactional sequences included in this chapter. Before he departed for Beijing, he shared his reasons for returning to China and staying there for a semester. He noted that in Beijing, particularly living with a homestay family, 'every day you are surrounded by the language, and every day you use the language'. He also referenced his friends' successful experience in learning Chinese in Beijing for a year, and envisioned the outcome of his study abroad:

> I think if I do this for a semester, and keep learning Chinese, then I will become definitely proficient. And that's, you know, that's my first goal to become proficient, so I can actually use it, instead of just going on holiday. (John, pre-departure interview)

Analytic Approach and Research Questions

From sociolinguistics, we borrowed Bucholtz's (2003) notion of authentication as agentive processes in which a genuine or credible identity is asserted, in order to illustrate authenticity as an ideology and authentication as a social practice. We did so also to explore the meaning of authenticity from the perspective of participants, namely host families and student guests.

Therefore, throughout the paper, we address three interlocking questions:

(1) How was authenticity achieved through authenticating practices at homestays?
(2) What features or practices were authenticated in the unfolding process of everyday homestay interaction?
(3) What sociocultural meanings or attributes were ascribed to the authenticated features and practices?

A close analysis showed that among the conversational recordings involving Chinese authenticity, the most salient type of authentication (Bucholtz, 2003) is the juncture when hosts explicitly evaluated students' performance. Within each instance of authentication, metalinguistic, metapragmatic[3] or metacultural communication underscores particular linguistic and cultural practices of the students, while creating opportunities for language and culture learning. Having identified these interactional sequences, we then attempted to pinpoint some of the underlying ideologies that drive the valorization of particular speech forms and cultural practices.

Findings

This section details our findings on the two students' homestay interactions that involve authenticating practices. In ordinary scenarios of eating and playing, student sojourners exchanged their thoughts, feelings and conditions with their homestay hosts. The give-and-take of daily matters was a forum for authenticating practices where the hosts were instantiated as the primary arbiters of authenticity, and students were set up as performers whose linguistic and sociocultural practices were evaluated on the basis of local ideologies and the hosts' metacommunicative awareness of sounds, words or cultural practices.

Sound

Authenticating practices are instruments of identity construction. These instruments are not necessarily systematic assessments, however. Rather, they are essentially idiosyncratic and idealistic. Through idealization, a new identity may be ascribed to learners if their performance conforms to the ideals of Chineseness. In this respect, identity is similar to authenticity. Both inhere in specific actions, interactions and situations (cf. Bucholtz & Hall, 2004). In Excerpt 8.1, a Chinese identity was ascribed to the focal student, John, as he was experimenting with a unique phonological feature of Beijing Mandarin. Elly, John's peer, was invited to play poker with John and his host mother at home. Given that they were playing poker according to their newly acquired Chinese rules, Elly was not able to figure out when she needed to show her card. After John's reminder, Elly presented her cards and apologized for her slowness.

Excerpt 8.1

```
1   Elly:   duìbuqǐ
            sorry
            sorry
2   Mom:    méi guānxi
            not matter
            it's all right
3   Elly:   [@@]
4   John:   [méi guān]xi
            not matter
            it's all right
5   Mom:    uh [[jiùshi]]
                exactly
            uh, exactly
6   John:   [[méishì]]r a
            be:all:right:[ɹ] PRT
            it's all right r
7   Mom:    méishìr
            be:all:right:[ɹ]
            it's all right r
8   Elly:   @@@@
9   Mom:    xíngr wǒmen xiànzài zhōngwén xué  de    jiù    [búcuò   le]
            okay   we     now    Chinese   learn  CSC  exactly pretty:good PRT
            okay, we now have learned Chinese pretty well
10  John:                                                  [@@@]
11  Mom:    dōu     yǐjīng [[hěn ]]búcuò    le       [3@@3]
            already already very pretty:good PRT
            already pretty good
12  John:                  [[uh]]           [3uh3]
                            INT              INT
                           uh, uh
13  Mom:    <F<HI méishìr HI>F>
                be:all:right:[ɹ]
                it's all right r
14  Elly:   uhn
```

15 **Mom**: ér yīn   chūlái   le
         [ɻ]:sound come:out PRT
         r-sound comes out already
         zhōngguó de   ér yīn chūlái le
         China   ASSOC [ɻ] sound come:out PRT
         Chinese r-sound comes out already

In this sequence, the authenticating practice centered on the phonological feature of the retroflex vowel [ɻ] in Beijing Mandarin. The vernacular, *jing qiang* (Beijing accent), is particularly associated with this subsyllabic retroflex [ɻ] attached to the syllable final, causing the final to be rhotacized (Chao, 1968; Li & Thompson, 1981; Zhang[4], 2005, 2008). After repeating the host mother's 'it's all right', John offered an alternative form *méishì* (Turn 6) to convey the same illocutionary force of soothing Elly's discomfort. John's *méishì* ended with an approximated Beijing retroflex vowel [ɻ], although his retroflex was hardly comparable to his host mother's shown in the rest of the transcript. After hearing John's retroflex, the host mother first repeated John's *méishìr* (Turn 7) and then offered her compliment on the student's Chinese learning. Although initially it might not have been clear if the compliment should go to Elly or to John, this was later clarified when the host mother repeated John's utterance. This time her voice exhibited an emphatic quality (i.e. a loud volume at a high pitch level) in Turn 13. Ultimately, the host mother's reformulation of the utterance (Turn 15) not only provided an account for the compliment to John but, more importantly, authenticated John's utterance with a retroflex vowel [ɻ] as a salient feature of Chinese.

While the use of rhotacization, namely the occurrences of retroflex vowel [ɻ], is commonly discussed in lay and academic discourses as a phonological feature of Northern Mandarin varieties, particularly Beijing Mandarin, the host mother subjectively authenticated this phonological feature as representing 'Chinese' through her self-initiated reformulation in Turn 15. In this way, the ideology of Chineseness is based on the process of *erasure* (Irvine & Gal, 2000) in which sociolinguistic variations such as Chinese from other locales are made invisible. The semiotic process of erasure is one type of essentialism through which a social group is clearly delineated and becomes inherently homogenous (Bucholtz, 2011).

Throughout the interaction, the reformulation (Turn 15), coupled with repetition (Turns 7 and 13) and emphatic voice quality (Turn 13), contributed to the authentication of John's utterance as pointing toward his linguistic identity as a speaker of 'real' Chinese. Therefore, rhotacization, a Beijing dialect feature and sociolinguistic style, derived a new meaning in this specific situation through its association with Chinese identities in general. It should be emphasized that the meaning of John's rhotacization (i.e. Chineseness) was coproduced between his host mother and him. While John produced the retroflex vowel, it was his host mother who oriented to it, and authenticated it, as a feature of 'real' Chinese.

Word

Authenticating acts denaturalize a speech form by connecting it to a social, symbolic value. For example, in the preceding case, John's retroflex vowel [ɹ] was valorized as an essentially Chinese sound. Excerpt 8.2 is another case in point. In response to the host mother's inquiry about his internship experience of the day, Sam was able to borrow a metaphorical expression 'harvest' from his host mother's utterance and incorporate the expression into his reply. His hosts then recognized Sam's metaphorical expression 'harvest a lot' as a particularly genuine turn of phrase in Chinese. The extent to which the genuineness was manifested was expressed through a verbal compliment 'yes, very good' and a numerical assessment 'one hundred'. To recall, Sam had arrived in China with an (estimated) Advanced level of proficiency in Chinese.

Excerpt 8.2

1 **Mom:**   Sam   jīntiān zài bàngōngshì
              (name) today at   office
              Same today at office
              juéde
              think
              (do you) think
              yǒu shōuhuò ma?
              have harvest PRT
              any harvest?
2 **Sam:**   shōuhuò
              harvest
              harvest
              shì shénme
              is what
              what is (harvest)?
3 **Mom:**   mh
              you learn something
              it means
4 **Sam:**   duì
              yes
              yes
              [uhn]
5 **Mom:**   *[you] learn learn learn learn learn learn anything?*
6 **Sam:**   duì wǒ shì uhn
              yes I   am IINT
              yes, I   am uhn
              kěyi shuō shōuhuò hěn duǎ?
              can say   harvest very many
              can (I) say harvest a lot?'

7   **Mom**: [en en   en   en]
            INT INT INT INT
            yeah, yeah, yeah, yeah
8   **Dad**: [en en   en] duì duì hěn hǎo
            INT INT INT yes yes very good
            yeah, yeah, yeah, yes, yes, very good
            nǐ   gāngcái shuō de   nàge shōuhuò hěn duō
            you just   say NOM that harvest very many
            the 'harvest a lot' you just said
            jiùshì hěn hěn zhōngwén
            just very very Chinese
            it's very very Chinese
9   **Sam**: hm
10 **Dad**: duì jiù xiàng zhōngguórén <@shuō de@>
            yes just like Chinese   say NOM
            yes, just like (what) Chinese (would) say
11 **Sam**: hm
            wǒ [yào <F jì   zhe F>]
            I   want:to remember PRT
            I have to remember (it)
12 **Mom**:   [duì shuō de] fēicháng   hǎo
                   yes say CSC exceptionally good
                   yes, (you) said (it) exceptionally well
13 **Dad**: hm
14 **Mom**: fēicháng   hǎo   *one hundred*
            exceptionally good one hundred
            exceptionally well, one hundred
            one [*hundred*] e
            one hundred INT
            one hundred, uh
15 **Dad**:   [@@]
16 **Sam**: *[2 five hundred bucks 2]*
17 **Mom**: [2 éi   nàge fēnr 2]
                 INT that score
            uh, the score
18 **Dad**: *score*
19 **Mom**: fēnr *score*?
            score score
            score, score
            I- I can give you one hundred
            @@@@@
20 **Sam**: xièxiè
            thank
            thanks

Here, the host mother invited Sam to talk about what he had learned during the day, but the metaphorical expression of 'harvest' posed a challenge to Sam's comprehension of the question. More specifically, the metaphor 'harvest' is associated with two well-known proverbs in Chinese 一分耕耘，一分收获 (one cultivation, one harvest) 'no pain, no gain' and 要怎麼收获，先怎麼栽 (how to harvest depends on how to cultivate) 'you reap what you sow'. All of these expressions fall under the conceptual metaphor MAKING EFFORT IS CULTIVATING CROPS, implying responsibility on the part of the student. With the assistance of literal translation in English, Sam turned the interaction into a learning opportunity. In Turn 6, Sam reacted to the host mother's question in Chinese but through direct translation of the English phrase 'yes, I am', making this utterance ungrammatical. He then recycled the word 'harvest' from his host mother and asked if it would be okay to say 'harvest a lot'. This triggered the host parents' series of tokens of agreement 'yeah' (Turns 7 and 8) and responsive assessment 'yes' (Turn 8). Later, the host father explicitly noted that what Sam had just said is exactly like what a Chinese person would say. In response (Turn 11), Sam prosodically and lexically marked his positive stance toward being authenticated as a speaker of Chinese. Following the verbal assessment, a numerical value was assigned to Sam to show the degree of Chinese authenticity with regard to what he had just said. In Turns 14 and 19, the score of 100 was repeated several times. Numbers are often associated with surgical logicality devoid of subjectivity and bias, and provide us with a precise, rationalistic means of accounting for the world (Stafford, 2010[5]); however, in Excerpt 8.2 the assigned number word was loaded with emotion as the host mother creatively expressed her excitement and commended Sam for his successful use of the metaphor. Through a great amount of Chinese–English code-switching, as well as verbal and numerical evaluations from the hosts, Sam's use of the metaphorical expression was very positively evaluated. The utterance, 'harvest a lot', became a stylistic linguistic resource for evoking Chineseness, and it was marked as worth remembering.

Cultural practice

In Excerpts 8.1 and 8.2, speech forms (phonological and metaphorical features) were valorized to index individual speakers' awareness, beliefs and dispositions toward the essentialized nature of being Chinese. However, authenticating acts also extend beyond language per se and may index cultural practices that are identified as representing Chineseness. Excerpt 8.3 shows how authentic Chinese identity was invoked in the host family's affective response to the student's culinary preference. Positive and negative affective responses are 'building blocks of identities' (Ochs & Capps, 1997: 86). Excerpt 8.3 exemplifies this notion by showing a trajectory of authentication: cultural practice–affect response–social identification. The focal student, John, was engaging in the family mealtime talk with his host parents. At the dinner table, the host mother took a positive affective stance toward John's culinary preference for avoiding eating meat every day.

Excerpt 8.3

1 **John**: kěshì wǒ juéde
   but   I think
   but I think
2 **Mom**: hm
   INT
   hm
3 **John**: búyòng
   need:not
   no need
   měi měi   tiān búyòng chī ròu
   every every day need:not eat meat
   (to) eat meat every every day
4 **Mom**: búyòng chī ròu
   need:not eat meat
   no need to eat meat?
5 **John**: mh
   INT
   mh
   uh wǒ wǒ hén xǐhuān ròu dànshì
   INT I I very like meat but
   uh, I I like meat very (much) but
   búyòng měi tiān chī
   need:not every day eat
   no need to eat (meat) every day

   ((Several utterances omitted))

6 **Dad**: kànlái nǐ   hái bú shì
   it:seem you still not are
   it seems you are still not
   zhēnzhèng de měiguó háizi
   genuine NOM American kid
   real American kids
   měiguó   háizi tiāntiān   dōu xiǎng chī ròu
   American kid every:day all want eat meat
   American kids want to eat meat every day
7 **Mom**: ā
   INT
   yeah
8 **John**: mh
   INT
   mh

9   **Dad**:   zhīdào ba?
             know   PRT
             do (you) know (this)?
10   **Mom**: nà   nǐ   jiù [xiàng zhōngguó háizi @@]@   [[@@@@]]
             then you just like   Chinese   kid
             then you are just like Chinese kids
11   **Dad**:   [měi tiān jiù xiǎng dōu xiǎng chī] [[@@@@]]
                          every day just want all want eat
                          just want, just want to eat (meat) every day
12   **John**: mh
13   **Mom**: nàme wǒ wǒmen John   jiù   xiàng zhōngguó de   xiǎohái
             then ou- our   (name) just like Chinese ASSOC kids
             then ou- our John is just like Chinese kids
14   **John**: mhhm

In discussing culinary practices with his host mother, John expressed his stance toward eating meat (Turn 1–5), which he enjoyed very much but considered unnecessary for everyday meals. In Turn 6, John's identity as an American child was challenged by the host father: John did not conform to an essentialized model of authentic American children who, according to the host father, attempt to eat meat every day. The host father extended this opposition between preference and dispreference for eating meat every day to the level of contrastive national identities – American versus Chinese children. Following the denial of John's American identity, the host mother reauthenticated John's eating preference as more closely aligning with Chinese children's eating habits (Line 10). Later in her repair (Line 13), the inclusive first-person plural possessive pronoun 'our' (i.e. 'our John') suggested a role for authenticity through endearment. The endearment here displays that an authenticating act is often an affect-loaded, discriminatory act. Predilection for avoiding daily meat consumption was positively acknowledged and valorized, and John was invited to become part of the host family through the endearing pronoun 'our'. The positional identity of being Chinese was thus discursively constructed and interactionally solidified.

Difference and sameness in all aspects of living in the world are constantly encountered by study abroad students and their hosts. Discourses of polar contrasts, such as contrasting habits of meat consumption in America and China, are not uncommon. Within these discourses, food and eating are polarized to index unique ways of being in, and belonging to, a nation, such that frequent consumption of meat is ascribed to the identity of authentic Americans, and that avoidance of overeating meat represents Chinese identity. Essentialist readings, as argued by Bucholtz and Hall (2004), are inescapable in the articulation of authentic identities. In the case above, it was the essentialization that Americans and Chinese are comparable and contrastable on the scale of food consumption. Authentication and essentialization thus work in tandem as a form of social identification. In Excerpt 8.4, Sam was authenticated as an American, because of his proclivity for drinking cool milk, which his host mother categorized as being an American trait.

Excerpt 8.4

1 **Sam**: nǐ nǐ hē   guò liáng niúnǎi ma?
you you drink ASP cool milk PRT
have you you drank cool milk?

2 **Mom**: wǒ wǒ wǒ [wǒ bù] néng hē nàme   liáng de
   I   I   I   I not can drink like:that cool NOM
I I I I can't drink (milk) that is so cool

3 **Sam**: [wǒ]
I

sh shìjie shìjiè shàng méiyǒu hěn name   hǎo de   *feeling*
wor world world in   no:exist very like: that good NOM feeling
there is no such a good feeling in the wor world world

nǐ hē   yī ge hěn gāo de
you drink one CLF very tall NOM
(when) you drink a tall

4 **Mom**: èn
INT
mh

5 **Sam**: píng yi liáng niúnǎi
bottle one cool milk
a bottle of cool milk

shì hǎo <@ hén hǎo @>
is good   very good
(it)'s good, very good

((several utterances omitted))

6 **Mom**: shì zhèyàng de   Sam
is this:way NOM (name)
Sam, (let's) put it this way

zhōngguó zhōngguórén cóng xiǎo a
China   Chinese   from little PRT
from little Chine Chinese

jiù   xíguàn   chī rè de   dōngxi
already be:used:to eat hot NOM thing
have been used to eating hot (food)

7 **Sam**: uhhnh

8 **Mom**: jiù chéng xíguàn le
then become habit PRT
(it) then becomes a habit

měiguórén kěnéng cóng xiǎo jiù   hē liáng chī liáng de ba
American might from little already drink cool eat cool NOM PRT
from little Americans might have been used to drinking cool, eating cool (food)

yě xíguàn   le
also be:used:to PRT
(they) also become used to (cool food).

The conversation was initiated through Sam's query about the host mother's experience of drinking cool milk, and it then continued with his affective display of his enormous enjoyment of drinking cool milk through hyperbole 'no such a good feeling in the wor world world' in Turn 3. Note that the omitted utterances between Turns 5 and 6 were exchanges between the host mother, host brother and Sam on the two hosts' negative dispositions toward drinking cool milk, the reason being that cool milk upsets their stomach. The host mother then provided an account for avoiding cool milk (Turns 6–8), which transported the previous discussion on subjective experiences to a discourse of polar contrasts at national levels. This time, Americans were associated with cool food, and Chinese were connected to hot food. Homogenizing identity within a nation and heterogenizing identities across countries together form acts of authentication. Through such acts, Sam was positioned within the frame of homogenized American habits, the host mother and brother embraced the regimented Chinese habit, and a reductive binary was established. The two poles are separate and incommensurable, they contrast national identities and, more importantly, they evoke inequalities with regard to the choice of associated social values. Excerpts 8.3 and 8.4 illustrate how American identity is associated with unhealthy foodways, specifically over consumption of meat and drinking cool milk, both considered by the Chinese hosts to imperil one's health. The Chinese hosts, therefore, positioned themselves as the norm from which all others diverge (cf. Bucholtz & Hall, 2004). Polar-contrast discourses that arise out of essentialization and authentication create ideological inequalities and reflect folk perceptions of authentic cultural practices.

Discussion and Conclusions

In this chapter, we have examined the question of authenticity in study abroad settings from the perspective of participants' own authenticating practices, examining specific interactional sequences where the students' performances and preferences were publicly evaluated as more or less authentically Chinese. Authentication is not a process of veracity attesting. It is a modality for subjectivity making and identity inscribing based upon participants' social histories, and local ideologies, including folk beliefs about cultural practices, national identities and language. Authenticity is a constellation of authenticating acts whereby an identity is asserted through idealizing, homogenizing, heterogenizing or essentializing the semiotic behavior of the participants. In our data, the host families positioned themselves as the ultimate arbiters of authenticity. As authoritative speakers of the language and experts on culinary practices, they determined what represented Chinese authenticity and concomitantly rejected what was considered to be inauthentic Chinese. In appraising Chineseness, the hosts displayed idiosyncratic beliefs and values. They may have also *erased* (Irvine & Gal, 2000) internal differences in favor of idealized and homogenized versions of linguistic and cultural practices that could serve as emblems of group membership (Kroskrity, 2000). In our examples, the Beijing retroflex vowel, a metaphorical expression and food consumption were essentialized and idealized as linguistic and cultural practices that iconically signified Chinese membership. The semiotic process of erasure is a ubiquitous and important precondition for comparing and contrasting the two oppositional groups in homestay lives: Chinese versus Americans. When American student sojourners appropriate elements of Chinese languaculture and incorporate them, whether intentionally or not, into their daily linguistic and cultural practices, they are positively authenticated as being Chinese. When their performance conflicts with the ideological construal of their hosts, a distance may be created by their hosts to assert the essential difference between the two social groups, such that Chinese behave in one way and Americans in another. Differences are thus ascribed to social groups whereas similarities are attributed to individual conformity.

From a practical perspective, authentication orients the students toward the values shared in homestays and the norms of authenticity embedded within the natural conditions of ordinary Chinese. The host families voice those linguistic and cultural presuppositions through explicitly assigning national identities to speech forms and culinary preferences. In this light, discourses of authenticity enact and socialize abstract notions of Chineseness. The homestay is a unique, complex, sociocultural site where local ideologies are generated and commented upon, and the homestay hosts are empowered to provide explicit instruction based on their folk linguistic and cultural assumptions (cf. Cook, 2006), despite any idiosyncratic qualities of these assumptions. The student sojourners assume double duties to observe and to participate in the course of local Chinese ideologies. Whether they eventually adopt or reject these ideologies, or incorporate these elements of linguistic and cultural practices into their communicative repertoires, depends on the identities they wish to display.

Despite the positive evaluations that our learners of Chinese sometimes received, their hosts' authenticating practices may also, paradoxically, have positioned them as societal outsiders. Authenticating discourses are no doubt relatively rare among interactants who identify as belonging to the same group. For instance, among inhabitants of Beijing, the use of a retroflex vowel or of a conventionalized metaphor would be relatively unlikely to elicit comment. Authenticating discourses, therefore, underscore the students' temporary conformity to the hosts' ideas and experiences. This suggests that students' linguistic and cultural practices often do not, or at least are not expected to, conform to the ideals of the community. Studies in Japanese homestays also showed that talking and acting like Japanese are not expected by some homestay hosts. When it occurred, the behavior was deemed unnatural and overaccommodating (Iino, 2006), or caused students to be identified as strange foreigners (*henna gaijin*) (Cook, 2006). Although our study showed that talking and acting like Chinese sometimes received a positive response from homestay hosts, it is possible that authentication ultimately creates a challenging dilemma between students' desire to be positively identified as community members and their desire to maintain the identities associated with their origins.

Such personal conflicts can perhaps be mitigated if learning Chinese can be conceived as a process of *hybridization* (McDonald, 2011: 2), which creates 'linguistic and cultural hybrids' who can comfortably navigate and mediate between different cultures. McDonald argued that a university Chinese teaching program should turn students into sinophones who develop hybrid identities, and establish reference points for themselves, in and beyond the sinophone world. This conceptualization of studying Chinese also applies to study abroad students, as it might be unrealistic for them to speak Chinese indistinguishably from local Chinese or to be wholeheartedly accepted as insiders. Both are perhaps unattainable even by L1 speakers of Mandarin Chinese when they migrate from one sinophone society to another, such as from Taipei to Beijing. If this is the case, a sinophone in this increasingly globalized world needs to develop the capability to operate effectively, comfortably and fluently across linguistic and cultural borders (McDonald, 2011). To cultivate such hybrid identities, we suggest that students may benefit from learning the relation between aspects of languaculture and the representation of different social identities (Kinginger, 2013, 2014). Explicit instruction that aims to make such a connection, similar to authenticating practices, needs to consider the indexicality of linguistic-cultural practices and the associated identities and ideologies, rather than simply the referential meanings of sounds, words and grammar. van Compernolle (2014) and Henery (2014) have shown us that principled, concept-based approaches to indexicality can orient students to sociolinguistic, stylistic variations as resources for constructing social identities, distance and power (e.g. the French *tu/vous* system).

The limitations of this study, of course, are many, since we concentrated on the most salient type of authenticating acts in our data – authentic identities ascribed to homestay students by their hosts. Further studies might consider other types of authentication whereby student sojourners articulate an authentic identity they choose to inhabit, such as remembering as an authenticating act in the pursuit of true selves (Ochs & Capps, 1997). Another pressing need is for studies that explore the connection between authenticating practices and students' development of identity across time, which are challenging to document but highly desirable in understanding the impact of authentication in the long run. This chapter is meant to be a stepping stone to these unaddressed issues. To move forward, this chapter shows that folk beliefs of authenticity are ideologically achieved through authenticating practices, on the basis of which participants make sense of their homestay interactions.

Appendix A: Transcription Conventions

The following conventions are adopted in transcribing the interactional data. For detailed descriptions of the features, please refer to Du Bois *et al.* (1993).

:	speaker identity/turn start	@	laughter
?	appeal	<@ @>	laugh quality
Italic	English code-switching	<HI HI>	higher pitch level
[ ];[[ ]];[2 2]	overlap	<F F>	loud volume

Appendix B: Grammatical Glosses

ASSOC	associative
ASP	aspect
BA	ba construction
CLF	classifier
CRS	current relevant state
CSC	complex stative construction
INT	interjection
NOM	nominalizer
POSS	possessive
PRT	particle

Acknowledgment

Research for this chapter was funded in part by a grant from the Confucius Institute and in part by a grant from the US Department of Education Grant (CFDA 84.229, P229A060003–08) to the Center for Advanced Language Proficiency Education and Research (CALPER), College of Liberal Arts, Pennsylvania State University. However, the arguments presented here do not necessarily represent the policy of the Department of Education, and one should not assume endorsement by the Federal Government.

Notes

(1) As the editors of the volume pointed out, from a conversation analytic perspective, the IRE pattern is a question-answer adjacency pair with an optional evaluation as the third turn. At issue is the way power is negotiated (or not), i.e. who initiates questions, and if the learner's second turn does not include a follow up, then he or she is helping to co-construct a power imbalance in the interaction. In addition, IRE or QA-with a closing third turn might not necessarily originate in the classroom but is instead an everyday interactional pattern that has been adopted in classroom interaction, albeit in an imbalanced way.

(2) In Chomskian views and their interpretations within applied linguistics, the native speaker is an idealized monolingual within a homogenized speech community, whose pure grammatical competence serves as a model for language learners. In elaborating a definition of communicative competence that has informed language teaching for decades, Hymes (1972) argued against prioritizing grammatical competence over other sociocultural or discourse-level features for the purpose of understanding communication. Communicative competence 'involves knowing not only the linguistic code, but also what to say to whom, and how to say it appropriately in any given situation' (Saville-Troike, 2003: 18).

(3) 'From a semiotic point of view, all such [pragmatic] meanings can be described as rules linking certain culturally constituted features of the speech situation with certain forms of speech. To give those rules, or talk about them, is to engage in "meta-pragmatic discourse"' (Silverstein, 2001: 382–383). See also van Compernolle's study (this volume) addressing the role of metapragmatics in authenticating identities.

(4) Zhang (2005, 2008) showed that rhotacization in Beijing Mandarin is a salient sociolinguistic variable that reflects authentic Beijing-ness. In particular, the use of rhotacization is associated with a male Beijing-smooth-operator persona that indexes streetwise characteristics, such as being able to talk one's way out of situations. In her study (Zhang, 2005) on the construction of a professional identity among young Beijing business professionals, she found an interesting pattern involving rhotacization between professionals working in foreign and state-owned businesses, and between male and female professionals in both types of companies. While professionals working for international cooperation minimized their rhotacization in order to project a cosmopolitan professional identity, male professionals used the rhotacized style more frequently than did female professionals. Zhang suggested that this is due to the well-known association of the phoneme with the image of the local male Beijing-smooth-operator.

(5) Stafford (2010) argued that unlike Western folk beliefs, where numbers are a way of avoiding subjectivity and saying exactly what we mean, in everyday life in China and Taiwan numbers are often emotionally loaded and important in conceiving life experience, such as in Chinese fengshui (geomancy) or haggling over the price in order to arrive at 'good-sounding-numbers'. As such, Chinese folk mathematics expresses a fundamental interest in qualitative patterns rather than in quantities per se.

References

Bucholtz, M. (2003) Sociolinguistic nostalgia and the authentication of identity. *Journal of Sociolinguistics* 7 (3), 398–416.

Bucholtz, M. (2011) *White Kids: Language, Race, and Styles of Youth Identity*. New York: Cambridge University Press.

Bucholtz, M. and Hall, K. (2004) Language and identity. In A. Duranti (ed.) *A Companion to Linguistic Anthropology* (pp. 369–394). Oxford: Blackwell.

Bucholtz, M. and Hall, K. (2005) Identity and interaction: A sociocultural linguistic approach. *Discourse Studies* 7 (4–5), 585–614.

Bucholtz, M. and Hall, K. (2008) Finding identity: Theory and data. *Multilingua* 27, 151–163.
Chao, Y. (1968) *A Grammar of Spoken Chinese*. Berkeley, CA: University of California Press.
Chun, E.W. (2004) Ideologies of legitimate mockery: Margaret Cho's revoicing of mock Asia. *Pragmatics* 14 (2), 263–289.
Cook, H. (2006) Joint construction of folk beliefs by JFL learners and Japanese host families. In M.A. DuFon and E. Churchill (eds) *Language Learners in Study Abroad Contexts* (pp. 120–150). Clevedon: Multilingual Matters.
Dewey, D.P., Bown, J. and Eggett, D. (2012) Japanese language proficiency, social networking, and language use during study abroad: Learners' perspectives. *Canadian Modern Language Review/La Revue Canadienne Des Langues Vivantes* 68 (2), 111–137.
Du Bois, J.W., Schuetze-Coburn, S., Cumming, S. and Paolino, D. (1993) Outline of discourse transcription. In J.A. Edwards and M.D. Lampert (eds) *Talking Data: Transcription and Coding in Discourse Research* (pp. 45–87). Hillsdale, NY: Lawrence Erlbaum.
Eckert, P. (2003) Elephants in the room. *Journal of Sociolinguistics* 7 (3), 392–397.
Eckert, P. (2012) Three waves of variation study: The emergence of meaning in the study of sociolinguistic variation. *Annual Review of Anthropology* 41, 87–100.
Ellis, R. (1997) *Second Language Acquisition*. New York: Oxford University Press.
Freed, B.F., Segalowitz, N. and Dewey, P. (2004) Context of learning and second language fluency in French: Comparing regular classroom, study abroad, and intensive domestic immersion programs. *Studies in Second Language Acquisition* 26 (2), 275–301.
Henery, A. (2014) Interpreting 'real' French: The role of expert mediation in learner observations, understandings, and use of pragmatic practices while abroad. Unpublished PhD dissertation, Carnegie-Mellon University, Pittsburgh, PA.
Hymes, D. (1972) On communicative competence. In J. Pride and J. Holmes (eds) *Sociolinguistics: Selected Readings* (pp. 269–293). Harmondsworth: Penguin.
Iino, M. (2006) Norms of interaction in a Japanese homestay setting – toward two way flow of linguistic and cultural resources. In M.A. DuFon and E. Churchill (eds) *Language Learners in Study Abroad Contexts* (pp. 151–173). Clevedon: Multilingual Matters.
Irvine, J.T. and Gal, S. (2000) Language ideology and linguistic differentiation. In P. Kroskrity (ed.) *Regimes of Language: Ideologies, Polities, and Identities* (pp. 35–83). Santa Fe, NM: School of American Research Press.
Johnstone, B. and Kiesling, S.F. (2008) Indexicality and experience: Exploring the meanings of /aw/-monophthongization in Pittsburgh. *Journal of Sociolinguistics* 12 (1), 5–33.
Kinginger, C. (2009) *Language Learning and Study Abroad: A Critical Reading of Research*. Basingstoke: Palgrave Macmillan.
Kinginger, C. (2013) Identity and language learning in study abroad. *Foreign Language Annals* 46 (3), 339–358.
Kinginger, C. (2014) Student mobility and identity-related language learning. *Intercultural Education*; doi: 10.1080/14675986.2015.992199.
Kinginger, C., Lee, S.-H., Wu, Q. and Tan, D. (2014) Contextualized language practices as sites for learning: Mealtime talk in short-term Chinese homestays. *Applied Linguistics*; doi: 10.1093/applin/amu061.
Kroskrity, P.V. (2000) *Regimes of Language: Ideologies, Polities, and Identities*. Santa Fe, NM: School of American Research Press.
Li, C.N. and Thompson, S.A. (1981) *Mandarin Chinese: A Functional Reference Grammar*. Los Angeles, CA: University of California Press.
Marriott, H. (1993) Acquiring sociolinguistic competence: Australian secondary students in Japan. *Journal of Asian Pacific Communication* 4 (4), 167–192.
Marriott, H. (1995) The acquisition of politeness patters by exchange students in Japan. In B.F. Freed (ed.) *Second Language Acquisition in a Study Abroad Context* (pp. 197–224). Philadelphia, PA: John Benjamins.

McDonald, E. (2011) *Learning Chinese, Turning Chinese: Challenges to Becoming Sinophone in a Globalized World*. New York: Routledge.
Niedzielski, N.A. and Preston, D.R. (2000) Folk linguistics. *Trends in Linguistics: Studies and Monographs 122*. Berlin: Mouton de Gruyter.
Ochs, E. and Capps, L. (1997) Narrative authenticity. *Journal of Narrative and Life History* 7, 83–90.
Regan, V., Howard, M. and Lemée, I. (2009) *The Acquisition of Sociolinguistic Competence in a Study Abroad Context*. Bristol: Multilingual Matters.
Reyes, A. (2005) Appropriation of African American slang by Asian American youth. *Journal of Sociolinguistics* 9 (4), 509–532.
Saville-Troike, M. (2003) *The Ethnography of Communication: An Introduction* (3rd edn). Oxford: Blackwell.
Shenk, P.S. (2007) 'I'm Mexican, remember?' Constructing ethnic identities via authenticating discourse. *Journal of Sociolinguistics* 11 (2), 194–220.
Siegal, M. (1996) The role of learner subjectivity in second language sociolinguistic competency: Western women learning Japanese. *Applied Linguistics* 17, 356–382.
Silverstein, M. (2001) The limits of awareness. In A. Duranti (ed.) *Linguistic Anthropology: A Reader* (pp. 382–401). Malden, MA: Wiley-Blackwell.
Silverstein, M. (2003) Indexical order and the dialectics of sociolinguistic life. *Language & Communication* 23 (3), 193–229.
Stafford, C. (2010) Some qualitative mathematics in China. *Anthropological Theory* 10 (1–2), 81–86.
van Compernolle, R.A. (2014) *Sociocultural Theory and L2 Instructional Pragmatics*. Bristol: Multilingual Matters.
Wilkinson, S. (2002) The omnipresent classroom during summer study abroad: American students in conversation with their French hosts. *Modern Language Journal* 86 (2), 157–173.
Zhang, Q. (2005) A Chinese yuppie in Beijing: Phonological variation and the construction of a new professional identity. *Language in Society* 34 (3), 431–466.
Zhang, Q. (2008) Rhotacization and the 'Beijing smooth operator': The social meaning of a linguistic variable. *Journal of Sociolinguistics* 12 (2), 201–222.

9 Metapragmatic Talk and the Interactional Accomplishment of Authenticity in Study Abroad

Janice McGregor

Introduction

Folklinguistic knowledge, or the commonplace, everyday beliefs that people have about language, language learning and language use (see Niedzielski & Preston, 2000), tends to uphold the native speaker of a given language as the owner of an idealized and complete linguistic competence that the second language (L2) learner should strive to emulate (Kramsch, 1997, 2008). In institutional contexts, administration, faculty and students contribute to this view by endorsing study abroad (SA) as the main path towards more authentic and complete L2 competence. My own experiences of learning German demonstrate that even highly skilled and motivated learners may not grasp that interacting in an L2 is a social practice that requires collaborative meaning making and negotiation with others instead of memorization and one-sided participation. At the start of my time abroad, I hoped to pass for German in conversations with locals, and I attempted to imitate their utterances and interactive practices. I wanted to be viewed as a natural, genuine speaker of 'pure vernacular' (Eckert, 2003: 392) in everyday interactions, although I soon realized that being an authentic speaker involved far more than uttering words and phrases that corresponded to native-like practices. I had to learn how to be authentically 'me' in German and go beyond simply mimicking local practices. I had to learn how to articulate and negotiate my own thoughts, ideas and perspectives with others. I also had to learn how to manage my interlocutors' beliefs, ideas and reactions to my perspectives as they unfolded in the context of an interaction.

Considering that quotidian folklinguistic assumptions about language learning and use are frequently present in the linguistic landscape of SA promotion materials, it is perhaps not surprising that I desired to be authentically German without having examined my thoughts, beliefs and L1 socialization. Students who yearn for native-like L2 fluency are often sold cosmopolitan, worldly identity trajectories, although they may not understand what meaningful language learning and use actually involve. As an L2 learner in an SA context, regardless of whether or not my German was improving, I rarely talked about my L2 competence in terms of its development, relying instead on discourses of deficit and incompleteness. While there is no room to elaborate on such discussions here, the fact that language learning processes are frequently and strategically essentialized in order to get students abroad is an issue that requires further investigation.

Much scholarship in second-language acquisition (SLA) has reflected and contributed to the folklinguistic belief that the native speaker owns the notion of 'enoughness', that is, the benchmark for being viewed as a real or authentic speaker or community member (Blommaert & Varis, 2011). Early SLA studies in SA contexts, for example, sought to measure the linguistic development of large numbers of students in decontextualized settings in an attempt to ascertain whether they experienced major L2 gains while abroad. A consistent finding of this work has challenged the folklinguistic notion that studying abroad leads to advanced L2 competence, as scholars have discovered that sojourning students' L2 competence does not always become more native-like while abroad (Brecht *et al.*, 1995; Kinginger, 2004, 2008; Polanyi, 1995). Although traditional proficiency tests show that some students do make exceptional L2 gains, by now, we know that a consistent finding of research on students' linguistic achievements while abroad is one of individual variability (Kinginger, 2008, 2009). As a reaction to such research, scholars have investigated emic (participant-relevant) perspectives by exploring students' beliefs, goals and reflections on experiences in order to better understand the complex issues surrounding language use, identity and intercultural development in SA (see Jackson, 2008; Kinginger, 2004, 2008; McGregor, 2014; Müller, 2011; Pellegrino-Aveni, 2005). Most of these studies have brought into the discussion the myriad ways in which SA students orient to local participation and have helped promote the view that language learning and use are at all times complex undertakings that involve, at the very least, knowing how, when and why to say what to whom.

However, a dearth of scholarship still exists regarding SA students' participation in interactive practices as these unfold in conversation between two or more local individuals. Although the number of studies investigating naturally occurring interactions in SA has begun to increase, we still know very little about the ways in which sojourners co-construct and negotiate talk with local peers in conversation. In this chapter, I contribute to this growing area of research by investigating an SA student's talk-in-interaction with a local peer. I focus specifically on the use of metalinguistic talk (i.e. talk about language) and how it informs the ways in which the interlocutors collaboratively authenticate one another's knowledge. L2 learners have traditionally been conceived of as authentic when their L2 use corresponds to the native-like use of language at all levels (e.g. phonology, morphology, syntax, pragmatics) *or* when L2 use originates solely from their own choices (MacDonald *et al.*, 2006; van Compernolle & McGregor, this volume). As will be shown, I conceive of authenticity not as a fixed and complete end-state, but rather as an ongoing process of *authentication* that integrates a linking of both views.

L2 Interaction in Study Abroad

To date, research that addresses larger questions of L2 competence in SA has investigated primarily non-conversational data, with the exception of a few studies that analyze naturally occurring conversation and interactive practices in SA (see Lee & Kinginger, this volume; Masuda, 2011; Shively, 2013a, 2013b, 2015; Taguchi, 2014). Because it is often assumed that language learners in SA contexts participate regularly in conversations with local peers, there is a great need for researchers to record and collect naturally occurring interactions in SA and carefully analyze these data. One study by Levine (2009) has identified talk-about-language as a social and discursive practice occurring in interaction that would benefit from further investigation.

Levine (2009) examines the use of metalinguistic L2 learner talk, or what he calls 'talk-about-language', in interactions between SA students and experienced German speakers in settings in which the acquisition of forms was not the sole focus. In this way, Levine distinguishes talk-about-language from the more pedagogically driven concept of 'focus-on-form' (see Long, 1991). In an instance of talk-about-language, a student's goal may be related to participating in authenticating practices in order to create intersubjective spaces with interlocutors and not to acquire particular linguistic forms. Instances of talk-about-language appear to be embodied and situated activities (van Lier, 2002: 146) related to a learner's past, present and future place in the second language and culture, that is to say, their ongoing L2 socialization. These events also arise from their own context and legitimize the L2 learner's position in a new speech community. Levine's research therefore promotes a dialectical conceptualization of authenticity that both corresponds to local German norms and arises from a learner's own agentive choices. The results of Levine's study demonstrate that L2 learner talk-about-language plays an important role in the students' socialization into a new language and culture, since metalinguistic talk also informs participants' knowledge of how particular interactional resources and strategies are employed by all participants in local discursive practices (Hall *et al.*, 2011).

Addressing the development of interactional competence of L2 learners of Japanese, Taguchi (2014) investigates a common feature in Japanese conversations – incomplete sentences. In tracing both quantitative and qualitative changes in the use of incomplete sentences in peer interactions by L2 learners of Japanese during a three-month semester abroad, Taguchi shows that the learners' knowledge about organizing and adjoining incomplete sentences sequentially actually served as a resource that the learners employed mutually and reciprocally in their practice of joint meaning making. This finding is compelling since authentic language competence is often said to correspond to syntactically complete, idealized native language use. However, Taguchi shows that the collaborative use of incomplete sentences in interaction greatly informed the development of the learners' L2 interactional competence.

In a study investigating the development of humor in conversation in SA, Shively (2013a) analyzes interactional data and finds that friendship, time and close relationships allow for her participant to become more successful in using humor in L2 interactions with local interlocutors. Notably, this study highlights the importance of *revoicing* in learners' development of humor in an L2 (emphasis mine). A speaker revoices a word when she reproduces a word or phrase used by a local peer in her own speech, with her own intentions and stance (Shively, 2013a: 933). This finding highlights the need for scholars to reconceptualize authentic language use as dialectic or unified whole; that is, L2 use is authentic when it corresponds to local linguistic and interactive practices and originates from the L2 user and her history, socialization and knowledge.

These studies promote the need for more research that identifies what SA students are actually *doing* in interaction with local peers during a sojourn abroad and how this informs our understanding of how learner and competence authenticity is accomplished in interaction (see also Lee & Kinginger, this volume). In this chapter, I therefore identify instances of talk-about-language (Levine, 2009) in order to better understand what learners are accomplishing with this talk. The research questions are as follows:

(1) Does talk-about-language feature prominently in naturally occurring interactions between an SA student and local peers? If so, what (e.g. social, discursive) functions does this talk have?
(2) Does talk-about-language inform the participants' collaborative authentication of one another's knowledge? If so, how?

L2 Competence

A brief history

A discussion of what comprises L2 competence is in order, since the term has been dealt with in different ways. Anthropological linguist Dell

Hymes (1972) proposed the term communicative competence as a reaction to the work of formal linguist Noam Chomsky. Chomskyan views of an L2 learner's linguistic knowledge paralleled that of an internal black box, since his theories of what comprised linguistic competence intentionally left out considerations of social knowledge about how and when to use utterances appropriately (Chomsky, 1965). While Hymes argued that language structure and its acquisition could never be examined without contextual consideration, Chomsky believed that an innate, internal mechanism was sufficiently able to account for the processes of language acquisition. Since then, a number of models have been proposed by applied linguists (see Canale, 1983; Canale & Swain, 1980; Celce-Murcia, 1995, 2007; Celce-Murcia et al., 1995) to articulate what comprises communicative competence. Canale and Swain (1980) and Canale (1983) were the first to propose a model for communicative competence in the context of language learning and pedagogy. They departed from Hymes's work by stating that a model of communicative competence must involve more than just grammatical and sociolinguistic competence. By adding strategic and eventually discourse competence to their model of communicative competence, their work reflected Hymes's primary concern that social knowledge about language use be considered. Yet they were not able to account for the interrelated nature of the model's four components, something that Celce-Murcia et al. (1995) set out to address in an updated model of communicative competence. Celce-Murcia et al. directly addressed this shortcoming by proposing that a core or central competence, namely discourse competence, could better account for the interrelationships between the components of their model. Canale and Swain's grammatical competence was also reconceptualized as linguistic competence to account for structural components *and* a language's sound system and lexicon. While these are certainly strengths of their updated model, at the time, Celce-Murcia et al. still did not address the jointly constructed nature of language use in conversation and interaction in which learners both gain and deploy new interactional resources that occur in conversation with others. Celce-Murcia (2007: 48) revisited these questions 10 years later and proposed an updated model of communicative competence that incorporated what she called a 'hands-on' component – interactional competence. According to Celce-Murcia, this component addresses knowledge regarding how to perform common L2 speech acts and speech act sets. It also addresses conversational competence, or how to deal with openings and closings, turn-taking, interruptions, back-channeling, and so on.

Nevertheless, familiar issues are still at the heart of Celce-Murcia's most recent model of communicative competence. While the model and its components' interrelationships have been made much more explicit and are better able to address the complexity involved in language learning and pedagogy, the model nevertheless promotes a view of knowledge and action as separate components. For example, Celce-Murcia's descriptions of the sociocultural and interactional competence components do not address the co-constructed nature of language use in interaction. Proposing, for example, that L2 learners require knowledge about how to perform common L2 speech acts does not address the fact that speakers are co-participants in the collaborative construction of those acts and may only come to understand what is socioculturally appropriate in a particular context through participation in interactions. For this reason, in the current study, I consider interactional approaches to language use since these are best suited to addressing the collaborative nature of talk and authentication in conversational contexts. Interactional approaches allow for the investigation of L2 learner talk-in-interaction with others, including how learners collaboratively construct talk via the use and negotiation of interactional resources (e.g. acknowledging an interlocutor's utterance, stance display, demonstrating alignment with one's interlocutor, negotiation of meaning, metalinguistic talk) that are considered vital for the successful participation in and co-construction of interactive practices.

Interaction, sociality and indexicality

Participation in interactions involves two or more individuals co-constructing meaningful talk that is goal-directed. Goal-directed here refers to the fact that speakers in conversation with one another are typically aware of possible trajectories that would allow them to jointly move the episode towards completion. As an example, van Compernolle (2015) writes that a supermarket customer in the United States often hears a cashier utter, 'how are you doing today?' while checking out. An experienced shopper in this context would know the possible goal-directed conversational trajectories that would bring this service encounter interaction to its successful completion (i.e. the series of actions that constitute the event, including scanning one's store card, hearing the total, paying for the groceries, closing the interaction with a leave-taking sequences, and so on). In other words, interactional co-participants draw on sets of interactive practices – the conventionalized, yet flexible routines that are recognized by interactants as corresponding to some speech event – as a way to accomplish their goals.

Interactive practices can involve topic initiation and continuation including how topics are managed and can also involve the syntactic and lexical choices that inform or result from the management of initiated topics. They also include participation structures, for example, how turns are taken in an interaction. These practices may contribute to how interlocutors negotiate a shared understanding of a topic, aim to make episodes mutually intelligible and organize the interaction in a way that moves it towards completion. Typical agendas, contexts and participant roles within a particular context inform how we respond and view interactions, as well as how we will participate in similar episodes in the future. For this reason, successful participation in local L2 interactions requires that students do more than reach or attain a prescribed proficiency level, or just learn to speak (Hall, 1995: 218). In this way, an L2 interactional competence framework represents an important departure from the aforementioned models of communicative competence. Interacting with others requires not just social-context-specific knowledge of what it means to take part in a particular type of interaction, especially as it relates to the roles and interactional responsibilities (e.g. question-asking versus question-answering) of those involved. Interacting with others also requires an awareness of the sociocultural constructions that are collaboratively developed, maintained and (re)-negotiated by those involved in engaging in these particular practices. In other words, a person's interactional competence is never complete since it constitutes the joint creation of a form, interpretation, stance, disposition, identity, activity, action, emotion or other culturally relevant reality (Jacoby & Ochs, 1995). L2 learner interactional competence must therefore at all times underlie and result from successful interaction, since learners use resources (e.g. metalinguistic talk, repair) garnered from interactive practices with other interlocutors (Hall 1993, 1995).

Using these resources plays a crucial role in the development of authentic ways of doing talk and communication in SA as well. And developing authentic ways of participating in L2 talk while abroad must include 'knowing how to index another person in an interaction', since knowing how to address others is typically viewed as 'fairly indispensable to basic social talk' (Kinginger & Farrell, 2004: 37). At first glance, it appears as though learning how to index another person in German is not a supremely complicated undertaking. Sociolinguistic descriptions in beginner German language textbooks typically and clearly mark the second-person pronoun *Sie* as formal and the second-person pronoun *du* as informal. Students are told that *Sie* indexes formality, deference and/or age and social difference and *du* indexes informality, solidarity and/or intimacy (see Kinginger & Belz, 2005). Students are therefore taught that the usage of second-person pronouns *du* or *Sie* links to macro-sociological categories typical of what Silverstein (2003) and van Compernolle (2014) call first-order indexicality (e.g. age, setting, appearance, level of formality, and so on). Yet there may be other local meanings associated with the use of these forms that textbooks do not elaborate on. These other meanings and their interpretations are typically discovered by learners who, while using the L2 in a local context, experience some kind of conflict that demonstrates their choice of address form was inappropriate for that particular context. Silverstein (2003) and van Compernolle (2014) describe these more particularized meanings as existing at the level of second-order indexicality, since first-order levels do not account for the local differences that affect the meanings and interpretations of the use of *du* or

Sie. The L2 learner has to come to more particularized understandings about what these forms index at the local level in their specific context in order to use these forms in a more authentic way. Third-order indexicality refers to explicit metadiscourse about these meanings that points to larger macrosociological ideologies. At this level, discussions hail cultural value systems that go well beyond simple mappings of form and meaning. Issues related to indexicality emphasize the need to go beyond just discussions of form and function. In order to understand how SA students participate in L2 talk, we must also come to know how they unite their understandings of first-order indexical uses of *du* and *Sie* with local, particularized meanings typical of second-order indexicality.

Authenticity

The aforementioned conceptualizations of language use and interaction are a departure from traditional views of what constitutes an authentic L2 speaker. In the general sociolinguistics literature, Bucholtz (2003) has argued that scholars need to reconceptualize authenticity as the product of individuals' participation in interactive practices rather than a trait characteristic of an individual that preexists interaction. By extension, L2 learners may be conceived of as authentic speakers of the language they are learning as they actively negotiate community practices with others and learn how to use language and interact in a way that corresponds to local patterns of L2 use. Extending scholarship in philosophy (Cooper, 1983) to applied linguistics, MacDonald *et al.* (2006) have critiqued the ways in which authentic competence and authentic learners have been conceptualized in SLA, noting that text, competence and the language learner have often been conceived of as authentic if they correspond to the native-like use of language at all levels (e.g. phonology, morphology, syntax, pragmatics). Text, competence and the language learner have also been conceived of as authentic when language, performance and interpretation originate solely from the speaker's own choices. MacDonald *et al.* (2006: 255) claim that these two views of authenticity should no longer be considered separately, suggesting that measuring nonnative speakers' L2 competence without investigating how language users orient to both themselves and others in interaction can lead to a 'poverty of performance' and a 'poverty of interpretation' (MacDonald *et al.*, 2006: 256). As L2 learners negotiate their own knowledge in interaction with others, they elicit and 'try on' new, local interactive practices. Since learners actively participate in interactions by using talk-about-language and other strategies that shape the interaction in order to collaboratively develop a shared knowledge of the world with their interlocutor(s) (Young, 2011), scholarship should synthesize both notions of authenticity as a united whole. I argue here that participation in local interactive practices and the collaborative construction of intersubjective spaces between

SA students and local peers is both the locus and product of L2 interactional competence. In this way, interactional competence is viewed as mediational in nature, since it facilitates the collaborative accomplishment of talk and is also facilitated by the resources that become available in the interaction (van Compernolle, 2015: 281). For this reason, it becomes necessary to reconceptualize authenticity as a dialectical process of *authentication*. This view addresses the joint accomplishment of interlocutors in interaction with others, since interactants – regardless of 'native' or 'nonnative' status – cannot legitimize themselves as authentic speakers (in the L1 or L2) without the authentication (or lack thereof) of the interlocutor(s). Both aspects are at all times a part of the dynamic, authentication process.

Data Collection and Analysis

The data in this study come from one participant's recorded interactions during his SA year in Marburg, Germany. Luke (a pseudonym) participated in a direct exchange program to Marburg, Germany, from a mid-sized state university in the Northeastern United States. He submitted recordings of naturally occurring conversations as a part of a larger project on language learning and community participation in SA. During the study, I also collected language history questionnaires and language proficiency evaluations, which were administered at three different times during his year abroad: at the beginning of the first and second semesters and the end of the second semester. The naturally occurring conversational data were recorded by Luke during his final two months in Germany. I gave him a small digital recorder and asked him to record conversations with local peers whenever German was being used primarily. He subsequently sent me his data files via email. I transcribed the data using a transcription system that can be found in the Appendix. In transcribing and analyzing the data, I found instances of talk-about-language and other resources frequently found in L2 talk (e.g. word coinage, language switches, clarification requests) that helped establish how he was (or was not) participating in local interactions.

The language history questionnaires that I collected provided a better sense of Luke's experiences with German as he embarked on the year abroad. The language proficiency evaluation was administered in order to demonstrate that traditional proficiency exam results cannot tell us how L2 learners use language in interaction locally and collaboratively accomplish authenticity. The proficiency evaluation was comprised of a number of cloze tests ranging from elementary to advanced. This test is commonly used as a diagnostic placement test in language institutes in Germany; in fact, the University of Marburg's *Sprachenzentrum* (language center) used a similar evaluation in their placement process. Tables 9.1 and 9.2 demonstrate that

Table 9.1 Language proficiency evaluation scores

	Luke
1 (October 2009)	84.5
2 (April 2010)	115
3 (July 2010)	114

Table 9.2 Language proficiency evaluation rubric

Evaluation levels	Score
Elementary 1–Elementary 2	up to 50
Elementary 2–Elementary 3	up to 70
Elementary 3–Intermediate 1	up to 90
Intermediate 2–Intermediate 3	up to 110
Advanced	up to 120
Native-speaker level	over 120

Luke's language proficiency evaluation scores were consistently high in the second semester abroad (Advanced in both April and July).

As will be shown, Luke uses talk-about-language, specifically metapragmatic talk, in order to participate in local interactive practices and the process of authentication. In one interaction with a local German friend, Katrin, Luke initiates a discussion about formal and informal address form use in German through a personal anecdote about an error that he made in conversation with a local friend and her parents. He participates in the process of authentication by discussing his own experiences and negotiating his knowledge on address forms in both languages. He also negotiates Katrin's assessments, creating an intersubjective space in which both he and Katrin collaboratively articulate, analyze and re-orient to formal and informal address forms in German and American English.

Findings

Luke's 'faux pas': 'I met her parents and I said *du* to them.'

Luke, an advanced L2 learner, engages in a talk-about-language event that deals primarily with the concept and use of formal and informal address in German and American English. His interactions take place with Katrin, a local German student and friend. In Excerpt 9.1, Luke tells Katrin about an event from earlier in the week. The subsequent discussion causes him to rethink how formal and informal second-person pronouns (*du* and *Sie* 'you') are used in German.

Excerpt 9.1 Luke tells Katrin about an interaction he had in German

1	**Luke**:	ich hab (.) ihre eltern kennen gelernt (.) und ich hab sie geduzt
		I met her parents and I said du to them
2	**Katrin**:	mmja
		hmm yeah
3	**Luke**:	die haben mich aber auch geduzt
		but they said du to me too
4	**Katrin**:	ja
		yeah
5	**Luke**:	aber (.) julia hat sofort gesagt ↑nein nein nein nein nein
		but julia immediately said no no no no no!
6	**Katrin**:	oh: ((laughing))
		ohhh hahaha
7	**Luke**:	ich mein ohh: dann (.) so ein faux pas gemacht und
		I mean ohh then did such a faux pas and
8	**Katrin**:	ach quatsch
		oh nonsense
9	**Luke**:	aber das war es (.) ja also (..) solche sachen merk ich mir (1.0)
		but that was it yeah so I notice things like that
10	**Katrin**:	aber trotzdem
		but nevertheless
11	**Luke**:	ja (.) ich hab im xx also (.) wie ich gedacht habe war (.) die sind die eltern (.) von einer freundin (.) also
		yeah I'd xx so how I had thought about it was they are the parents of a friend so
12	**Katrin**:	ja aber trotz (.) also in deutschland würde man die immer siezen
		yeah but still well in Germany one would still say Sie to them
13	**Luke**:	ja ja ja (.) das weiss ich jetzt
		yeah yeah yeah I know that now

Luke begins this interactive episode by telling Katrin about a pragmatic error that he made while speaking: addressing his friend's parents with the informal second-person *du* form, when the *Sie* form would have corresponded to local German norms. In line 5, Luke talks about recognizing his error when Julia immediately and explicitly corrected him. Luke reasons that he said *du* to Julia's parents because he felt close to Julia. He then notes that this was a pragmatic faux pas on his part and Katrin responds by downgrading his assertion. In line 12, however, Katrin does reject Luke's rationale for having chosen *du*, noting that *du* does not, in fact, correspond to the most appropriate pragmatic address form choice in this context. In Excerpt 9.2, Luke continues to manage and negotiate this topic by extending the discussion of German address forms to other contexts.

Excerpt 9.2 *Luke and Katrin on addressing superiors in German*

1 **Luke**: es geht g genau so mit de (.) mit den dozenten ja die sagen
    it's the exact same with the with professors yeah they say
2 **Katrin**: aber das ist nochmal anders weil die dozenten kennst du (..) weil sie
    but that's different again because professors you know because they
    wirklich deine vorgesetzten sind
    really are your superiors
3 **Luke**: +^ jajaja aber ich meine es ist
    yeahyeahyeah but I mean it's
4 **Katrin**: +^ xx richtige authoritätsperson natürlich ist denn xx eltern (.) sind dann
    xx real people of authority of course that is because parents are
    eltern authoritäten aber das ist anders (.) die sind nicht so vorgesetzt (.)
    parental authority but that's different they are not really your superiors
    und die (.) sie xx
    and they they xx
5 **Luke**: +^ wo du du willst auch höflich bleiben
    although you you also want to remain polite
6 **Katrin**: +^ ja (.) auf der anderen seite wenn jemand sagt (.) du kannst mich duzen
    yeah on the other hand if someone says you can say du to me
    dann ist es höflich wenn man duzt
    then it's polite when you say du
7 **Luke**: oh (.) ist das so↺ (.) oh
    oh is that so↺ oh
8 **Katrin**: also bei den dozenten find ich ist es grenzwärtig aber bei den eltern zum
    well with professors I find it more borderline but with parents for
    beispiel
    example
9 **Luke**: solltest du das machen
    you should do that
10 **Katrin**: +^ mittlerweile duz ich sie aber also ein bisschen mulmig ist man dabei
    in the meantime I say du but well it's a bit one is a bit unsure
    noch dabei ((laughing))
    doing it hahaha

In Excerpt 9.2, Luke compares the selection of address form choice in two contexts: speaking with a friend's parents and speaking with university professors. Katrin quickly rejects his comparison and notes that when an authority figure offers the use of the informal address forms, it is considered rude not to comply. Luke's reaction in line 7 shows that he has not yet considered the implications of using a formal address form with someone who has articulated that they would prefer to be addressed informally.

The fact that Luke and Katrin, both experienced speakers of German and English, discuss complicated sociopragmatic issues related to indexicality and address form use stresses the fact that Katrin is actively authenticating Luke's identity as a German speaker. It is clear that Luke is able discuss the sociolinguistic conventions of address form use that are typically linked to first-order indexicality. Luke has no trouble with conventions that can be linked to macrosociological categories (van Compernolle, 2014: 50) such as age, setting, appearance, activity and level of formality when in interaction with others. By selecting *du* in interaction with Julia's parents, Luke indexes his belief that familiarity is appropriate in this context. This belief, however, does not correspond to local German interactive practices. Katrin and Luke discuss his first-order correlation and note the complex nature of address form choice, moving into the realm of second-order indexicality. Luke attempts to compare the use of *Sie* in conversation with friends' parents to the use of *Sie* in conversation with professors and Katrin problematizes this link straight away. Commenting on differences in authority and power between a student and professor, she articulates her view as to why choosing the appropriate German address form for one's friends' parents might actually be more challenging than selecting the appropriate German address form for professors. At this level, sociolinguistic conventions may turn into indexical resources for language users as speakers particularize and describe indexical meanings (van Compernolle, 2014), as can be seen here. A metapragmatic discussion about indexicality and address form choice ensues and Katrin comments on how difficult it is for her to say *du* to her friends' parents, even after they have offered her this informality. Generally speaking, Luke and Katrin's interactions show that in order to negotiate this slippery terrain, one must do more than just link ways of speaking to local German norms – one must also simultaneously produce, negotiate and reflect on one's choices and the social repercussions of these choices.

Re-orientations: 'I'm happy that we don't have something like that in English.'

In Excerpt 9.3, Luke comments on how happy he is that English makes no distinction between formal and informal second-person pronouns. Katrin, however, states that this lack of pronominal distinction confuses her, something that Luke had not previously considered difficult or problematic.[1]

Excerpt 9.3 Luke and Katrin negotiate formal and informal address in German and English

1 **Luke**: mm (.) ich bin froh dass s (.) wir (.) nicht so was (.) auf englisch haben
  mm I'm happy that we don't have something like that in English
2 **Katrin**: ja (.) mich hat das verwirrt dass es das nicht gibt
  yeah it confused me that it doesn't exist
3 **Luke**: +^oh↑¿
  oh¿¿

190 Authenticity, Language and Interaction in Second Language Contexts

4 **Katrin**: ja klar (.) weil für mich wars klar
well yeah because for me it was clear
5 **Luke**: +^aber w (.) du benutzt halt (.) du or you
but w you just use du or you
6 **Katrin**: ja aber dann muss ich überlegen nehm ich den vornamen oder nicht
yeah but then I have to consider do I use first names or not
7 **Luke**: oh
oh

Luke is surprised to hear that Katrin finds it easier to negotiate two address forms for the second-person pronoun. He assumes, until this moment, that everyone finds it easier to address others using English, since only one second-person singular pronoun exists. In this way, via third-order indexicality or 'explicit metadiscourse' about the pronominal address form system in German (van Compernolle, 2014: 51), Luke becomes aware of other potential indexical meanings according to different ways of viewing human relationships that he had not previously considered. He discovers that, for Katrin, the *du/Sie* system in German makes clear the kinds of appropriate interactional and relationship trajectories that are possible between two individuals.

Luke and Katrin eventually come to realize that American English does have other ways of dealing with address and that this kind of information is not always encoded in a second-person pronoun. In Excerpt 9.4, Katrin, who has thus far been positioned as the expert speaker in interaction with Luke, discovers that she too must re-orient to different ways of viewing address form use in American English and German. In line 9, Luke amends his statement from Excerpt 9.3, line 1, noting that American English does in fact have the same concept, although it is codified differently.

Excerpt 9.4 Luke and Katrin negotiate formal and informal address in German and English

1 **Katrin**: zum beispiel
for example
2 **Luke**: aja also es es gibt auch das gleiche
oh yeah well there there is also the same
3 **Katrin**: +^ja¿ (1.0) und zum beispiel von michelle (.) die eltern¿
yeah¿ and for example michelle the parents¿
4 **Luke**: mm
mm
5 **Katrin**: hätt ich nicht mit vornamen angesprochen zum beispiel
I would never have spoken to them with first names for example
6 **Luke**: aber
but

7	**Katrin:**	+^wenn du jetzt sagst (.) das sind die eltern von ner freundin
		when you say that's the parents of a friend
8	**Luke:**	mm
		mm
9	**Katrin:**	+^kann ich dann gar nicht die vornamen also hätt ich zum beispiel
		I can't use the first names at all so for example I would never have
		nicht gemacht
		done that
10	**Luke:**	dann (.) wenn du da zu weihnachen warst hast du
		then when you were there at christmas did you
11	**Katrin:**	ja
		yeah
12	**Luke:**	hättest du denn die mit (..) um mr and mrs martin angesprochen (.) ah die
		would you have addressed them with Mr And Mrs Martin uh the
		ganze zeitlang?
		whole time?
13	**Katrin:**	ja
		yeah
14	**Luke:**	die haben doch gesagt nein
		surely they said no
15	**Katrin:**	ich weiss nicht wie oft ich die direkt angesprochen habe weil meistens xxx
		I don't know how often I addressed them directly because mostly xxx
16	**Luke:**	+^aber die (.) die haben doch gesagt wie heissen sie denn
		but they they surely said what are their names then
17	**Katrin:**	uh ruth und (.)
		uh Ruth and…
18	**Luke:**	die haben go doch gesagt (.) du musst uns ruth nennen also (.) das sagt
		they surely said you have to call us Ruth I mean that's what
		man auf englisch ich weiss das denn
		one says in English I do know that
19	**Katrin:**	ja
		yes
20	**Luke:**	also weil also es ist denn das schafft viel distanz (.) wenn man
		because it's because it creates a lot of distance when one
		mr und mrs sagt
		says Mr and Mrs
21	**Katrin:**	ja aber
		yeah but
22	**Luke:**	+^viel also das ist ich würde sagen das ist eher stärker als Sie
		a lot so that is I would say it's even stronger than Sie
23	**Katrin:**	mmhm
		mmhm

In this interaction, Katrin states that she cannot address her American friend's parents using first names only. Luke questions her statement, positioning himself as an expert of American English. He has trouble accepting Katrin's statement and repeatedly expresses his doubt. At the end of line 25, Luke articulates his knowledge that '[the person's first name is] what one says in English I do know that', although in line 28 Katrin avoids aligning with Luke's comment. Luke then makes an important distinction between using Mr/Mrs in American English and *Sie* in German, saying that the use of Mr/Mrs actually creates more social distance than *Sie*. Katrin does not overtly align with this assessment; however, she does appear to consider the ramifications of not recognizing this other possible indexical meaning in her own interactions with friends' parents in the United States.

Excerpts 9.1–9.4 demonstrate that metapragmatic talk is a social and discursive practice in which Luke and Katrin co-construct new understandings of indexicality and address form in German and American English by discussing personal experiences and existing declarative knowledge. Both Katrin and Luke assume the position of expert at different points in the interactions, providing assessments of each other's address form choices. Such assessments lead to fruitful metapragmatic discussions regarding why certain address forms do or do not correspond to local patterns of use. Overall, Luke and Katrin begin to unite two elements: first-order knowledge about address form choice in German (e.g. *du* or *Sie*) and American English (e.g. first names or last names) and particularized second-order knowledge about the use of these forms in interactions with different interlocutors and how they may index different meanings. In addition, these metapragmatic events allow Luke and Katrin to discuss address form choice as it corresponds to local patterns of use and arises from their own choices. While Katrin initially has trouble aligning with the patterns of use that, according to Luke, correspond to local American English interactive practices, participating in metapragmatic discussions brings her to notice other ways of viewing address form indexicality and she rethinks the ways in which she interprets and deals with address form in American English.

Discussion

The findings of this study demonstrate how an SA participant uses interactional resources in order to manage his participation in a local interaction. Luke and Katrin engage in metapragmatic talk to collaboratively negotiate address form use via different indexicalities in order to accomplish the local social and conversational goals. Both interlocutors engage in processes of authentication regarding their knowledge about address form use in German and English. In what follows, I respond to the research questions posed earlier in this chapter.

Functions of talk-about-language

In interaction with his local German friend Katrin, Luke initiates and negotiates complex metapragmatic events related to indexicality and address form in German and American English. Luke's pragmatic misstep with Julia's parents, described via first-order indexicality, is problematized by Katrin, who demonstrates that how we assign meaning to address forms may change in different interactional contexts with different power dynamics. This particular talk-about-language action sequence constitutes a collaborative practice in which the interlocutors co-create safe spaces for negotiating meaning of address form in German and American English. Crucially, Luke does not engage in talk-about-language in order to acquire new forms or elicit the 'right' answer. Instead, Luke and Katrin's negotiation of appropriate address form use leads them to new understandings of how second-order indexical meanings can be associated with other ideological depictions (via third-order indexicality). In this way, they authenticate one another's L1 and L2 pragmatic and interactional competencies through the use of metapragmatic discourse and talk-about-language serves as a way for Luke and Katrin to re-build intersubjectivity. It is important to note that in interactions, as long as intersubjectivity is being maintained, there is typically no need for speakers to collaboratively pursue authentication via talk-about-language. In this case, it is clear that with regard to beliefs about address form use in German and English, intersubjectivity was not being maintained. For this reason, metapragmatic talk served as a way for them to reconstruct a shared understanding and authenticate one another's knowledge about the use of address form in German and English.

Talk-about-language and authentication

Talk-about-language events allow Luke to negotiate talk in ways that go beyond traditional notions of authenticity. Luke's data show how metapragmatic discussions about conversational missteps and conceptual understandings can lead interlocutors to re-orient to previous assumptions about form and function. Luke and Katrin work collaboratively to authenticate one another's utterances, as they manage their own agentive choices and appeal to personal experiences dealing with complicated concepts as well as how these correspond to local interactive practices. In collaboratively synthesizing their understandings of concept and experiences with language use, Luke and Katrin show that talk-about-language events can promote the collaborative accomplishment of authentic ways of 'doing being' an L2 user. By uniting their own choices about when and how to use appropriate forms with their understandings of how the forms are linked to local practices, they come to new understandings of not just form and function, but also their orientations to each other and social interactions more generally. What is more, Luke and Katrin authenticate each other's knowledge of *du/Sie* and other address strategies through their interactions, hailing larger cultural value systems that necessarily inform and shape their knowledge and use of address strategies in both languages.

Conclusions

The findings of the present study highlight the role of talk-about-language in the cooperative accomplishment of authentic ways of learning and speaking in interactions during SA. My participant, Luke, uses talk-about-language as a way to create an intersubjective space in which he both legitimizes his own knowledge about address form use in German and English and negotiates Katrin's knowledge of these forms and their actual use. A clear implication of the results of this study is that scholars need to continue to investigate how language learners use the L2 in interaction with local others while abroad, since interlocutors orient to interactive events differently depending on context, ideology and power structures in play. For this reason, more data from a variety of SA contexts are needed. Do participants take part in local communities while abroad? What participant roles are available to SA students in their local communities? Do participants actually have the opportunity to participate in local interactions? If so, how do they participate in interaction with local peers? Do the participants and their interlocutors collaboratively accomplish authentic ways of using the L2?

Prospective SA students would thus benefit from doing being authentic speakers by participating regularly in interactions with experienced speakers (both in the L1 and L2) before going abroad. These prospective SA students could simultaneously take part in guided activities in which they discuss and analyze their own conversational transcripts, recordings or videos. Drawing students' attention to what they accomplish in interaction (via talk-about-language or other strategies) may help students recognize collaborative work in talk and could serve as an encouragement for them to actively search out similar experiences while abroad. As has been noted elsewhere, participation in interactive practices is neither static nor fixed and the collaborative negotiation of local L2 community practices is at all times the reason for and the result of participants' developing L2 interactional competencies. For this reason, more pedagogical interventions are needed that promote dynamic and collaborative uses and views of L2 learning and use. If L2 learners experience meaningful participation in interaction with other speakers pre-sojourn, they will become aware of need to consider the collaborative and dynamic nature of L2 learning and use.

Appendix: Transcription Conventions

The following conventions were adopted in transcribing the interactional data.

(.)	brief pause
(1.0)	longer pause; measured in seconds
italics	English gloss

+^	overlap
○	whispering
:	elongation
((laughing))	laughter
↑	higher pitch level
?	rising intonation
xx	unintelligible

Note

(1) This can be ascribed to the folklinguistic belief that simpler constructions are easier to learn and use, regardless of the language. As Slobin (1987) notes, however, language learners tend to select the most available means possible in their mother tongue and may have a hard time giving up long-held beliefs about language that are entrenched in their 'thinking-for-speaking' patterns. In this way, they are guided in how they choose to talk about experience.

References

Blommaert, J. and Varis, P. (2011) 'Enough is enough': the heuristics of authenticity in superdiversity. *Tilburg Papers in Culture Studies*, 2.

Brecht, R.D., Davidson, D. and Ginsburg, R. (1995) Predictors of foreign language gain during study abroad. In B. Freed (ed.) *Second Language Acquisition in a Study Abroad Context* (pp. 37–66). Philadelphia, PA: John Benjamins.

Bucholtz, M. (2003) Sociolinguistic nostalgia and the authentication of identity. *Journal of Sociolinguistics* 7 (3), 398–416.

Canale, M. (1983) From communicative competence to communicative language pedagogy. In J.C. Richards and R.W. Schmidt (eds) *Language and Communication* (pp. 2–27). London: Longman.

Canale, M. and Swain, M. (1980) Theoretical aspects of communicative approaches to second language teaching and testing. *Applied Linguistics* 1, 1–47.

Celce-Murcia, M. (1995) The elaboration of sociolinguistic competence: Implications for teacher education. In J.E. Alatis, C.A. Straehle and M. Ronkin (eds) *Linguistics and the Education of Language Teachers: Ethnolinguistic, Psycholinguistic, and Sociolinguistic Aspects. Proceedings of the Georgetown University Round Table on Languages and Linguistics, 2005* (pp. 699–710). Washington, DC: Georgetown University Press.

Celce-Murcia, M. (2007) Rethinking the role of communicative competence in teaching. In E. Alcon Soler and M.P. Safront Jorda (eds) *Intercultural Language Use and Language Teaching* (pp. 41–57). Dordrecht: Springer.

Celce-Murcia, M., Dörnyei, Z. and Thurrell, S. (1995) A pedagogical framework for communicative competence: A pedagogically motivated model with content specifications. *Issues in Applied Linguistics* 6 (2), 5–35.

Chomsky, N. (1965) *Aspects of a Theory of Syntax*. Cambridge, MA: MIT Press.

Cooper, D.E. (1983) *Authenticity and Learning: Nietzsche's Educational Philosophy*. London: Routledge and Keagan Paul.

Eckert, P. (2003) Elephants in the room. *Journal of Sociolinguistics* 7 (3), 392–397.

Freed, B.F. (1995) *Second Language Acquisition in a Study Abroad Context*. Philadelphia, PA: John Benjamins.

Hall, J.K. (1993) The role of oral practices in the accomplishment of our everyday lives: The sociocultural dimension of interaction with implications for the learning of another language. *Applied Linguistics* 14, 145–167.

Hall, J.K. (1995) (Re)creating our worlds with words: A sociohistorical perspective of face-to face interaction. *Applied Linguistics* 16, 206–232.

Hall, J.K., Hellermann J. and Pekarek Doehler, S. (eds) (2011) *L2 Interactional Competence and Development*. Bristol: Multilingual Matters.

Hymes, D. (1972) On communicative competence. In J.B. Pride and J. Holmes (eds) *Sociolinguistics* (pp. 269–293). Harmondsworth: Penguin.

Jackson, J. (2008) *Language, Identity and Study Abroad: Sociocultural Perspectives*. London: Equinox.

Jacoby, S. and Ochs, E. (1995) Co-construction: An introduction. *Language and Social Interaction* 28 (3), 171–183.

Kinginger, C. (2004) Alice doesn't live here anymore: Foreign language learning as identity (re)construction. In A. Pavlenko and A. Blackledge (eds) *Negotiation of Identities in Multilingual Contexts* (pp. 219–42). Clevedon: Multilingual Matters.

Kinginger, C. (2008) Language learning in study abroad: Case studies of Americans in France. *Modern Language Journal*, Monograph, 1.

Kinginger, C. (2009) *Language Learning and Study Abroad: A Critical Review of Research*. Basingstoke: Palgrave Macmillan.

Kinginger, C. and Belz, J. (2005) Socio-cultural perspective on pragmatic development in foreign language learning: Microgenetic case studies from telecollaboration and residence abroad. *Intercultural Pragmatics* 2, 369–421.

Kinginger, C. and Farrell, K. (2004) Assessing development of metapragmatic awareness in study abroad. *Frontiers: The Interdisciplinary Journal of Study Abroad* 10, 19–42.

Kramsch, C. (1997) The privilege of the nonnative speaker. *Modern Language Journal* 112 (3), 359–369.

Kramsch, C. (2008) Ecological perspectives on foreign language education. *Language Teaching* 41 (3), 389–408.

Levine, G. (2009) L2 learner talk-about-language as social discursive practice. *L2 Journal* 1 (1), 19–41.

Long, M. (1991) Focus on form: A design feature in language teaching methodology. In K. de Bot, R.B. Ginsberg and C. Kramsch (eds) *Foreign Language Research in Cross-cultural Perspective* (pp. 39–52). Amsterdam: John Benjamins.

MacDonald, M.N., Badger, R. and Dasli, M. (2006) Authenticity, culture, and language learning. *Language and Intercultural Communication* 6 (3–4), 250–261.

McGregor, J. (2014) 'Your mind says one thing but your emotions do another': Language, emotion, and developing transculturality in study abroad. *Die Unterrichtspraxis/Teaching German*, 47, 109–120.

Masuda, K. (2011) Acquiring interactional competence in a study abroad context: Japanese language learners' use of the interactional particle *ne*. *Modern Language Journal* 95 (4), 519–540.

Müller, M. (2011) Learners' identity negotiations and beliefs about pronunciation in study abroad contexts. Unpublished doctoral dissertation, University of Waterloo.

Niedzielski, N.A. and Preston, D.R. (2000) Folk linguistics. *Trends in Linguistics: Studies and Monographs 122*. Berlin: Mouton de Gruyter.

Pellegrino Aveni, V. (2005) *Study Abroad and Second Language Use: Constructing the Self*. New York: Cambridge University Press.

Polanyi, L. (1995) Language learning and living abroad: Stories from the field. In B.F. Freed (ed.) *Second Language Acquisition in a Study Abroad Context* (pp. 271–291). Philadelphia, PA: John Benjamins.

Silverstein, M. (2003) Indexical order and the dialectics of sociolinguistic life. *Language and Communication* 23 (3), 193–229.

Shively, R. (2013a) Learning to be funny in Spanish during a semester abroad: L2 humor development. *Modern Language Journal* 97 (4), 930–946.

Shively, R. (2013b) Out-of-class interaction during study abroad: Service encounters in Spain. *Spanish in Context* 10 (1), 53–91.
Shively, R. (2015) Developing interactional competence during study abroad: Listener responses in L2 Spanish. *System* 48, 86–98.
Slobin, D.I. (1987) Thinking for speaking. *Proceedings of the Thirteenth Annual Meeting of the Berkeley Linguistics Society*, 435–444.
Taguchi, N. (2014) Development of interactional competence in Japanese as a second language: Use of incomplete sentences as interactional resources. *Modern Language Journal* 98 (2), 518–535.
van Compernolle, R.A. (2014) *Sociocultural Theory and L2 Instructional Pragmatics*. Bristol: Multilingual Matters.
van Compernolle, R.A. (2015) *Interaction and Second Language Development: A Vygotskian Perspective*. Philadelphia, PA: John Benjamins.
van Lier, L. (2002) An ecological-semiotic perspective on language and linguistics. In C. Kramsch (ed.) *Language Acquisition and Language Socialization: Ecological Perspectives* (pp. 140–164). London: Continuum.
Young, R.F. (2011) Interactional competence in language learning, teaching, and testing. In E. Hinkel (ed.) *Handbook of Research in Second Language Teaching and Learning* (Vol. 2; pp. 426–443). London/New York: Routledge.

10 Focus on Form in the Wild

Gabriele Kasper and Alfred Rue Burch

Introduction

Learning requires attention to the thing that is being learned. Supported by a large body of research, an influential and longstanding direction in the study of instructed additional language (L2) learning derived from this requirement is an instructional principle called 'Focus on Form' (FonF; Doughty & Williams, 1998). FonF implies that during an ongoing meaning-oriented activity, a student's attention is directed to the form of the utterance (Long & Robinson, 1998), such as a selected word, its pronunciation or morphology, other grammatical features, or indeed sociolinguistic, discourse and pragmatic indicators.

Spurred by the interactionist hypothesis of second-language acquisition (SLA) (Mackey *et al.*, 2012), studies abound on how FonF is implemented through teaching materials and interactional arrangements, and what effect on L2 learning it has. Yet much less research has been devoted to the role of attention to language when L2 speakers learn another language in their lives outside organized instruction (see Barron, 2003; Hassall, 2006 for some exceptions). It is true that from its inception, SLA has been interested in 'spontaneous' language learning and development in immigrants' and sojourners' social environments at work and in their communities, with variable attention to the nexus of social context, language use and learning (Block, 2003; Klein, 1986; Norton, 2000; Perdue, 1993; Schmidt, 1983; Schumann, 1978).

A conversation-analytic (CA) perspective on SLA (CA-SLA) has pulled into view moments where participants turn to learning in the midst of pursuing some other activity in their lifeworld. 'Language learning in the wild' has become a lively research direction within CA-SLA (Brouwer, 2003; Greer, 2013; Ishida, 2009, 2011; Käänta *et al.*, 2013; Kurhila, 2001, 2006; Theodórsdóttir, 2011a, 2011b; Theodórsdóttir & Eskildsen, 2011; Wagner, 2016). Yet neither the older research strand on spontaneous L2 learning nor the recent studies on L2 learning in the wild have engaged with FonF. There are valid reasons for this. One is, of course, that the older research on spontaneous L2 learning predates the formulation of the FonF principle. But that does not account for the lack of uptake of FonF in the literature on spontaneous L2 learning since the 1990s. Rather, it appears that research on FonF has been confined to classrooms and the laboratory because these environments allow researchers to systematically manipulate learners' attention through teaching arrangements and experimental design. At the same time, directions in non-instructed SLA with an explicitly social orientation (e.g. Block, 2007; Norton, 2000) have shown little engagement with cognitive issues in L2 learning.

In the history of SLA, the dearth of research on FonF in the wild is not without irony. It was Schmidt and Frota's seminal study (1986) on Schmidt's learning of Brazilian Portuguese while he was living in that country that first formulated the need for learners to 'notice the gap' as a necessary condition for L2 learning. As is well known, this study became the cornerstone of the noticing hypothesis (Bergsleithner *et al.*, 2013; Schmidt, 2001), the crucial theoretical foundation of FonF as a principle of language pedagogy. Yet even the extensive classroom literature has barely begun to explore how attention to language form is generated, sustained and abandoned in face-to-face interaction, and what the consequences of these actions are. Studies under the interactionist hypothesis have typically focused on predetermined actions such as (teacher) corrections of student errors (recasts, Lyster & Saito, 2010) and have not examined how students may direct their attention to language form through other actions, or how resources other than language afford FonF. Put differently, interactionist research has sought to answer the classic question of how teachers' preplanned pedagogical actions affect student responses and learning outcomes, but the students' agentive participation and the competencies that make teachers' and students' language-oriented actions possible in the first place have largely remained under the radar.

For CA research on L2 learning in the wild, a major concern is to examine the linkage between participants' orientation to language as they strive to maintain or restore intersubjectivity and shifts from pursuing the activity at hand to L2 learning. Perhaps researchers investigating L2 learning in the wild have avoided pointing out the links to FonF in standard SLA in order to clearly demarcate CA's praxeological stance from the cognitivist conceptualization of L2 learning that underwrites the notion of FonF. Extending a proposal by Fasel Lauzon and Pekarek Doehler (2013) to respecify FonF as a principle of second-language pedagogy, we suggest that gains can be made from respecifying FonF from a praxeological perspective in settings specialized for language learning as well as in social activities in the wild. This respecification makes visible two kinds of connections: connections between L2 learning as a social activity in diverse social settings, and connections between CA-SLA and other SLA traditions that examine FonF in L2 learning.

Our interest in this chapter is in seeing how FonF comes about in the course of ordinary social activities that are not arranged for language learning. The analytical project is to make visible how, and with what consequences, the participants generate, sustain and abandon attention to language form through their coordinated actions in the ongoing social activity. The connection with the theme of this volume is: what are the competencies that L2 speakers and their interlocutors engage when they turn their attention to language form? In what sense are these competencies 'authentic'? How do they relate to the competencies that people engage to participate in social pursuits other than teaching and learning languages?

To begin, we will consider how CA analysis may afford a lens on the topics of authenticity in the essay by MacDonald et al. (2006) that are pertinent to this chapter. After describing how learning is understood in CA, we will unfold the notion of interactional competence as the condition that makes learning in interaction possible. The centerpiece of the chapter is the analysis of an extended segment of mundane conversation in which the participants shift the focus of their talk from an everyday topic to language form in order to address a gap in the L2 speaker's lexicon of Japanese. In the course of plugging the gap collaboratively, the L1 speaker runs into a problem writing the character (*kanji*) of a synonym. After the L2 speaker practices the conjugation of the new word, the L1 speaker returns to her writing difficulty. When the L2 speaker shows that she recognizes the *kanji*, the L1 speaker treats the reversal of epistemic status as incongruent with the normative distribution of category-bound predicates: as a literate L1 speaker of Japanese she is supposed to know *kanji* whereas the L2 speaker is not expected to have that knowledge. From a purely cognitive concern with understanding, knowing and learning a word that comes up in the talk, the interaction thus shifts to knowing *kanji* as an issue of moral rights and obligations. The chapter ends with some thoughts about what can be gained for SLA theory and the practices of language education by respecifying FonF as proposed in the analysis.

Authenticity

Authenticity is not a concept used in CA, but the notion can usefully be inspected from a CA perspective. MacDonald et al. (2006) problematize the idea of authenticity as a stable property of (abstract and concrete) objects – *authenticity of correspondence (text authenticity, competence authenticity, learner authenticity)* and *authenticity of genesis (classroom authenticity)* (the distinction between the two forms of authenticity is attributed to Cooper, 1983). Instead they propose to ask whose text, whose competence and whose meaning defines authenticity in the domain, and what makes classroom texts authentic. In the context of language learning in the wild, *authenticity of genesis*, defined as the *site* of learning, is a moot point since the domain in which learning takes place and the target domain are one and the same, that is, the L2 speaker's lifeworld. In the sense of the *processes* through which learning takes place, *authenticity of genesis* makes relevant a consideration of how learning is conceptualized and investigated in CA-SLA. The crucial point here is that for CA and cognate traditions there is no learning mechanism separate from or in addition to the sense-making procedures and interactional competencies through which social members, including very young children, manage their participation in social life. Language, culture and interaction are learnable because they are on constant public exhibition in the 'objective production and objective display of commonsense knowledge of everyday activities as observable and reportable phenomena' (Garfinkel & Sacks, 1970: 342) and the 'inferential visibility of moral conduct' (Edwards, 1997; Kasper & Wagner, 2014: 194). Consequently, the interactional competencies that enable interaction also enable learning, whether in the wild (Ishida, 2009, 2011; Kääntä et al., 2013; Theodórsdóttir, 2011a, 2011b; Wagner, 2016) or in classrooms (Lee, 2006; Macbeth, 2000; Majlesi & Broth, 2012; Mori & Hasegawa, 2009). For researchers and practitioners who are concerned with learning and development in any arena of social life, it is therefore critical to have an explicit, empirically grounded understanding of how interactional competence can be conceptualized (an ontological question) and how it can be apprehended (an epistemological and methodological question).

Interactional Competence

At the most general and abstract level, interactional competencies are the socially and culturally available practices that people use to manage diverse social undertakings, from everyday activities in the home to frequent and infrequent institutional interactions (classroom lessons or weekly meetings at the workplace versus a citizenship interview, for instance) and arrangements for research such as survey interviews and laboratory experiments. These visibly displayed competencies are authentic, that is, real and consequential for the participants in the ongoing interaction. There is no external warrant of authenticity by teachers, researchers or other parties. What is real and consequential for the participants is not necessarily correct, appropriate or effective for them. With displays of non-understanding, corrections and other forms of repair, participants can treat something that the other party said or did, or that the speaker said or did themselves, as incorrect, inappropriate or ineffective. That does not make that bit of conduct any less authentic than behavior that is tacitly treated as correct, appropriate and effective (tacitly, because normative behavior usually goes unnoticed). Normative and non-normative conduct are produced by the same interactional methods.

Partly under the influence of CA, interactional competence made an early appearance in applied linguistics (Hall, 1993, 1999; He & Young, 1998; Kramsch, 1986; Schmidt, 1983). A sustained effort to specify interactional competence in L2 use, learning and development across a range of social settings has been under way since the mid-2000s and is documented in several book publications (Gardner & Wagner, 2004; Hall *et al.*, 2011; Hellermann, 2008; Nguyen, 2012; Nguyen & Kasper, 2009; Pallotti & Wagner, 2011). To be interactionally competent in a particular activity – dispensing medicines (Nguyen, 2012), participating in professional meetings (Ford, 2008), teaching English for specific purposes (Okada, 2015) – requires that participants collaboratively organize their undertaking through activity-specific configurations of interactional methods, primarily turn-taking and action sequences, and vocal and non-vocal resources assembled as local, contextually sensitive practices (Young & Miller, 2004). To the extent that interaction is *talk*, language or languages are an important type of resource. Yet when participants cannot draw on a shared linguistic repertoire, or when that repertoire is very limited, they still interact successfully. Preverbal children (e.g. Lerner *et al.*, 2011) are as much competent interactants as are adults with language impairments (Goodwin, 2006). From an evolutionary perspective, Levinson (2006: 42) notes that language is the explicandum, not the explicans: humans did not evolve language, then get involved in a special kind of social life; it was just the reverse. Language must have evolved *for* something for which there was a ready need – that is, for communication in interaction.

The primacy of interaction over language (Levinson, 2006; Schegloff, 2006) has significant implications for understanding language learning and development, and for designing instructional interventions to promote L2 learning. From the empirical literature, Levinson (2006: 45–46) assembled the properties of a universal 'interaction engine' that is foundational to interactional competence. Below we provide our version of Levinson's list. In addition to the generic interactional organizations – turn-taking, sequence organization and repair – features of the machine include the following:

(1) Recipients respond to actions not behaviors. In order to respond to an action, the recipient must interpret the observable behavior at the sequential moment it appears.
(2) Actions are *recipient designed* (Sacks & Schegloff, 1979; Sacks *et al.*, 1974); that is, they are produced for a specific co-participant. Recipient design takes into account the recipient's knowledge, interests, identities and stances. Therefore a recipient can presume that the action addressed to them is designed to be interpretable specifically for them.
(3) From (1) and (2), it follows that interaction is cooperative in the sense that participants ineluctably listen to, interpret and recipient design actions in turns and sequences. Participants also organize their actions in ways that contribute to the larger undertaking. Cooperation in this sense is a system constraint that operates entirely independently of individual motivation or volition. It does not mean that interaction is harmonious.
(4) Interaction is intensely orderly, but the interaction order is contingent, 'governed not by rule but by expectation' (Levinson, 2006: 45). Interaction cannot be planned out in advance.

(5) Interaction is organized through complementary relational discourse identities (Zimmerman, 1998) such as speaker-listener, teller-recipient, questioner-answerer. The turn-taking mechanism (Sacks *et al.*, 1974) makes alternating discourse identities available. The reciprocity of discourse identities is constrained in formal institutional talk (Heritage & Clayman, 2010).
(6) Interaction self-generates participation structures (Goffman, 1981; Goodwin, 2007) that regulate access and discourse identities, and reflexively transform as the activity progresses.
(7) Interaction is closely timed. Responses are expected to come immediately (although see Mushin & Gardner, 2011, for a cultural adaptation). Delays generate inferences that non-normative circumstances are at play (see Bilmes, 2014, on the difference between silence and delay).
(8) Interaction in face-to-face situations is multimodal. Participants use gesture, facial expression, posture, spatial orientations and materials in the environment to produce actions, identities, stances and social relations (Streeck *et al.*, 2011). Whether or not they include verbal resources, multisemiotic practices are laminated in dense simultaneous and sequential configurations (Goodwin, 2013). These resources and practices exponentially increase the complexity of interaction, but the richness of resources and their contingent assembly on a moment-by-moment basis in no way invalidates Sack's insight that there is 'order at all points' in interaction (Sacks, 1992: 484).

As our analysis will show, the interaction engine propels participants' activity-specific interactional competencies. It is visibly at work not only when the participants get on with the activity at hand, but it also generates shifts to language form and sustains *in situ* language learning when language resources are lacking. Through their unproblematic and problematic understandings, the recipient design of their turns, and their coordinated nonvocal actions, the participants can be seen to mutually 'authenticate' (Bucholtz, 2003) their participation in the activity from moment to moment and the transformations of the participation structure. Based on data from mundane talk involving an L2 speaker of Japanese, we will analyze how the participants engage multisemiotic practices as they achieve, maintain and abandon FonF, and what activities precede and follow the language-focused actions.

Method

Participants and setting

The focal participant in this study is Peony (pseudonym), an L2 speaker of Japanese. Peony had lived and worked in Tokyo for roughly two years prior to the recording of the data. Having grown up bilingually as a speaker of Taiwanese and Mandarin, she also has a high level of ability in English and is learning Japanese. Based on a corpus of around 14 hours of video-recorded conversations, the larger study investigates how Peony interacts with various co-participants in a range of everyday settings in Japan. In the data for this study, Peony's co-participant is Keiko, an L1 speaker of Japanese who also speaks English as a second language. The two women have known each other for a number of years and get together socially. In the excerpts analyzed below, Peony and Keiko are talking over tea and dessert at a café. In accomplishing this everyday activity, they draw on resources from different semiotic fields (Goodwin, 2013): linguistic and non-linguistic vocalizations; embodiment, including gesture, posture and facial expressions; and technologies such as smart phones, tablets and writing. The semiotic fields that the participants attend to simultaneously and successively are as much afforded by the setting ('brought along') as they produce the setting in the first place ('brought about', Giddens, 1976). Setting can thus be understood as the emerging and constantly evolving 'contextual configurations' (Goodwin, 2013) from which social actions and activities are built.

Data collection and transcription

The interaction was recorded by Peony with a digital voice recorder and a video camera as part of a longitudinal study of her everyday interactions in Japanese, conducted by the second author. The method of entrusting the research participants themselves with the data collection, without the researcher present (Cook, 2008; Ishida, 2009, 2011; Theodórsdóttir, 2011a, 2011b), is common in studies of second-language interaction and learning outside classroom settings ('remote observation method', Iino, 1999; see also Lee & Kinginger, this volume; McGregor, this volume). Peony's conversation with Keiko would have occurred regardless of the data collection or research agenda. The researcher chose neither the setting nor the topics for the conversation, or the focal participant's interlocutors.

As is standard practice in CA, the transcription of the talk adopts the conventions developed by Gail Jefferson (e.g. Jefferson, 2004). There is no equivalent standard for transcribing non-vocal aspects such as gesture, gaze and physical actions. The conventions used in this study have been developed by the second author, based on various systems in the literature on CA and multimodal analysis (see Appendix A). Data are analyzed from the complementary perspectives of CA (Sacks, 1992; Sidnell & Stivers, 2013), membership categorization analysis (MCA, Sacks, 1992; Stokoe, 2012), and multimodal analysis (Streeck *et al.*, 2011).

Analysis

Prior to the excerpts analyzed here, Keiko introduced the topic of *shootengai*, translated here as 'shopping arcade', also referred to as 'covered market' in English vernacular. These shopping quarters are common throughout Japanese metropolitan areas. They generally house a variety of small retail stores, including locally owned food, clothing, electronics and stationary shops as well as more specialized vendors. The most notable and defining features of *shootengai* are: (a) they are located on streets (unlike markets and malls); (b) these streets are generally restricted to pedestrian traffic (like pedestrian zones); and (c) they are in large part covered to provide protection from the elements (unlike pedestrian zones). *Shootengai* are part of the cultural geography of urban Japan. As such, any resident of urban areas in Japan is expected to know about them.

FonF: A lexical gap in Peony's knowledge of Japanese

Before the beginning of Excerpt 1, Peony brings up the *shootengai* in Kichijoji, a popular and fashionable neighborhood in West Tokyo outside the urban center (Figure 10.1). In so doing, she displays her knowledge of the cultural geography of the area and shows herself as a culturally competent member. Keiko comments upon how lively and popular (*sakaeteru*) the *shootengai* in Kichijoji is, which is where we pick up the conversation. As we see below, Peony does not know the word *sakaeru*, which leads to an extended language-focused sequence aimed at helping Peony to understand the word and plug her knowledge gap. To this effect, the participants mobilize laminated configurations of semiotic resources to implement such generic actions as repair, word definitions and epistemic status checks. These actions work as methods to accomplish intersubjectivity, language learning and the construction of memberships in social categories.

In Excerpt 10.1, Peony and Keiko successively transition from the conversation about the mutually known *shootengai* to language teaching and learning. In this process, they construct an asymmetrical epistemic relationship in the domain of language knowledge about Japanese.

Excerpt 10.1 [ARB-P20140110 41:28]

```
036    K     ↑kichijooji wa moo, sakaeteru yo ↑ne¿
              PLACE      TOP IP  bustling   IP  IP
              The one in Kichijoji is really bustling, isn't it?

037          (0.3)
```

```
038    P      sakae:¿
              bustl-
              bustl-

       k      +RH down
039    K      +sakaeteru.
              bustling
              Bustling.

040           (0.9)

041    P      akai.=
              red
              Red ((MISREPETITION))

042    K      =sakaeteru tte yuu no wa↓:,  (0.4) hanjoo shiteru,
              bustling   QT  say NOM TOP          prosperous do

       k      +GZ>slightly left
043           [+aato
                and
              Bustling is.... it's prosperous, and...

       p      +nod
044    P      [+°°↑uh↓°°

045           (1.3)

       k                       +GZ>P
046    K      °>nan no,<° +sakaeteru to shiranai?
               what         bustling QT  know-NEG
              What's that. You don't know bustling?

047           (0.7)

048    P      [°°(    )°°

       k                   +GZ>right
049    K      [sakaeru +tte::
               bustle   QT
              So bustle is...

050           (0.3)

       k      +GZ>table
       k      +RH traces part of 栄
       p                       +GZ>K's tracing-----
051    K      +kanji wa, +(0.4) koo yuu yatsu.
              character TOP     this kind thing
              The kanji is... like this.
```

```
        k    GZ>P, traces the final two strokes slowly
        p    body turns right (to bag), brings up paper
052          (2.2)

        k    +body turns left (to bag)
053     K    +(tatoeba/a pen) (0.6) pen ne?
              for example      pen IP
             (for example / a pen) ... a pen?
```

Figure 10.1 Shootengai in Kichijoji (photo courtesy of Jun Kametani)

In line 36, Keiko offers an assessment of the shopping arcade in Kichijoji by describing it as **sakaeteru** ('lively' or 'bustling'). With the interactional particle **yo ne**, Keiko treats the assessed object as equally available to Peony and invites a second assessment (Hayano, 2011). This action reveals two expectations on Keiko's part about Peony's epistemic access: that Peony knows the shopping arcade in Kichijoji, and that she knows the lexical item **sakaeteru**. Peony first responds by 'sounding out' (van Compernolle, 2010) **sakaeteru** with a partial repetition and rising intonation that marks the word as troublesome. After a delay (line 38), Keiko treats the other-initiation of repair as a hearing problem by repeating the word in full with falling intonation (line 39). In so doing, Keiko orients to the preference for trying the easiest solution to an other-initiation of repair first (Svennevig, 2008). Yet the repetition does not result in understanding. After a lengthy pause (line 40), Peony repeats the word as **akai**, which means 'red'. In response, Keiko treats Peony's misrepetition as evidence that Peony does not recognize **sakaeteru**. As a method to resolve the problem, Keiko offers a definition of the lexical meaning of **sakaeteru** (line 42). Specifically, she provides a synonym based upon Chinese morphology (**hanjoo shiteru**), similar to how one might provide a synonym in English by using a word deriving from Greek or Latin. By drawing on Chinese morphology rather than offering a native Japanese-based synonym or using descriptive practices to get the meaning of the problematic word across, Keiko reveals her assumption that Peony, as a competent speaker of Mandarin, will recognize the Chinese-based word as a matter of category-bound knowledge.[1]

Peony's quiet 'uh' in line 44 and the ensuing 1.3 second pause show that Keiko's attributions are not working out. Resorting to another tact, Keiko makes an 'explicit epistemic status check' (Sert, 2013) by asking whether Peony knows the word. Taking the ensuing silence as a disconfirmation, Keiko provides the citation form of the word **sakaeru** (rather than the stative form **sakaeteru** used earlier), followed by the quotative particle **tte**, a turn format (line 49) that projects further talk about the word. While the talk up to this point was directed towards plugging a gap in Peony's lexical knowledge of Japanese in order to solve an understanding problem and resume the topical talk about the Kichijoji shopping arcade, the activity is now completely shifting towards the lexical item as the topic of the talk. In line 51, Keiko turns to a common cultural practice for achieving word recognition among speakers of languages who share a writing system based on Chinese characters, such as Japanese and Mandarin (see Appendix A for a description of *kanji* and Chinese characters). Using her right index finger, she partially traces the *kanji* on the table (line 51, see also Figure 10.2) while Peony maintains her gaze on Keiko's hand. With these coordinated actions, the participants engage in a shared constellation of resources that includes their knowledge of *kanji* as well as the embodied action of tracing the relevant character out.

Figure 10.2 Trace of sakaeru, line 051

As Keiko is tracing the character, she also provides the indexical description **koo yuu yatsu** 'like this', which treats her tracing of the character under Peony's gaze as a sufficient recognitional. However, before Keiko finishes tracing the final two strokes, Peony has turned away to get her notepad from her bag (line 52, see also Figure 10.3). With this action, Peony shows that recognition has not been achieved. Keiko follows suit with a complementary search in her bag while formulating her search target, **pen ne?** 'a pen?'. The ordered search actions project another endemic practice, sedimented from prior use between Peony and other interlocutors, namely to write a character on paper in order to accomplish word recognition.

While the excerpt exposes a gap in Peony's lexical knowledge, it illustrates at the same time the interactional competencies that are brought to bear by both Peony and Keiko as they collaboratively navigate an emerging language-related topic as the primary concern of their talk. By first treating a lexical trouble source as a hearing problem, the participants aim for achieving understanding as a condition for advancing the talk about their current topic. When the trouble reveals itself as a lexical gap, they deploy a sequence of sequences (Schegloff, 2007) to level the knowledge asymmetry. These ordered sequences are built upon each other through multiple semiotic resources, beginning with a definition of the item's lexical meaning in

Figure 10.3 Trace of sakaeru, line 052

210 Authenticity, Language and Interaction in Second Language Contexts

Japanese through embodied actions such as tracing the *kanji* on the table and accessing the material tools for subsequently writing it. With these mutually recognized and tightly coordinated practices, the participants jointly authenticate FonF as an emergent, discursively achieved activity.

FonF: A successful and a problematic use of *kanji*

Excerpt 10.2 picks up the talk a few lines later as Keiko writes the *kanji* on the paper that Peony has provided. While they are working towards

Excerpt 10.2 [ARB-P20140110 42:12]

```
        p       GZ>paper
        k       writing (栄 sakae)
068             (2.9)

069     K       sa[kaeru.
                bustle
                Bustle.

070     P       [a- aa. (0.2) sagae, hai. (0.2) agae¿
                              *bustle yes         *bustle

        k       +GZ>P
071     K       +sakaeru.
                bustle
                Bustle.

072             (0.3)

        p       +nod
073     P       +uh uh [uh.

        k               +GZ>paper +pen>paper
074     K               [+sakaete, +ato wa >°nan dakke na°<=
                         bustling  and TOP  what COP  IP

        k               +GZ>outside
075             =[+muzukashii kanji=wakaranai naa.
                   difficult character understand-NEG IP
                It's bustling, and, what was that. I don't know that hard kanji.

        p               +GZ>K>paper
076     P       =[+uh:::.
```

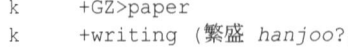

```
        k       +GZ>paper
        k       +writing (繁盛 hanjoo?)                          +GZ>P
```

Focus on Form in the Wild   211

```
077   K     +nanka, konna, koo nan, (0.4) >nanka< koo [nan,+
              something this way this NOM    something this NOM
            Like, this, this way... like this way,

       p                                              +nod
078    P                                              [+a- a- (0.2)

       p                            +GZ>K
079          uh::. (0.2) >wakaru [+wakaru.<
                         understand understand
             uh... I got it, I got it.

       k                       +BH slightly up
080    K                       [+sono-
                                that
             That-

081          (0.4)

082    P     ippai [(aru) hito¿
             many   *exist person
             There are a lot of people

       k                  +BH wave up toward face
083    K                  [minna-+
                           everyone
             Everyone-

084          (0.2)

       k     +nod
       k     +LH down
       k          +RH waving toward self      +RH circle out
085    K     +soo,=+ippai >hito ga kite, ippai< +ka::u?
             yeah  many   person SUB come-CONT, many buy
             Yeah, a lot of people come, and they buy a lot of stuff?

       p     +nod
086    P     +hai.
             yes
             Yes.

       k     RH down
087          (0.3)

       k     +GZ>slightly left
       k             +GZ>P
       k                  +RH PRD up, downbeats moving right
088    K     +toka .hh (.) +>omise ga< ippai narande[te,
             and           shop SUB    many line up-CONT
             And the shops are all lined up

089    P                                        [nn nn [nn

       k                                               +GZ>RH
       k                                               +RH shake
090    K                                               [+>hito ga
                                                        person SUB

       k     +GZ>P  +RH circling              +RH down
       p                      +nodding
```

```
091            +ippai,=+nigiwat-  +(0.3) >kiteru<=[nigiwa-tteru +basho.=
               many    crowded           coming   crowded       place
               There are a lot of people, it's crowde- ... they come. It's a crowded place.

                p                                            +nod
092             P                                            [+hnn:::.

093     P    =↑aa:::[:: nigiwatteru¿
                       crowded
             hnnn, aa::: it's crowded?
```

achieving mutual understanding, Keiko shows uncertainty about how the character she is writing to enable Peony to recognize the word is actually written. Peony provides a candidate understanding of the word in her own formulation.

As projected by the participants' getting pen and paper in Excerpt 10.1, Keiko writes the *kanji* for *sakae* (栄) under Peony's watch, followed by saying the citation form **sakaeru**. As Keiko completes the first mora (**sa**) (see Appendix B for a description of mora), Peony overlaps with a claim of recognition (**a- aa.**), suggesting that she has now identified the meaning of the character. Yet she still has not grasped the phonological form of the word, as shown by her non-target-like repetitions (line 70) and Keiko's correction (line 71). Rather than attempting to repeat the word yet another time, Peony claims recognition (**uh uh uh**) (line 73) without demonstrating that she has actually grasped the word (Sacks, 1992). However Keiko treats the recognition claim as a sufficient warrant of understanding to consider the matter resolved.

Keiko now continues the language-focused activity by picking up the Sino-Japanese synonym for *sakaeru* from her turn in line 42, *hanjoo* 'prosperous'. In contrast to her confident writing of the character for *sakae* when it turned out that Peony did not know the word, Keiko prefaces her writing of the character for *hanjoo* by assessing it as difficult (**muzukashii**) and makes a 'claim of insufficient knowledge' (Sert & Walsh, 2013) with the assertion that she does not know how to write it (line 75). Simultaneous with writing the character (supposedly *hanjoo*, although this is hard to tell from the camera angle), Keiko audibly displays her focus on the activity of writing by saying **nanka, konna, koo nan, (0.4) >nanka< koo nan,** 'like, this, this way … like this way'. The verbalizations treat the writing as effortful and solitary and signal to Peony that turn taking is temporarily put on hold.

When Keiko finishes writing and directs her gaze to Peony as a method to re-establish turn taking and solicit a response, Peony again claims recognition with a nod and vocalizations that index a change in epistemic state (**a- a-**), followed by repeated claims to understanding with **wakaru, wakaru** 'I got it, I got it'. She then upgrades her understanding *claim* to a *display* of understanding (Koole, 2010; Sacks, 1992) by providing a candidate definition with **ippai (aru) hito?** 'there are a lot of people' (line 82). Keiko agrees with Peony's definition by nodding and the agreement token **soo** 'yeah'. Next she reformulates and expands upon Peony's formulation while Peony supplies recipient tokens (lines 85–93). In her response **ippai >hito ga kite, ippai< ka::u?** 'a lot of people come, and they buy a lot of stuff?' (line 85) Keiko treats the structural resources of Peony's preceding turn as a 'public substrate' (Goodwin, 2013: 9) that she selectively reuses and transforms to build a more specific description of the shopping arcade as **sakaeru.** Building upon the prior formulation, Keiko says >**hito ga ippai, =nigiwat- (0.3) >kiteru <=nigiwa-tteru basho.** 'There are a lot of people, it's crowde- ... they come. It's a crowded place.' (lines 90–91), and once again recycles a version of these prior turns, this time adding to the description yet another near-synonym for *sakaeru*, **nigiwatteru** 'crowded'. Peony latches on a recognition claim **aa::::** and repeats **nigiwatteru** with slightly rising intonation (line 93), thus offering her understanding up for confirmation.

In this excerpt, the participants again achieve understanding through the practice of writing a problematic lexical item with its *kanji*. Keiko's claim that she does not know how to write the character proves inconsequential since Peony is able to recognize it. Through candidate understandings and reformulations, the participants accomplish a shared understanding of two near-synonyms for **sakaeru** 'bustling', the initial trouble source and knowledge gap in Peony's lexical repertoire of Japanese, **hanjoo suru** 'prosperous' and **nigiwatteru** 'crowded'. They thus generate multiple occasions for focus shifts to the written form and to near-synonyms in the talk. Following Peony's show of understanding after the *hanjoo* sequence, it is noticeable that Keiko's descriptions specifically characterize the *shootengai* in Kichijoji rather than offering abstract definitions of **sakaeru**. With the shared semiotic repertoire in place, the participants show themselves ready to shift their talk entirely back to its previous topical focus.

FonF: Doing conjugation

However, in Excerpt 10.3, Peony returns to a focus on the initial trouble source, the lexical item *sakaeru*. In particular, she is seeking to confirm the difference between the citation form and the stative form of the verb.

Excerpt 10.3 [ARB-P20140110 42:33]

```
        k                       +click pen, pen PNT>forward
        k                                   +RHIF PNT>forward
094     K           [soo soo.=+shichijooji +tte:,
                    yeah yeah PLACE         QT

        k     +RHIF PNT>P    +RH down
```

```
095              [+>soo yuu toko<+ [deshoo?
                    that kind place COP
                 Yeah yeah. Shichijoji is that kind of place, right?

096       P     [uhn.             [sakaeru:?
                 yeah              bustle
                 Yeah... bustle?

          k     +nod
097       K     +°n[n.°
                 Yeah.

          p            +RHIF forward down
098       P     [+saeteru?
                   *bustling
                 Bustling ((MISREPETITION))

099       K     [sakaeteru.
                 bustling
                 Bustling

          p      +nod
          p      +RH>cheek
100       P     [+hai hai.
                 yes yes
                 Yes, yes.

101             (0.3)

          p     +GZ>paper
          p     +LH>paper          +LH retract
          k           +GZ>paper
102       P     +saka:e+teru. [uh: +sakaeteru.
                 bustling           bustling
                 Bustling. Uhh, bustling.

          k                       +clicking pen
103       K                      [soo. +sakaeteru.
                                   yeah bustling
                 Yeah. Bustling.

          k     writing (さかえる sakaeru?)
104             (0.3)

          p     +nod
105       P     +↑uhn.

          k     writing
106             (3.4)

107       P     nn::.
```

```
         k       writing, hands paper to P
108              (4.1)

         p                       +RH>paper, puts paper in front of her
         p                       +nod
109      P       ↑nn::, sakaeru. [+nn nn nn.
                         bustle
                 Yeah, bustle. Yeah yeah yeah.

110      K                       [nn::.

111              sakaeru.
                 bustle
                 Yeah. Bustle.

         p               +GZ>K+       +GZ>paper
         p               +RH taps paper
112      P       hhyeah, +kichijooji +(0.3) [sakaeru.
                          PLACE              bustle
                 Hhyeah, Kichijoji... bustle.

113      K                               [sakaeru...
                                          bustle
                 Bustle.
```

After affirming Peony's understanding of **nigiwatteru**, Keiko brings the talk back to the topic of Kichijoji (pronouncing the place name with a non-standard initial voiceless alveolo-palatal sibilant) by describing the location with the anaphoric reference **soo yuu toko** 'that kind of place' (line 95) and soliciting agreement from a position of epistemic primacy with the stance marker **deshoo** (Cook, 2012). Peony agrees with the assessment shortly after Keiko produces the place name, showing her (correct) expectation of where the turn is heading. Yet overlapping with the turn-final **deshoo**, Peony says **sakaeru:¿**. Although the word meaning could be heard as a second assessment, the citation form and rising intonation treat the item as a learning object. The talk reverts again to its previous language focus as Peony solicits confirmation of the word form. Following Keiko's confirmation, Peony manipulates the word form by saying **saeteru¿**, ostensibly an unsuccessful attempt at producing the stative form *sakaeteru* (see Appendix B for the difference between citation and stative forms of verbs in Japanese). Keiko aligns with Peony's treatment of the current activity as *doing conjugation* (see Brouwer, 2004, on *doing pronunciation* in L2 talk) by correcting the mispronunciation to **sakaeteru**. (line 99). After the correction, Peony practices the form by repeating it twice (line 102), the second time in overlap with Keiko's affirmation of the form practice. At this point, the correction sequence is complete and the talk could return to the topic of Kichijoji. Yet Keiko treats Peony's knowledge of the trouble source item as still at risk. Launching a post-completion sequence (Schegloff, 2007), she writes what appears to be the citation form *sakaeru* in hiragana. When

216 Authenticity, Language and Interaction in Second Language Contexts

Keiko hands Peony the paper, Peony emphatically affirms her recognition of the word with a high-pitched turn-initial affirmation token and repetition of the citation form. In overlap with a series of turn-final affirmation tokens (line 109), Keiko re-affirms Peony's recognition display by repeating Peony's preceding turn. Now that the parties have mutually reaffirmed that they have reached a shared understanding of *sakaeru*, Peony signals with a turn-initial code-switched **hhyeah** that she is ready to leave the vocabulary activity behind after applying the citation form *sakaeru* to describe the place referent Kichijoji (line 112), in overlap with Keiko's collaborative completion of the turn.

Excerpt 10.3 is framed by both participants' attempts to return the topic from a language-focused activity to the talk about a mutually known locality. After Peony insists on practicing the morphology of *sakaeru* and so resumes the FonF, Keiko engages yet another writing practice to secure Peony's knowledge of the target item by writing it in hiragana. Following a strong recognition display, Peony's application of the target item to characterize the shopping arcade shows her readiness to end the vocabulary learning activity and resume the disrupted everyday talk. Yet this time around, it is Keiko who launches a language-focused topic.

FonF: Keiko's uncertain knowledge of a *kanji*

Up to now, the participants have treated Peony's preoccupation with learning a new word as par for the course. Her lexical gap generated an epistemic asymmetry between Keiko as expert and occasioned teacher of Japanese and Peony as a novice and student. In common sense understanding, these complementary knowledge statuses are normatively associated with the categories of L1 speaker and L2 speaker, respectively. For the participants as well, the association of category membership and knowledge is self-evident. But we also observed that on one occasion, Keiko showed having trouble writing a character. As the talk returns to the writing of that 'difficult' character in Excerpt 10.4, the knowledge asymmetry between Peony and Keiko reverses.

Excerpt 10.4 [ARB-P20140110 42:46]

```
113    K                          [sakaeru.=>demo ko-< tabun=
                                   bustle   but this-  maybe

       p       +GZ>K
       k       +GZ>paper
       k       +LH across table>paper
       k               +body left (to bag)
114            =+>kono< kanji +$machigaeteru$. [>tabun.<
               this character mistaken              maybe
       Bustle. But this- maybe this character is wrong. Maybe.
```

Focus on Form in the Wild   217

```
         p                            +GZ>paper
         p                            +mouth agape
115      P                            [+khh

         k    +GZ>P              +body left, pulls out tablet
116      K    +shoobai hanjoo no +(hoo chotto imi shirabete).
              commerce prosperity GEN one little meaning look-up-CONT

117           .hh de, muzukashii hoo yatta ↓no.=
                  and difficult one do-PST NOM
              I looked up the prosperity related to commerce and, and chose the difficult one.

         p                   +RH>pen               +writing
118      P    =muzukashi-. (.) +a- wakaru okuru. (0.3) +tabun chi-
              difficult.          understand send        maybe *

119           kore
              this
              Difficult. a- I got it (*I got it) (0.3) maybe th- this.

         k    GZ at tablet
120           (0.7)

         k    GZ at tablet
121      K    hon↑too?
              really
              Really?

         p    GZ>K
122           (0.6)

         k    +leans in, GZ>paper
         p    +hands paper across table
123      P    +tabun kore?
              maybe this
              Maybe this?

124           (0.6)

         k         +GZ>P                   +lean in (tablet>chest)
         p         +pulls paper back +GZ>paper
125      K    SOO. +$NANDE SHITTERU  +NO, A [+YABAI.$
              yeah why know          NOM  ah  terrible
              Yeah! How do you know that!?! Oh my god.

         p                                  +pen>paper
126      P                                  [+ŭŭ:::

         p    writing
127      P    [nn:::

         p    writing
         k     +GZ>paper
128      K    [+.hhh $chotto matte, doo yatte kaiku n¿$
                      little wait   how do    *write
              Hold on, how do you write that?
```

```
              p        writing
    129                (0.4)

              p        writing
    130       P        kore no::¿
                       this GEN
                       This one?

    131                (0.4)

              p        writing
              p        GZ>paper
    132       K        soo:: soo soo sonna $kanji, sonna [yatsu:$
                       yeah  yeah yeah that-kind character that-kind one
                       Yeah yeah yeah. That kind of character, that one.

              p                                          +GZ>K
              p                                          +RH tap on paper
    133       P                                          [+sakaeru?
                                                          bustle
                       Bustle?

              k        +nod
    134       K        .hhh +soo.=
                            yeah
                       Yeah.

              p        +GZ>paper
              p        +pen>paper
    135       P        =+soo.+kono kanji?=
                             yeah this character
                       Yeah. This character?

    136       K        =eru [eru.
                        eru  eru
                       Eru, eru ((final two hiragana of sakaeru, repeated))

              p        writing
    137       P        [aa/::\:: hai. °(yeah, sa[kaeru)°
                                 yes            bustle
                       aa::::: yes. Yeah, bustle.
```

Gazing at the paper in front of her, Keiko admits that one of the characters she wrote might be wrong. With this admission she invokes her earlier assessment of the character for *hanjoo* 'prosperity' as difficult and the claim that she does not know it (lines 74–75). She then accounts for the possible mistake by describing how she came to write that particular character. With the account – to gloss, she looked up the characters for *hanjoo* and chose the one most related to commerce, which also happened to be the most difficult character to write (lines 116–117) – Keiko orients in various ways to her epistemic status and to shared knowledge of *kanji*. First, by returning the talk to the writing of the character and accounting for its possible incorrectness, Keiko shows her understanding that it is her epistemic obligation (Stivers *et al.*, 2011) to provide Peony with correct information about Japanese and her category-bound obligation as an educated L1 speaker of Japanese to have the required literacy skills to do so. Secondly, by describing how she selected the *kanji* from the online dictionary, she implies that she was not able to retrieve the character from her own knowledge but had to rely on the online dictionary as distributed memory (Hutchins, 1995, 2006). This method to access the character is treated as a taken-for-granted cultural practice[2] by both Keiko and Peony. Thirdly, by describing how she selected the character, Keiko presumes that Peony knows that there are multiple homonyms pronounced as *hanjoo*. This presumption trades on knowledge about the structure of *kanji* that is shared by literate users of Japanese and Chinese, namely that homophony is prevalent in Chinese.

At first Peony affiliates with Keiko's stance by repeating **muzukashii** 'difficult' (line 118). Yet as her next action, she produces a clipped change of state token (**a-**) and claims to know which character is the correct one. As she begins to write the character, she announces a proposal by saying 'maybe this'. While Peony is writing, Keiko maintains her gaze on her tablet even when she responds to Peony's announcement with a display of skepticism (**hon ↑ too¿** 'really'¿, line 121). Having finished writing, Peony hands the paper to Keiko while repeating 'maybe this¿' to solicit Keiko's response to her proposal (line 123).

After a short pause as she reads what Peony has written, Keiko produces a response turn in a markedly louder voice. As projected by Peony's solicit, she first affirms that Peony has written the character correctly. Her next actions display surprise at Peony's knowledge of the character. With **NANDE SHITTERU NO** ('How do you know that') Keiko uses a reverse polarity question (Koshik, 2005) that treats Peony's knowledge of a character that Keiko does not know as contravening the normative distribution of category-bound knowledge. Without formulating the category, Keiko implicitly categorizes Peony as *hen na gaijin*, a 'strange foreigner' (Nishizaka, 1999), who shows category-incongruent and therefore illegitimate access to a knowledge domain that should be under Keiko's control instead (cf. Bucholtz & Hall, 2005, for the notion of 'illegitimizing' identities). The following assessment **A YABAI** ('Oh my God', lit. 'terrible') upgrades Keiko's stance on the reversal of epistemic status relations. After a further, weaker surprise display (**chotto matte,** 'wait') Keiko requests that Peony show her how to write the character (line 128). The demonstration (lines 129–132) ends with Keiko's emphatic recognition of the character. In the next sequence, the participants revert to their normative epistemic relationship. Peony once again solicits affirmation of the character for *sakaeru* ('bustle'), and Keiko reminds Peony to add the hiragana える (*eru*) to the character, which Peony registers as something she did not consider.

Post-FonF: The morality of knowing *kanji*

In the last portion of the excerpt, Keiko returns to expressing surprise about what she treats as non-normative distribution of knowledge between her and Peony. The association of epistemic rights and obligations with membership in cultural communities occupies most of the ensuing talk.

Excerpt 10.5 [ARB-P20140110 42:46]

```
            k                                             +GZ>P
138   K                            [yaba:i, [chotto +matte=
                                    terrible  little wait
            Oh my god. Hold on!

139   P                                       [aa:::

140   K    =nande pioni $kakete watashi wa kake[↑nai$ .hhh
            why   NAME  write-can I       TOP  write-can-NEG
            Why can you write it and I can't?

            p                                       +GZ>K
            p                                       +smiles
141   P                                       [+yay::::: .

142   K    YA[BAI.
              terrible
            My god!

            p    +RH out toward K, retract
            p          +GZ>down
            p          +folding paper
143   P    [+gamba[+tte:::: .
              work hard
            Work hard!

            k                   +head rest on RH
            k                   +GZ>outside
144   K              [>are, +atashi< nihonjin dakke [naa.
                       IP    I        Japanese person IP  IP
            Huh? But I'm Japanese.

            p                                       +GZ>K
145   P                                       [+$motto
                                                more

            k    +GZ>P
146         +gambaru.$ hh
              work hard
            Work harder!

            k          +head tilt right
            k          +GZ>tablet
147   K    [$iya are, +okashii na. .hh
              bad that, strange  IP
            That's bad. Strange.

            p    folding paper
            p    +GZ>paper
148   P    [+((laugh))
```

```
         k    GZ at tablet
         p                   +puts pen down on K's side of table
149      K    dokka icchatta. +(1.4) kakeru.=↑pin sugoi ne,=
              where go-PST-totally IP  write-can NAME amazing IP

150           yoku kanji ka[keru ne.
              well characters write-CAN IP
              Where on earth did it go. (1.4). You can write, you're amazing. You can
              write the characters well, huh?

         p                       +GZ>K
151      P                       [+a kanji a- (0.2) kanji ga a- a- um (0.3)
                                    character       character SUB

         k    +GZ>P
152           +kantan.
              easy
              The characters are (0.2) the characters are a- a- um (0.3) easy.

         k    GZ>tablet
153           (0.5)

154      K    °nn:[:.°

         p            +RHIF PNT>throat
         p                   +GZ>down
         p                   +RH>down
         k                   +GZ>P       +GZ>tablet
155      P    [+watashi +(iru) ni +(0.6) watashi ni:
               I         *    for         I    for
              For me. (0.6) For me.

156           (0.5)

         k    +slight nod
157      K    +nn::.

         p                       +GZ slowly>K
         k                           +GZ>P
158      P    sonna- (0.4) ni: uh +muzuku+shik- (0.6)
              that much             difficult-*NEG

159           muka [a-
                   *
              They really aren- that hard (0.6) har-

         k                           +GZ>tablet
160      K    [>muzukashiku<nai? [pin+chan ni totte,=
                difficult-NEG      NAME       for
              They're not hard? For you,

         p                       +shakes head
161      P                       [+°muzukashikunai°
                                    difficult-NEG
              Not hard.
```

```
162    K         =muzukashi[kunai?=
                 difficult-NEG
                 Not hard?

       p                       +nod
163    P                       [+uhn. =nn.
```

In the beginning of the excerpt, Keiko upgrades her earlier surprise response (line 125). Repeating the negative assessment **yaba:i** 'terrible' and using a reverse polarity question (line 140; Koshik, 2005), she implicitly categorizes Peony and herself as members of different cultural communities who normatively have access to exclusive knowledge territories. Specifically, she treats Peony's demonstrated ability to write in Japanese, and her own lack of that ability on this particular occasion, as category incongruent, as epistemic trespassing on Peony's part and failure on her part to live up to her epistemic obligations to Peony. Peony responds with humor, first with a celebratory **yay::::** and, after Keiko again expresses surprise, by teasing her with **gambatte:::::** 'work hard'. The appeal to 'work hard' (often translated as 'good luck') is common in Japanese, especially in educational settings or other situations that require effort, used to encourage the recipient to persist and do their best in the face of a difficult task. It is not a routine response to a self-deprecation. An expected second pair part would have been a disagreement with, or minimization of, Keiko's negative self-assessment (Pomerantz, 1984). Instead the encouragement to 'work hard' agrees with Keiko's assessment and thus aligns with Keiko's censuring herself for being a 'bad Japanese'. Such an action could be disaffiliative, but as Peony's turn is produced in a light tone and with a smile, it comes off as a friendly tease. Prefaced with a response that shows mild surprise (**are,** 'huh?'), Keiko further steps up her account of why the knowledge asymmetry between her and Peony diverges from the normal. She now goes on record with her appeal to contrasting cultural membership by explicitly categorizing herself as Japanese (>**atashi**< **nihonjin dakke naa.**, line 144). With the self-categorization, Keiko invokes Peony's identity as non-Japanese and the contrasting epistemic responsibilities associated with their cultural identities. In this way Keiko further takes herself to task for not knowing the character. Her self-blame gets another, upgraded tease in which Peony urges Keiko to **motto gambaru** ('work harder') while maintaining her smile. Keiko affiliates with the tease by assessing her knowledge gap as **iya** 'bad' and **okashii** 'strange' while smiling together with Peony. With the joint smiling and Peony's laughter during Keiko's self-deprecation, the participants accomplish a good natured and lighthearted 'matching stance' (Couper-Kuhlen, 2012). In an effort to restore her tainted expertise as a writer of Japanese, Keiko downgrades the problem by claiming that the characters 'went somewhere' (line 149), implying that she knew them at some point.

In the remainder of the excerpt, the topical focus shifts from Keiko's difficulty writing in the character to Peony's ability to do so. Keiko initiates the topic shift by complimenting Peony on her ability to write the characters (lines 149–150). Peony rejects the compliment by assessing the characters as easy (**kantan**) and, when Keiko acknowledges the rejection without conveying understanding (line 154), provides an account for her assessment. Claiming that the characters are easy *for her* (line 155), Peony invokes her identity as an L1 speaker of Mandarin for whom writing Chinese characters is a taken-for-granted ability, an account that Keiko accepts after some reluctance, as her repeated other-initiations of repair (lines 160, 162) indicate. As they are reaching agreement on Peony's account, both participants reuse the lexical item *muzukashii* 'difficult' from Keiko's earlier assessment of the character (line 117). In this way they overtly set themselves into opposing relations towards the assessment object: the character for hanjoo is *muzukashii* 'difficult' for Keiko but *muzukashikunai* 'not difficult' for Peony. At the end of the talk initiated by Keiko's description of the shopping arcade in Kichijoji, the participants have reversed their relative epistemic statuses entirely. From an L2 speaker turned language learner at the moment she shows her non-understanding of a word in Japanese that she did not know, Peony assumes the status of expert in *kanji* when Keiko takes up the complementary status of a less knowledgeable writer of Japanese.

Despite occasional moves by both participants to return the talk to the shopping arcade, for the better part of their conversation their focus remains on the word meaning, the phonological, morphological and written forms of the original trouble source item in two writing systems, and the difficulty writing the *kanji* for the related Sino-Japanese word. The sustained and repeatedly reentered FonF on form is accomplished through the dense coordination of multisemiotic practices such as showing attentiveness and inattentiveness through gaze, affiliation through smiling, body movements for searching, tracing a character on the table, writing *kanji* on paper, selecting *kanji* from an online dictionary, and using Japanese as a resource to jointly accomplish actions and as an object for learning.

Discussion and Conclusions

We observed how in ordinary conversation, a lexical understanding problem prompts participants to shift from achieving intersubjectivity in talking about a mundane topic in their shared lifeworld to the spoken and written forms of the lexical item and its synonyms. In the course of a sustained interactional focus on the learning object that involves word definitions and form practice, a problem with writing the character of a synonym generates a concern with category-bound distributions of epistemic rights and obligations, which are taken as an occasion for doing friendship with good natured teasing. The participants accomplish these contingently emerging activities with laminations of resources from a range of semantic fields. The dense configurations of resources in particular sequential environments become interpretable as actions that are visibly designed for the co-participant. Earlier action configurations, most notably the turns including a form of the lexical item *sakaeru* and Keiko's assessment of the *kanji* for *hanjoo* as *muzukashii* 'difficult', are treated as public substrates that are transformed to fit the interactional project at hand. Through the same interactional competencies, driven by the relentless workings of the interaction engine, the participants achieve intersubjectivity, establish and maintain a joint focus on language form through learning and teaching, invoke memberships in social categories, and construct social relations. The participants visibly engage in these undertaking not only *with* but *for* each other and in so doing mutually authenticate their contributions every step of the way.

The FonF in the wild activity we observed in this conversation was sustained over multiple turns and re-entered several times after the participants had resumed their talk about the shopping arcade. Peony's and Keiko's extended engagement with a learning object contrasts with a case reported by Theodórsdóttir (2011b), in which the participants maintain FonF for no more than a two-turn insert sequence in order to establish the meaning of a critical lexical item that the L2 speaker is uncertain about. In Theodórsdóttir's study, the participants are buying and selling bread in a bakery in Iceland. It could therefore be argued that with the quick return to the main activity, the L2 Icelandic-speaking customer and L1 Icelandic-speaking salesperson show their orientation to getting on with the commercial transaction (other customers waiting in line, etc.), whereas our participants are having a leisurely talk in a coffee shop and are therefore afforded the latitude to linger on matters of language form and their wider repercussions. While this is entirely plausible, it is not the case that social setting determines the length and quality of FonF on form in the wild. In an episode recorded in a supermarket in Denmark, Wagner (2016) shows that an L1 Danish-speaking customer and an L2 Danish-speaking clerk engage in extended side sequences between the customer's initial request for a sales item and the successful completion of the transaction. Here the shift to FonF is first prompted by the customer, who treats the clerk's initial problem with hearing the reference to the product as indicating a lexical gap, while the clerk orients to remembering where the product is located. Similarly to Peony's and Keiko's conversation, the participants make relevant normative associations between social category membership and epistemic status, but in the supermarket episode it is the L2 speaker who treats that association as problematic.

For participants in social activities in the wild, then, it is possible to shift their joint attentional focus to language form as an opportunity for language learning and teaching, augmenting the L2 speaker's knowledge of grammar, lexis and pronunciation, confirming or correcting uncertain knowledge and even engaging in formal practice. For SLA, the purchase of studying the social organization of FonF in the wild is, minimally, to get detailed insight into how FonF emerges while participants are pursuing activities in their lifeworld, how FonF is afforded through actions and multisemiotic practices, and how the participants treat the form-focused project as completed and shift their interactional concerns back to their main pursuit.

But there is more to gain. A praxeological perspective on cognition and on knowing, using and learning languages shows that these matters are interrelated with memberships in social categories and category-bound epistemic rights and obligations. As such they have an ineluctable moral dimension. In this study (but not in Wagner, 2016), the moral dimension of language-focused interaction is backgrounded as long as social category incumbencies and knowledge distribution are tied together as normatively expected: Keiko shows herself as an expert and occasioned teacher of her first language, and Peony shows herself as relative L2 novice and eager student. When language status and knowledge become dissociated at the moment that Keiko admits to a gap in her knowledge of a *kanji* that Peony recognizes unproblematically, the morality of knowing and not-knowing the character becomes a strongly foregrounded issue for the participants, made relevant and consequential through Keiko's self-reprimand and formulation of contrasting memberships in cultural categories, and Peony's teasing. For SLA and language education, these connections are worth giving serious consideration to because they shed important light on the conditions and practices of language learning as a social undertaking.

Appendix A: Transcription Conventions

For the transcription of talk

TOP	topic marker
GEN	generative marker
COP	copula
FIL	non-lexical filler
POL	politeness marker
FP	final particle
1P	first person pronoun
,	continuing intonation
.	final intonation
¿	rising intonation
॰	slightly rising intonation
↓word	abruptly falling intonation

wo:rd	lengthening of the previous sound
=	latching (no space between sound before and after)
[	overlap
(0.7)	pause timed in tenths of seconds
(.)	micropause, shorter than 0.2 seconds
°word°	speech which is quieter than the surrounding talk
WORD	speech which is louder than the surrounding talk
bold	talk
talk	translation
*	unglossed particle

For the transcription of embodied action

H	hand(s)	F	finger
R	right	IF	index finger
L	left	2Fs	index & middle fingers
B	both	3Fs	index, middle & ring fingers
GZ	gaze		
+	place where action begins, description of action		
+	place where action begins in relation to talk		
/	stroke or beat of gesture		
—-	holding gesture or gaze in place		

Palm positions

PRD	prone down	(palm facing ground)
SPU	supine up	(palm facing up)
SPV	supine vertical	(palm facing in)

Appendix B: Japanese Language

I. Writing

Japanese utilizes a number of different writing systems, including *kanji*, *hiragana*, *katakana* and *roomaji*. As only *kanji* and *hiragana* are at issue in the current data, we will provide only a brief explanation of the relevant concerns.

Kanji (literally 'Chinese characters'), and ideographic and logographic characters which have primarily been borrowed from Chinese. Japanese and the various Chinese languages (including Mandarin and Cantonese among others) use these characters, which provides for a shared resource between speakers of the languages. However, there are some constraints that arise from the cross-linguistic use of *kanji* that are relevant to the data in this chapter.

(1) While the characters tend to have only one reading in Chinese, they can have multiple readings in Japanese. Some, the *onyomi*, are derived from Chinese, but have been adapted to the phonotactic constraints of Japanese. *Kunyomi*, on the other hand, are native Japanese readings that are not related to Chinese.
   (a) In relation to the characters discussed in the data, the Japanese word *sakaeru* is *kunyomi* (native reading). The *onyomi* of the character is *ei*, while the Mandarin pronunciation is *róng*. Notice that while the *onyomi* is derived from Chinese, the derivation may not be obvious to the average speaker – beyond the sound changes to fit Japanese phonotactics, both languages have undergone diachronic changes since the time that the *kanji* were borrowed.
(2) Even though a word is written with *kanji*, some Japanese words do not exist in Chinese and vice-versa. For example, the word *hanjoo* ('to be prosperous') is written in Japanese with the characters 繁盛 or 繁昌. However, these compounds are not used in Mandarin.
(3) *Kanji* have undergone various degrees of simplification in Japanese and Chinese. In Taiwan, traditional unsimplified characters are used, while in Japan, somewhat simplified forms are used. Mainland China uses a much more simplified system. This is illustrated by the character for *sakaeru* here:

Taiwan	Japan	Mainland China
榮	栄	荣

Hiragana are representations of *mora* (Vance, 1987), which are combinations of vowels, consonants plus vowels, or in the case of double consonants or final nasals, a single consonant. In the case of *sakaeru*, the word would be written in *hiragana* as さかえる. In general, *hiragana* are used to represent grammatical elements that would otherwise not be written in *kanji*; thus *sakaeru* is usually written as 栄える, where the *kanji* is used for the verb root, and the *hiragana* are used for elements that would be subject to sound change in conjugation. *Hiragana* are also used when the a person does not know or forgets the *kanji*, or uses them for the sake of brevity, as when writing memos.

II. Grammar

Both of the words at issue in the data, *sakaeru* and *hanjoo suru*, are stative verbs; that is, while they are grammatically verbs, they describe a state. When written in dictionaries or otherwise referenced in citation forms, they appear as written here. However, in mundane discourse, both generally appear in their stative/progressive forms, *sakaeteiru* and *hanjoo shiteiru*, both of which are contracted by omitting the *i* that appears before the verb ending *-ru*.

Acknowledgments

The authors thank the editors for their helpful comments on an earlier version of this chapter.

Notes

(1) In Mandarin, the word *hanjoo* (繁盛) is not used, but the characters would be read as *fánshèng*. The word that is used in Mandarin (繁栄) is pronounced as *fánróng* in Mandarin and as *hanei* in Japanese – not necessarily recognizable across the languages.
(2) By this we mean that for the participants, electronic resources such a smartphones and tablets are readily available tools that they use as unremarkable resources to pursue their project of the moment. Reflexively, with their self-evident use of digital media to solve a local language problem, Keiko and Peony show themselves as members of a shared contemporary culture.

References

Barron, A. (2003) *Acquisition in Interlanguage Pragmatics: Learning How to Do Things with Words in a Study Abroad Context*. Amsterdam: John Benjamins.
Bergsleithner, J.M., Frota, S.N. and Yoshioka, J.K. (eds) (2013) *Noticing and Second Language Acquisition: Studies in Honor of Richard Schmidt*. Honolulu, HI: University of Hawai'i, National Foreign Language Resource Center.
Bilmes, J. (2014) Preference and the conversation analytic endeavor. *Journal of Pragmatics* 64, 52–71.
Block, D. (2003) *The Social Turn in Second Language Acquisition*. Edinburgh: Edinburgh University Press.
Block, D. (2007) *Second Language Identities*. London: Continuum.
Brouwer, C.E. (2003) Word searches in NNS–NS interaction: Opportunities for language learning? *Modern Language Journal* 87, 534–546.
Brouwer, C.E. (2004) Doing pronunciation: A sequence of novice–expert interaction. In R. Gardner and J. Wagner (eds) *Second Language Conversations* (pp. 93–113). London: Continuum.
Bucholtz, M. (2003) Sociolinguistic nostalgia and the authentication of identity. *Journal of Sociolinguistics* 7, 398–416.
Bucholtz, M. and Hall, K. (2005) Identity and interaction: A sociocultural linguistic approach. *Discourse Studies* 7, 585–614.
Cook, H.M. (2008) Language socialization in Japanese. In P. Duff and N. Hornberger (eds) *Encyclopedia of Language and Education, Vol. 8: Language Socialization* (2nd edn) (pp. 313–326). New York: Springer.
Cook, H.M. (2012) Language socialization and stance-taking practices. In A. Duranti, E. Ochs and B. Schieffelin (eds) *The Handbook of Language Socialization* (pp. 296–321). Malden, MA: Blackwell.
Cooper, D.E. (1983) *Authenticity and Learning: Nietzsche's Educational Philosophy*. London: Routledge and Keagan Paul.
Couper-Kuhlen, E. (2012) Exploring affiliation in the reception of conversational complaint stories. In A. Peräkylä and M.-L. Sorjonen (eds) *Emotion in Interaction* (pp. 113–146). Oxford: Oxford University Press.
Doughty, C.J. and Williams, J. (1998) Pedagogical choices in focus on form. In C.J. Doughty and J. Williams (eds) *Focus on Form in Classroom Second Language Acquisition* (pp. 197–262). New York: Cambridge University Press.

Edwards, D. (1997) *Discourse and Cognition*. London: Sage.
Fasel Lauzon, V. and Pekarek Doehler, S. (2013) Focus on form as a joint accomplishment: An attempt to bridge the gap between focus on form research and conversation analytic research on SLA. *International Review of Applied Linguistics* 51, 323–351.
Ford, C.E. (2008) *Women Speaking Up: Getting and Using Turns in Workplace Meetings*. New York: Palgrave.
Gardner, R. and Wagner, J. (eds) (2004) *Second Language Conversations*. London: Continuum.
Garfinkel, H. and Sacks, H. (1970) On formal structures of practical action. In J.C. McKinney and E.A. Tiryakian (eds) *Theoretical Sociology* (pp. 338–366). New York: Appleton-Century-Crofts.
Giddens, A. (1976) *New Rules of Sociological Method*. London: Hutchinson.
Goffman, E. (1981) *Forms of Talk*. Philadelphia, PA: University of Pennsylvania Press.
Goodwin, C. (2006) Human sociality as mutual orientation in a rich interactive environment: Multimodal utterances and pointing in aphasia. In N.J. Enfield and S.C. Levinson (eds) *Roots of Human Sociality* (pp. 97–125). Oxford: Berg.
Goodwin, C. (2007) Interactive footing. In E. Holt and R. Clift (eds) *Reporting Talk: Reported Speech in Interaction* (pp. 16–46). Cambridge: Cambridge University Press.
Goodwin, C. (2013) The co-operative, transformative organization of human action and knowledge. *Journal of Pragmatics* 46, 8–23.
Greer, T. (2013) Establishing a pattern of dual-receptive language alternation. *Australian Journal of Communication* 40, 47–62.
Hall, J.K. (1993) The role of oral practices in the accomplishment of our everyday lives: The sociocultural dimension of interaction with implications for the learning of another language. *Applied Linguistics* 14, 145–167.
Hall, J.K. (1999) A prosaics of interaction: The development of interactional competence in another language. In E. Hinkel (ed.) *Culture in Second Language Teaching and Learning* (pp. 137–151). Cambridge: Cambridge University Press.
Hall, J.K., Hellermann, J. and Pekarek-Doehler, S. (eds) (2011) *L2 Interactional Competence and Development*. Bristol: Multilingual Matters.
Hassall, T. (2006) Learning to take leave in social conversations: A diary study. In M.A. DuFon and E. Churchill (eds) *Language Learners in Study Abroad Contexts* (pp. 31–58). Clevedon: Multilingual Matters.
Hayano, K. (2011) Claiming epistemic primacy: *yo*-marked assessments in Japanese. In T. Stivers, L. Mondada and J. Steensig (eds) *The Morality of Knowledge* (pp. 58–81). Cambridge: Cambridge University Press.
He, A.W. and Young, R. (1998) Language proficiency interviews: A discourse approach. In R. Young and A.W. He (eds) *Talking and Testing: Discourse Approaches to the Assessment of Oral Proficiency* (pp. 1–24). Amsterdam: Benjamins.
Hellermann, J. (2008) *Social Actions for Classroom Language Learning*. Clevedon: Multilingual Matters.
Heritage, J. and Clayman, S. (2010) *Talk in Action: Interactions, Identities and Institutions*. Malden, MA: Wiley-Blackwell.
Hutchins, E. (1995) *Cognition in the Wild*. Boston, MA: Massachusetts Institute of Technology Press.
Hutchins, E. (2006) The distributed cognition perspective on human interaction. In N.J. Enfield and S.C. Levinson (eds) *Roots of Human Sociality* (pp. 375–398). Oxford: Berg.
Iino, M. (1999) Language use and identity in contact situations. In L.F. Bouton (ed.) *Pragmatics and Language Learning* (Vol. 9; pp. 129–162). Urbana, IL: Division of English as an International Language, University of Illinois at Urbana-Champaign.
Ishida, M. (2009) Development of interactional competence: Changes in the use of *ne* in L2 Japanese during study abroad. In H.t. Nguyen and G. Kasper (eds)

Talk-in-interaction: Multilingual Perspectives (pp. 351–387). Honolulu, HI: University of Hawai'i, National Foreign Language Resource Centre.

Ishida, M. (2011) Engaging in another person's telling as a recipient in L2 Japanese: Development of interactional competence during one-year study abroad. In G. Pallotti and J. Wagner (eds) *L2 Learning as a Social Practice: Conversation Analytic Perspectives* (pp. 45–56). Honolulu, HI: University of Hawai'i, National Foreign Language Resource Center.

Jefferson, G. (2004) Glossary of transcript symbols with an introduction. In G.H. Lerner (ed.) *Conversation Analysis: Studies from the First Generation* (pp. 131–167). Philadelphia, PA: John Benjamins.

Kääntä, L., Jauni, H., Leppänen, S., Peuronen, S. and Paakkinen, T. (2013) Learning English through social interaction: The case of Big Brother 2006, Finland. *Modern Language Journal* 97, 340–359.

Kasper, G. and Wagner, J. (2014) Conversation analysis in applied linguistics. *Annual Review of Applied Linguistics* 34, 171–212.

Klein, W. (1986) *Second Language Acquisition*. Cambridge: Cambridge University Press.

Koole, T. (2010) Displays of epistemic access: Student responses to teacher explanations. *Research on Language and Social Interaction* 43, 183–209.

Koshik, I. (2005) *Beyond Rhetorical Questions*. Amsterdam: John Benjamins.

Kramsch, C. (1986) From language proficiency to interactional competence. *Modern Language Journal* 70, 366–372.

Kurhila, S. (2001) Correction in talk between native and non-native speakers. *Journal of Pragmatics* 33, 1083–1110.

Kurhila, S. (2006) *Second Language Interaction*. Amsterdam: John Benjamins.

Lee, Y.-A. (2006) Towards respecification of communicative competence: Condition of L2 instruction or its objective? *Applied Linguistics* 27, 349–376.

Lerner, G.H., Zimmerman, D.H. and Kidwell, M. (2011) Formal structures of practical tasks: A resource for action in the social life of very young children. In C. Goodwin, C. LeBaron and J. Streeck (eds) *Embodied Interaction: Language and Body in the Material World* (pp. 44–58). Cambridge: Cambridge University Press.

Levinson, S.C. (2006) On the human 'interaction engine'. In N.J. Enfield and S.C. Levinson (eds) *Roots of Human Sociality* (pp. 39–69). Oxford: Berg.

Long, M.H. and Robinson, P. (1998) Focus on form: Theory, research, and practice. In C.J. Doughty and J. Williams (eds) *Focus on Form in Classroom SLA* (pp. 15–41). New York: Cambridge University Press.

Lyster, R. and Saito, K. (2010) Effects of oral feedback in SLA classroom research: A meta-analysis. *Studies in Second Language Acquisition* 32, 265–302.

Macbeth, D. (2000) Classrooms as installations. In S. Hester and D. Francis (eds) *Local Educational Order* (pp. 21–71). Amsterdam: John Benjamins.

MacDonald, M.N., Badger, R. and Dasli, M. (2006) Authenticity, culture and language learning. *Language and Intercultural Communication* 6, 250–261.

Mackey, A., Abbuhl, R. and Gass, S.M. (2012) Interactionist approach. In S.M. Gass and A. Mackey (eds) *The Routledge Handbook of Second Language Acquisition* (pp. 7–23). Abingdon: Routledge.

Majlesi, A.R. and Broth, M. (2012) Emergent learnables in Swedish as second language classroom interaction. *Language, Culture and Social Interaction* 1, 193–207.

Mori, J. and Hasegawa, A. (2009) Doing being a foreign language learner in a classroom: Embodiment of cognitive states as social events. *International Review of Applied Linguistics in Language Teaching* 47, 65–94.

Mushin, I. and Gardner, R. (2011) Silence is talk: Conversational silence in Australian Aboriginal talk-in-interaction. *Journal of Pragmatics* 41, 2033–2052.

Nguyen, H.t. (2012) *Developing Interactional Competence: A Conversation-analytic Study of Patient Consultations in Pharmacy*. Basingstoke: Palgrave Macmillan.

Nguyen, H.t. and Kasper, G. (eds) (2009) *Talk-in-interaction: Multilingual Perspectives*. Honolulu, HI: University of Hawai'i, National Foreign Language Resource Center.

Nishizaka, A. (1999) Doing interpreting within interaction: The interactive accomplishment of a 'henna gaijin' or 'strange foreigner'. *Human Studies* 22, 235–251.

Norton, B. (2000) *Identity and Language Learning*. Harlow: Longman/Pearson.

Okada, Y. (2015) Contrasting identities: A language teacher's practice in an English for specific purposes classroom. *Classroom Discourse* 6, 73–87.

Pallotti, G. and Wagner, J. (eds) (2011) *L2 Learning as Social Practice: Conversation-analytic Perspective*. Honolulu, HI: University of Hawai'i, National Foreign Language Resource Center.

Perdue, C. (ed.) (1993) *Second Language Acquisition by Adult Immigrants. A Field Manual*. Strasbourg: European Science Foundation.

Pomerantz, A. (1984) Agreeing and disagreeing with assessments: Some features of preferred/dispreferred turn shapes. In J.M. Atkinson and J. Heritage (eds) *Structures of Social Action* (pp. 57–101). Cambridge: Cambridge University Press.

Sacks, H. (1992) *Lectures on Conversation, Vols I and II*. Oxford: Blackwell.

Sacks, H. and Schegloff, E.A. (1979) Two preferences in the organization of reference to persons in conversation and their interaction. In G. Psathas (ed.) *Everyday Language: Studies in Ethnomethodology* (pp. 15–21). New York: Irvington.

Sacks, H., Schegloff, E.A. and Jefferson, G. (1974) A simplest systematic for the organization of turn-taking for conversation. *Language* 50, 696–735.

Schegloff, E.A. (2006) Interaction: The infrastructure for social institutions, the natural ecological niche for language, and the arena in which culture is enacted. In N.J. Enfield and S.C. Levinson (eds) *Roots of Human Society* (pp. 70–96). Oxford: Berg.

Schegloff, E.A. (2007) *Sequence Organization in Interaction: A Primer in Conversation Analysis*. Cambridge: Cambridge University Press.

Schmidt, R. (1983) Interaction, acculturation and the acquisition of communicative competence. In N. Wolfson and E. Judd (eds) *Sociolinguistics and Second Language Acquisition* (pp. 137–174). Rowley, MA: Newbury House.

Schmidt, R. (2001) Attention. In P. Robinson (ed.) *Cognition and Second Language Instruction* (pp. 3–32). Cambridge: Cambridge University Press.

Schmidt, R. and Frota, S.N. (1986) Developing basic conversational ability in a second language: A case study of an adult learner of Portuguese. In R. Day (ed.) *Talking to Learn* (pp. 237–326). Rowley, MA: Newbury House.

Schumann, J. (1978) *The Pidginization Process: A Model for Second Language Acquisition*. Rowley, MA: Newbury House.

Sert, O. (2013) 'Epistemic status check' as an interactional phenomenon in instructed learning settings. *Journal of Pragmatics* 45, 13–28.

Sert, O. and Walsh, S. (2013) The interactional management of claims of insufficient knowledge in English language classrooms. *Language and Education* 27, 542–565.

Sidnell, J. and Stivers, T. (eds) (2013) *The Handbook of Conversation Analysis*. Oxford: Wiley-Blackwell.

Stivers, T., Mondada, L. and Steensig, J. (2011) Knowledge, morality and affiliation in social interaction. In T. Stivers, L. Mondada and J. Steensig (eds) *The Morality of Knowledge* (pp. 3–24). Cambridge: Cambridge University Press.

Stokoe, E. (2012) Moving forward with membership categorization analysis: Methods for systematic analysis. *Discourse Studies* 14, 277–303.

Streeck, J., Goodwin, C. and LeBaron, C. (eds) (2011) *Embodied Interaction: Language and Body in the Material World*. Cambridge: Cambridge University Press.

Svennevig, J. (2008) Trying the easiest solution in other-initiation of repair. *Journal of Pragmatics* 40, 333–348.

Theodórsdóttir, G. (2011a) Second language interaction for business and learning. In J.K. Hall, J. Hellermann and S. Pekarek Doehler (eds) *L2 Interactional Competence and Development* (pp. 93–116). Bristol: Multilingual Matters.

Theodórsdóttir, G. (2011b) Language learning activities in real-life situations: Insisting on TCU completion in second language talk. In G. Pallotti and J. Wagner (eds) *L2 Learning as a Social Practice: Conversation-analytic Perspectives* (pp. 185–208). Honolulu, HI: University of Hawai'i, National Foreign Language Resource Center.

Theodórsdóttir, G. and Eskildsen, S.W. (2011) The use of English in everyday Icelandic as a second language: Establishing intersubjectivity and doing learning. *Nordand Nordisk tidsskrift for andrespråksforskning* 6 (2), 59–85.

van Compernolle, R.A. (2010) Incidental microgenetic development in second-language teacher–learner talk-in-interaction. *Classroom Discourse* 1, 66–81.

Vance, T. (1987) *An Introduction to Japanese Phonology*. Albany, NY: State University of New York Press.

Wagner, J. (2016) Designing for language learning in the wild: Creating social infrastructures for second language learning. In T. Cadierno and S. W. Eskildsen (eds) *Usage-based Perspectives on Second Language Learning* (pp. 75–101). Berlin: De Gruyter Mouton.

Young, R.F. and Miller, E.R. (2004) Learning as changing participation: Discourse roles in ESL writing conferences. *Modern Language Journal* 88, 519–536.

Zimmerman, D. (1998) Identity, context and interaction. In C. Antaki and S. Widdicombe (eds) *Identities in Talk* (pp. 87–106). London: Sage.

11 Conclusions and Future Directions

Rémi A. van Compernolle and Janice McGregor

Introduction

As we noted in our Introduction, the chapters in this volume attest to the fact that authenticity lies at the intersection of many facets of second language (L2) development. Authenticity, it should be recalled, entails the appropriation of patterns of language and meaning that are recognizable within and across communities of speakers. This ties together the use of conventionalized linguistic, interactional and cultural practices as well as learners' own agentive actions – that is, authenticity of correspondence and authenticity of genesis (MacDonald *et al.*, 2006; and see Cooper, 1983 for the original discussion of correspondence and genesis in relation to authenticity). Further, authenticity is constructed, reified and/or challenged in performance – it involves the process of authentication (Bucholtz, 2003).

In this brief concluding chapter, we would like to synthesize the main lines of argumentation found throughout the volume as they relate to two principal themes: (1) patterns of language and patterns of meaning; and (2) agency, identity and culture. We then turn to a discussion of future directions for theory, research methods and pedagogy, before closing with a few final thoughts on authenticity in L2 studies and applied linguistics.

Patterns of Language and Patterns of Meaning

Patterns of language and meaning are dynamic. Languacultures (Agar, 1994) provide speakers with linguistic resources and conventions for meaning making that may be appropriated and reified in some instances, but challenged and modified in others. Authenticating patterns of language and meaning involves, on the one hand, the use of existing languacultural resources and, on the other, the *personalization* (van Compernolle, 2014: 76) of these resources as one's own.

Sociolinguistic authenticity was a central theme running throughout this book. Because language is variable from one context to the next, learners have to develop competencies in, and knowledge of, the patterns of meaning that are communicated through alternating forms. For example, van Compernolle and Henery's study (Chapter 2) highlighted the need to understand learners' understandings of, and motives for, using the French second-person pronouns *tu* and *vous*. This is because learners may be able to use forms in conventionally appropriate ways without understanding the significance of them or, conversely, they may use forms in ways that diverge from conventions precisely because they understand the potential effect such a use will have in a particular context. Similarly, van Compernolle (Chapter 4) showed that sociolinguistic authenticity can be accomplished as long as both patterns of language and patterns of meaning are recognizable within a community of speakers. Taguchi (Chapter 5) added the important observation that linguistic difficulty can lead some learners to avoid particular pragmatic forms that would be conventionally appropriate in favor of less appropriate, but linguistically less complex, alternatives. We can conclude from these three studies that the accomplishment of sociolinguistic authenticity involves knowledge of alternating patterns of language, an understanding of the social and cultural significance of the patterns in context, and the ability to put this knowledge to use in communication (e.g. processing constraints).

We have also seen that sociolinguistic authenticity results from, and is coproduced in, interactions with L2 community members, especially in study abroad contexts. Diao (Chapter 6) observed that peer socialization in study abroad can make sociolinguistic patterns visible to learners. Although the participant in her case study had already learned to use Chinese sentence-final particles, Diao showed how the learner's Chinese conversation partner socialized him into an understanding of the relevance and significance of the practice. Similarly, Lee and Kinginger (Chapter 8) documented how a Chinese learner's use of phonology and metaphor was authenticated by his host mother in a homestay study abroad context. The study by McGregor (Chapter 9) adds to these findings by focusing on interactional negotiation of expertise during metapragmatic talk, and how study abroad students and members of the host community can shift roles as experts and novices as they make cross-cultural comparisons. However, Fernández (Chapter 7) reminded us that socialization opportunities in study abroad settings are afforded and constrained almost by chance, as host community members may engage in communicative accommodation strategies that restrict learners' access to the patterns of language and meaning shared by the host community. Thus, these four studies show that, while interactions with peers and other members of host communities can be important contexts for authenticating practices and their development, there is no guarantee that this will occur, even if learners make gains in other domains of L2 learning (see also Kinginger, 2009).

Two chapters in the book explored authenticity beyond sociolinguistic issues. In his chapter, Williams (Chapter 3) offered an analysis of the authenticity of textbook explanations of auxiliary verb use in French and a proposal for a concept-based approach to teaching this grammar point. His shift in focus from rules-of-thumb to the concept of transitivity is an effective way of teaching auxiliary verb use because (1) it is based on a more complete and accurate description of language use (authenticity of correspondence), and (2) it has the potential to foster intentional, goal-directed use of the verbs in learners (authenticity of genesis). Thus, authenticity in grammar teaching must involve high-quality explanations of the language and at the same time push learners to appropriate the patterns of language and meaning as their own.

Kasper and Burch's study (Chapter 10) took on the cognitivist-interactionist approach to focus-on-form as a pedagogical practice from the perspective of conversation analysis and language learning 'in the wild' (i.e. in naturalistic, as opposed to classroom, settings). Because their data involved naturally occurring episodes of focus-on-form, the authors argued that authenticity of genesis was a non-issue. In other words, focus-on-form emerged authentically as the co-participants' own interactional practice, which was relevant to their real lifeworld. Authenticity of correspondence was linked to the ways in which co-participants negotiated and made relevant normative associations between social category membership (e.g. native versus nonnative speaker) and epistemic status (e.g. expert versus novice). The idea is that in naturalistic interaction (cf. classroom interaction), focus-on-form is accomplished as co-participants authenticate each other's actions as they attempt to maintain intersubjectivity.

Agency, Identity and Culture

Agency, identity and culture are intimately related concepts. Agency is socioculturally afforded (Ahearn, 2001) in that one's actions are everywhere and always mediated by the resources made available in one's cultural milieu. Likewise, identities are forged and performed in relation to the cultural means made available to people in their environment. These issues lie at the heart of authenticating L2 practices.

A common theme in several of the chapters was learner choice, conceived of as authenticity of genesis. The studies by van Compernolle and Henery (Chapter 2), Williams (Chapter 3), van Compernolle (Chapter 4) and Taguchi (Chapter 5) all point to the idea that agentive language use relies on conscious knowledge of the meaning and significance of the patterns of language learners are appropriating. This is because using language without the intention to make particular meanings and/or accomplish particular actions means that it is not the learner's own language. This was made especially clear in van Compernolle and Henery's exploration of French learners' orientation to, and use of, the pronouns *tu* and *vous*. Of course, as noted above,

Taguchi's study reminds us that learner agency can be constrained by L2 processing limitations. In other words, learners may know which forms they want to use and why, but they may simply have trouble producing them for whatever reason(s) (e.g. linguistic difficulty).

Related to learner choice is the issue of identity. Language style points to sociocultural membership categories (e.g. age, gender, education level) via multiple orders of indexicality (Silverstein, 2003). Consequently, as L2 learners develop their communicative abilities, they must also begin to make choices about the styles of language they intend to appropriate for use in different contexts as a means of self-identifying with and/or dissociating from various membership categories. Knowledge of variation in speech styles allows learners to make such choices deliberately (van Compernolle, Chapter 4; Taguchi, Chapter 5; Fernández, Chapter 7). Fernández's study is particularly illustrative of this point: one of her participants actively avoided the 'youngspeak' register befitting her externally perceived membership category (i.e. a young adult) because it did not align with her desired future identity as a Spanish teacher, which – to her mind at least – required the use of 'correct' or 'standard' Spanish.

Identities are also negotiated and authenticated *in situ*. The chapters by McGregor (Chapter 9) and Kasper and Burch (Chapter 10) showed how the epistemic statuses of 'expert' and 'novice' are not fixed in intercultural communication. Rather, who can be counted as the expert is something that emerges in the context of interaction in relation to the topic, participant knowledge bases and the experiences of the interactants. We have also seen how such identity-relevant issues as gender and sexuality can be authenticated, challenged and modified in interaction (Diao, Chapter 6). Lee and Kinginger's study (Chapter 8) also pointed out how a learner's use of salient sociolinguistic features and conceptual metaphors can be evaluated by members of the host culture, thereby authenticating the learner's development as one of the culture's members. Of course, the authors also reminded us that learners may assert their status as members of their home culture when challenging widely held negative stereotypes regarding cultural practices.

Future Directions

As a whole, this volume points to several directions for future research on authenticity in L2 contexts. In what follows, we provide a brief sketch of future work that centers on addressing authenticity in relation to theory, methods and pedagogy.

Theory

The point of departure for this volume was MacDonald *et al.*'s (2006) proposal of a dialectical view of authenticities of correspondence and genesis (Cooper, 1983). While each chapter in this volume has addressed the relationship between these two dimensions of authenticity, more work needs to be done. For example, there has been little discussion of how authenticity of correspondence can, or should, be operationalized. Should we base our understanding of conventions or normative use on grammar books, corpus data, sociolinguistic research, interactional analyses, or all of the above? Should correspondence be limited to perceived monolingual communities, or should multilingual data inform our conceptions of normative language use? Likewise, more research on and discussion of the operationalization of authenticity of genesis is warranted. We have seen in this book the use of various forms of external data (e.g. written responses, interviews) as means for understanding learners' L2 choices as well as reliance on an emic, or participant-relevant, approach to understanding authenticity of genesis as it emerges *in situ*. Future work would do well to examine and problematize how we understand language as the learner's 'own'.

Extending this line of inquiry will involve additional work theorizing the relationship between authenticity of correspondence and authenticity of genesis and their development. Following MacDonald *et al.* (2006), we proposed a dialectical unity of the two in our Introduction (van Compernolle & McGregor, Chapter 1). But the question of whether, and to what extent, one dimension of authenticity develops ahead of (i.e. leads) the other remains unaddressed. It would seem, in our opinion, that some development of authenticity of correspondence normally precedes the development of authenticity of genesis. In order to appropriate recognizable patterns of language and meaning as their own (authenticity of genesis), they must first begin to pick up the patterns of language and meaning that are recognizable in the languaculture they are studying or are immersed in (authenticity of correspondence). To be sure, we do not mean to suggest that language learners must acquire all possible patterns of language and meaning before they can begin the work of making them their own. Rather, as a dialectic, we assume that both influence each other in development. Consequently, we believe that while a learner most likely begins by picking up patterns of language and meaning (e.g. through instruction or incidental learning) without authenticity of genesis, the subsequent appropriation of such patterns as the learner's own results in a transformation not only of the previously picked up patterns but of those the learner will encounter in the future. And so it goes in a potentially endless cycle of appropriation and authentication. However, we hasten to remind the reader that we are simply speculating on the relationship between authenticity of correspondence and authenticity of genesis. Future work in this area would do well to explore how the two develop and influence each other across multiple time scales and in different contexts.

Methods

The chapters in this book have all used different methods for examining authenticity. Language use was analyzed in technology-mediated pedagogical tasks (van Compernolle & Henery, Chapter 2), sociolinguistic interviews (van Compernolle, Chapter 4) and naturalistic conversational settings (Diao, Chapter 6; Fernández, Chapter 7; Lee & Kinginger, Chapter 8; McGregor, Chapter 9; Kasper & Burch, Chapter 10). Language knowledge was evaluated through planning tasks (van Compernolle & Henery, Chapter 2), interviews (van Compernolle, Chapter 4; Taguchi, Chapter 5), discourse completion tasks (Taguchi, Chapter 5) and language tests (Williams, Chapter 3). This diversity speaks to the multidimensional nature of the object of study, and to the many ways in which researchers may approach the question of authenticity in relation to their foci of interest.

We believe that methodological diversity serves to enhance our understanding of L2 authenticity and its development. That said, we also believe that more reflection is needed in order to design research studies that afford access to three dimensions of L2 development: (1) knowledge of community-relevant patterns of language and meaning; (2) knowledge/awareness of one's use or avoidance of normative patterns; and (3) actual language use. Admittedly, the diversity of methodological approaches to, and theoretical perspectives on, examining authenticity will lead to differences in how these three dimensions of L2 development are operationalized, how data are collected and how data are analyzed. For instance, whereas several of the research traditions adopted in this book draw from multiple sources of data, conversation analysis (Kasper & Burch, Chapter 10) typically limits analysis to naturally occurring conversational data. The analytic mentality compels us to focus on participants' interactional displays of knowledge and awareness *in situ*, thus making additional sources of data unnecessary, or at least only ancillary to the examination of how participants '*do* authenticity' as social action. By contrast, as we saw in van Compernolle's study (Chapter 4), multiple research tools and external sources of data may be necessary in order to evaluate learners' knowledge of language and their orientations to using the L2 in relation to how they actually use the L2 in communication.

We would also like to see more focus on longitudinal studies of authentication processes. Indeed, although most of the chapters in this book have at least linked their findings to the notion of development, emphasis has been primarily on the *nature* of authenticity. While such research is of course useful for understanding authenticity in L2 contexts, we need research documenting how authentication occurs over time, in different contexts, and the impact that authenticating practices may have on learners' appropriation of patterns of language and meaning, their agency, their identities, and their relationship with, and possible integration into, the target languaculture. In keeping with our commitment toward promoting methodological diversity, we believe that various forms of longitudinal research can shed light on authentication processes. Ethnographic case studies have the potential to provide in-depth thick description and analysis of authentication processes. Larger scale research involving quantitative methods can reveal common trends and patterns across groups of learners. Pedagogical research could address the impact of instructional practices on authentication, and how authentication may be achieved through intentional instructional arrangements. And these are just a few of the ways in which the development of authenticity could be investigated in future research.

Pedagogy

Although pedagogy was the central focus of only one chapter in this book (Williams, Chapter 3), all of the contributions have implications for how we could conceptualize L2 instructional arrangements to support learners in authenticating their use of L2 patterns of language and meaning. As Williams pointed out, one place to begin is the design of concept-based instructional materials which include systematic, meaning-based explanations of L2 patterns (authenticity of correspondence) and which support learners in appropriating those patterns as their own (authenticity of genesis). We have also seen this in relation to concept-based pragmatics instruction (van Compernolle, 2014) in the chapter by van Compernolle and Henery (Chapter 2). Although the authors' focus was on the intersection of learners' orientations to and use of *tu* and *vous*, a major theme of the chapter was that pedagogy needs to give learners access to the underlying conceptual categories of meaning that are indexed by L2 forms.

Beyond materials and task design, several of the chapters have compelled us to think about the consequences of the interactions in which learners participate for the authentication of their use of the L2, their agency and their identities. In formal, structured educational environments, we should always keep in mind that teachers engage in authenticating practices that can expand or restrict learners' access to available patterns of language and meaning. Diao (Chapter 6) and Lee and Kinginger (Chapter 8) point toward the relevance of providing metapragmatic evaluations of learners' use of sociolinguistically and culturally marked L2 patterns so that learners come to understand the patterns of meaning they index. This can certainly be integrated into classroom interaction if space is made for developing sociocultural competencies (e.g. emphasis on sociolinguistics and pragmatics). Fernández's study (Chapter 7) reminds us of the way that 'experts' (e.g. native speakers or teachers) may inadvertently restrict access to potential objects of authentication for fear of confusing learners with unfamiliar L2 patterns. In the classroom this concern is understandable, but we should make efforts to expand, rather than limit, students' access to the range of resources that the languaculture makes available to its speakers for making meaning. In addition, the chapters by McGregor (Chapter 9) and Kasper and Burch (Chapter 10) highlight the need to recognize the fluid and dynamic nature of epistemic statuses such as 'expert' and 'novice'. While teachers are ostensibly positioned as experts in the classroom, students can enact this role too depending on the knowledge bases drawn on in the pursuit of social actions. Authenticating these roles relies on teachers abdicating some of the power and control in the classroom to make room for learners to take on more responsibility for directing the course of interaction and accomplishing learning tasks.

Final Thoughts

This volume is meant to serve as an opening to an extended conversation about the nature of authenticity and its development in L2 contexts. Framed around the dialectical unity of authenticity of correspondence and authenticity of genesis (Cooper, 1983; MacDonald *et al.*, 2006), the contributions to the book provide as a whole a brief sketch of the many different ways in which we can look at authenticity across different contexts of language learning, whether inside a classroom or outside it (e.g. study abroad).

We would like to close this chapter by highlighting four conclusions that we can draw from the diverse contributions included in this book.

(1) Authenticity in L2 learning and use is about language, but not just about its form in relation to expected, normative or conventional use. Authenticity in language involves an understanding of the patterns of meaning that mediate, and are mediated by, the patterns of language deployed during communication. Learners can choose to adhere to, or challenge, normative use to the extent that they control the patterns of language (e.g. processing constraints) and understanding their relation to recognizable patterns of meaning.

(2) Authenticity is not an end state of development. Rather, *authentication* (Bucholtz, 2003) is a nontelic process that occurs across multiple time frames, from the moment-to-moment unfolding of turns at talk through to ontogenesis, as learners forge their identities and sense of self in relation to the L2 they are appropriating. Because authentication is an ongoing process, a learner's in-the-moment status as an authentic speaker of the language and/or member of the second languaculture may be asserted, challenged or modified at any time.

(3) There are psycholinguistic issues related to the performance of authentic patterns of language. It is not enough to know the patterns and their meaning potential in context, because online processing difficulties (e.g. linguistic difficulty) may lead learners to opt for alternative, and perhaps less desirable, ways of using the L2. It follows that learners require opportunities to 'speed up' (Paradis, 2009), or 'accelerate' (van Compernolle, 2014), their access to their conscious knowledge of the patterns of language and meaning they wish to create during real-time communication in order to develop their abilities to authenticate their desired L2 communicative practices.

(4) Pedagogy can afford learners opportunities to gain access to the patterns of language and meaning that can be used in authentication processes. Instructional arrangements should engage learners in appropriating recognizable patterns of language and meaning as their own. This requires that pedagogical materials include accurate, or authentic, descriptions of relevant patterns of language and meaning in terms of correspondence to community practices as well as tasks that encourage learners to manipulate and take risks with those patterns in ways that are personally meaningful and significant to them in relation to their histories and projected futures as users of the language.

Taken together, these conclusions lead us to a conceptualization of authenticity that rejects the view that monolingual first-language speakers hold a monopoly on what can be counted as authentic. Other users of a language, including learners, can authenticate their use of, and identities in, languacultures beyond their first. Authentication processes are also collaboratively managed; therefore, a learner's authenticity can never be evaluated in isolation of specific contexts of L2 use. As work in this domain continues, we hope that the contributions to this book will spur additional insights into L2 authentication and its development across different contexts, languages and learners.

References

Agar, M. (1994) *Culture Shock: Understanding the Culture of Conversation.* New York: Morrow.
Ahearn, L. (2001) Language and agency. *Annual Review of Anthropology* 30, 109–137.
Bucholtz, M. (2003) Sociolinguistic nostalgia and the authentication of identity. *Journal of Sociolinguistics* 7, 398–416.
Cooper, D.E. (1983) *Authenticity and Learning: Nietzsche's Educational Philosophy.* London: Routledge and Keagan Paul.
Kinginger, C. (2009) *Language Learning and Study Abroad: A Critical Reading of Research.* Basingstoke: Palgrave/Macmillan.
MacDonald, M.N., Badger, R. and Dasli, M. (2006) Authenticity, culture, and language learning. *Language and Intercultural Communication* 6 (3–4), 250–261.
Paradis, M. (2009) *Declarative and Procedural Determinants of Second Languages.* Amsterdam: John Benjamins.
Silverstein, M. (2003) Indexical order and the dialectics of sociolinguistic life. *Language and Communication* 23, 193–229.
van Compernolle, R.A. (2014) *Sociocultural Theory and L2 Instructional Pragmatics.* Bristol: Multilingual Matters.

Index

accommodation strategies 136–142
agency 15–16, 63–64, 235–236
appropriateness 14–15, 31–32
authentic language 3–4
authentic speaker 4, 61–62, 155–156
authentication 4, 64, 152, 155–157, 170–172
authenticity of correspondence 1–3
authenticity of genesis 1–3

communicative competence 3, 181–182
concept-based instruction 12, 32 (note 1), 43–46

DCT (discourse completion task/test) 83–87

entextualization 113–114

focus on form 198–199

homestay 152–154

identity 64–65, 75–76, 142–147, 170–171, 235–236
indexicality 182–184
interactional competence 181, 201–203

mediation 11
metapragmatic talk 193
metapragmatics 4, 65

native speaker 3, 4, 110–112, 174 (note 2), 178

patterns of language 3–5, 11–14, 233–235
patterns of meaning 3–4, 11–14, 233–235
pragmatics 12–14, 31, 83–85

socialization 123–124, 179–180
sociolinguistics 61–62, 64, 66, 155–157, 184

verbalization 45

For Product Safety Concerns and Information please contact our EU Authorised Representative:

Easy Access System Europe

Mustamäe tee 50

10621 Tallinn

Estonia

gpsr.requests@easproject.com